WITHDRAWN

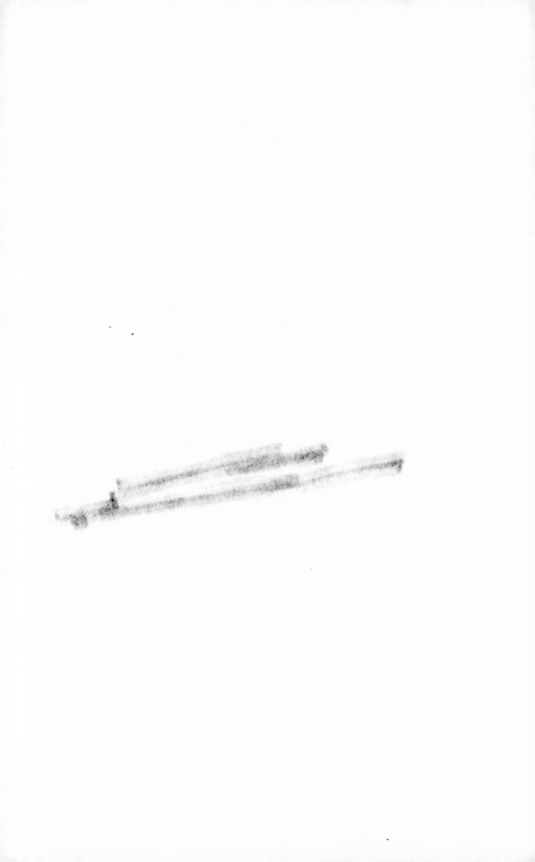

Old Believers *in* Modern Russia

Old
Believers
in Modern
Russia

Roy R. Robson

NORTHERN ILLINOIS UNIVERSITY PRESS

DeKalb 1995

© 1995 by Northern Illinois University Press

Published by the Northern Illinois University Press,

DeKalb, Illinois 60115

Manufactured in the United States using acid-free paper ∞

Design by Julia Fauci

Library of Congress Cataloging-in-Publication Data

Robson, Roy R.

Old Believers in modern Russia / Roy R. Robson.

    p.   cm.

Includes bibliographical references and index.

ISBN 0-87580-205-2 (alk. paper)

    1. Old Believers—Russia—History—20th century.

    2. Old Believers—Russia—History—19th century.

    3. Russia—Church history—1801–1917. I. Title.

    BX601.R58 1996   95-22663

    281.9′47—dc20   CIP

For Kim

Contents

Illustrations

Preface

In the broadest sense, this book is a study of how religion and culture interact. Specifically, it examines two major issues relating to the experience of Old Believers at the end of Russia's ancien régime. First, it seeks to prove that Old Believer traditions helped to create a "culture of community," not only distinct in organization and outlook from that of the Russian Orthodox church but also diverse in its many forms. Later chapters will show how this most traditional segment of Russian religious life interacted with the secular processes of modernization and change. It is necessary to realize even at the outset, however, that although the experience of the Old Believers was in many ways unified, it was never monolithic. While many significant traditions bonded the faithful to one another, other customs served to drive them apart and split their membership.

In order to analyze the life of the majority of Old Believers, I have consciously disregarded events that related to only small numbers of the faithful. While P. P. Riabushinskii and his Moscow merchant brethren became involved in national politics, for example, most Old Believers did not take part in Duma affairs. For that reason, and because other scholars have analyzed the political life of prominent Old Believers, I have chosen not to discuss the political situation of the Old Belief in the period between 1905 and 1917.

Official documents most often referred to Old Believers as *raskol'niki*—schismatics. The U.S. Library of Congress cataloging system still uses both "raskolniks" and "Old Believers." Old Believers, depending on the situation, called themselves *Starovery* (Old Believers), *Staroobriadtsy* (Old Ritualists), or, in rural areas or amongst themselves, simply *Khristiane* (Christians). On occasion, they also used the term *Drevnepravoslavnye*, usually translated as Old Orthodox (rather than Ancient Orthodox). Russian populist historians used Old Believer and Old Ritualist interchangeably. In these pages the term "Old Believer" will denote the specific, well-defined group, while "old ritual" (in small orthography) will often denote the movement itself.

The official church (also called the state church) will be called the "Russian Orthodox church." This was its formally recognized title. Using it does not imply that the Old Believers were *not* part of the Russian

Orthodox tradition. It does mean, however, that Old Believers in no way constituted a segment of the institution called the Russian Orthodox church. While the word "Nikonian" (after the patriarch Nikon, whose reforms touched off the original schism) has been used by Old Believers to denote the Russian Orthodox church, that term is in its own way as denigrating as "schismatic." Nevertheless, it is useful on occasion to be able to call "practices known in the official church after the reforms of the patriarch Nikon between 1654 and 1666" simply as "post-Nikonian" or even "Nikonian."

In general, footnotes and bibliographic entries for prerevolutionary books in Russian (and pre-1900 books in other languages) will cite only city and date of publication. For some Old Believer texts, where the publishing house is particularly important, I have added that information too. I have followed the Library of Congress system of transliteration. All dates are according to the Julian calendar, thirteen days behind the Gregorian.

I am fortunate to be working during a small renaissance in Old Belief studies and have enjoyed the support of numerous institutions and individuals. The IIE/Fulbright program and Boston College provided financial support to research and write the dissertation. The excellent staff at the Helsinki University Slavonic Library, a mecca for scholars, indefatigably located rare periodicals and liturgical texts. My fellow researchers in Helsinki and Moscow (especially during a notable seminar on Russian religious history) created a collegial and supportive environment in which my work took shape. I alone bear responsibility for errors in the text.

Archival research and manuscript preparation were supported by generous grants from the National Endowment for the Humanities and from the Joint Committee on the Soviet Union and its Successor States (of the Social Science Research Council and the American Council of Learned Societies), with funds provided by the U.S. Department of State under the Russian and Soviet Studies Research and Training Act of 1983 (Title VIII).

Sections of chapter 3 and chapter 4 have appeared in, respectively, the *Slavic Review* and *Seeking God: The Recovery of Religious Identity in Orthodox Russia, Ukraine, and Georgia,* edited by Stephen Batalden, and are used with permission.

This project would not have been completed without the support of Gregory L. Freeze, who pointed me toward sources, directed research, read drafts, and wrote countless letters of introduction. Members of my dissertation committee, Roberta Manning and Raymond McNally, championed my work and commented on the text. Robert Nichols served beyond the call of duty when reviewing an earlier version of the manuscript. Leonid Heretz—with good nature and remarkable speed—

checked Russian transliteration and gave advice on bibliographic style. Elena Borisovna Smilianskaia of Moscow State University aided this project in innumerable ways: finding sources, organizing field research, and commenting on early versions of the text. Everyone at Northern Illinois University Press, especially Mary Lincoln, has been professional and sympathetic in producing this volume. Since 1985, Michael B. Friedland has learned more about the Old Belief than any American historian could ever desire. His friendship and comments have been crucial to my work.

Finally, no such venture could have been completed without the support of my parents—Joe B. and Anita E. Robson—and the loyalty, intelligent input, and sacrifice of my wife, Kim.

Old Believers *in* Modern Russia

Now people only know how
To laugh at the ancient times;
They count the stars in heaven,
They see kingdoms on the moon.

Here they see forests and mountains,
Steppes, rivers, every grain; and
It affects them not; yet their gaze is fixed
On having coffee and tobacco.

Eternally the world flies
And turns day and night;
The tempter acquires those
Whose good deeds are very scarce.

—*From "On the Last Times,"*
an Old Believer Spiritual Verse

Studying *the* Old Believers

You say that I'm a schismatic,
I say: you're an Old Believer.
—*P. A. Viazemskii,*
"A Russian Romantic to a Russian Classicist"

 In 1974, while addressing a group of Russian Orthodox clerics, Aleksandr Solzhenitsyn condemned the church's position on Old Believers. Rather than praising churchly maintenance of Orthodox tradition, Solzhenitsyn commented that "in the Russia of the Old Believers the Leninist revolution would have been impossible." This statement struck a nerve even among Solzhenitsyn's most ardent admirers in the church, who countered that Old Believers preserved exactly the sort of ideological fanaticism and revolutionary zeal that characterized the Bolsheviks themselves.[1]

Solzhenitsyn's respondents, especially Russian Orthodox writers, showed remarkable constancy with the views of their clerical forebears. Rather than seeing the Old Belief as a shining example of Russian piety, these critics identified Old Believers as utopian extremists bent on schism from the mother church. Such a view of the Old Belief had originated centuries earlier at a time when the Russian church damned Old Believers as backward, ignorant, supremely superstitious, and stubborn peasants who could not differentiate between ritual and dogma. Old Believer *obriadoverie* (belief in ritual), according to this view, contrasted with the Russian Orthodox church's more enlightened differentiation between symbol and belief.[2]

Although the Old Belief has long aroused strong opinions, a tradition of historical research on Old Believers did not develop until the mid-nineteenth century. Early polemical arguments were undertaken by Russian Orthodox missionaries to the Old Belief,[3] but by the last years of Nicholas I's reign, both clerical and secular scholars had begun to analyze the Old Belief in more depth.

Church scholars focused on the events and themes of the original seventeenth-century Nikonian reforms, especially the ritual differences between the old and new rites. The most important revisions were the change in the spelling of Jesus' name, the number of repetitions of the word "alleluia," the translation of the creed from Greek to Church Slavonic, and the battle over how to form the fingers in making the sign of the cross.[4]

These church historians published considerable source material, but their analyses were less impressive.[5] Few ventured past the standard view that Old Believers were fanatic adherents of meaningless ritual distinctions. These scholars saw no need to study Old Believer attitudes in more detail, since fanaticism and ignorance seemed explanation enough for the Russian *muzhik*'s continued love of the Old Belief. The Holy Synod's general procurator wrote, as late as 1890, that "the characteristic lines of the contemporary schism *in its mass* appear as before—dark, careless and coarse stagnation in thought."[6] A priest complained that Old Believers showed only "pharisaism, secrecy, slyness, and more or less secret hostility and spite toward the Orthodox church and its servants."[7] The large missionary press that flourished after 1870—for example, the journals *The Missionary Review (Missionerskoe obozrenie)* and *The Fraternal Word (Bratskoe slovo)*—rarely provided a more nuanced view. Instead, missionaries assumed that Old Believers needed to be brought back to the mother church by "enlightenment" and "education."

Claiming that the heart of the schism lay in the ignorance of Russian peasants, the church jealously claimed to be the only legitimate form of Russian Orthodoxy. Old Believers, nevertheless, remained opposed to the Russian Orthodox church, rejecting its authority and, by extension, the state that sponsored it. One Russian Orthodox leader illustrated this obsession with legitimacy when describing Old Believers in his diocese:

> The head of the [Old Believers] of the Don diocese is the pseudo-bishop Spiridon. . . . Within his jurisdiction can be found up to fifty pseudo-pastors, among whom are several pseudo-archpriests, one pseudo-iguman, and one pseudo-archimandrite. About ten of the pseudo-pastors, among them the pseudo-iguman and pseudo-archimandrite reside not far from the residence of Spiridon.[8]

One is tempted to read the last phrase as "not far from the pseudo-Spiridon," to round out the author's emphasis on illegitimacy. The epigram beginning this chapter portrays the same idea: Old Believers somehow maintained reputations as both backward ignoramuses *and* rebellious schismatics.

In contrast to the church's view, secular historians of a populist bent created a different vision of the Old Belief. According to the populists, Old Believer history had only superficial connection to religious themes.

While populists recognized that the two-fingered sign of the cross provided a rallying cry, they believed that such a symbol obscured the real social, political, even economic rebellion at the root of the schism. According to populist scholars, underneath all the religious rhetoric Old Believers were really defending the ancient Russian traditions of self-governance, freedom from serfdom, and the primacy of local authority over central power on both the political and ecclesiastical level. The Old Believers showed their defiance of burgeoning western-inspired state power, these populists asserted, by wearing traditional clothing, praying according to the "ancient piety" (Russian Orthodoxy before the seventeenth-century reforms), and rejecting the power-hungry Nikon, as well as the secular authorities who stood behind him. Only this analysis, populist historians claimed, could explain both the ongoing allure of the Old Belief and the extreme prejudice directed against it by the Russian Orthodox church.[9]

The populist school of historiography held sway among secular Russian historians from the mid-nineteenth century far past the 1917 revolution. Its last great proponent, A. S. Prugavin, began to reintroduce the religious components of the Old Belief into what had previously been a secular analysis. "In [the schism's] own striking shape," he explained, "purely religious ideas and aspirations intermingle with purely cultural and social *(byt)* issues, so that it is frequently almost impossible to define where the first ends and where the second begins."[10] In a review of Old Believer historiography, Prugavin explicitly rejected materialism as the only avenue of discovery, hoping instead to analyze the "feelings and the heart" of the Russian peasantry by asking, "what does [the peasant] think? What does he believe? What does he not believe?"[11] Prugavin even praised the Slavophiles, who had collected certain poems, songs, and epics that held the key to understanding the peasants and, by extension, the Old Belief.[12]

With the exception of one short work by Prugavin—*Old Ritualism in the Second Half of the Nineteenth Century (Staroobriadchestvo vo vtoroi polovine XIX v.)*—both religious and secular historians concentrated on the earlier period in the history of the schism, the years before the middle of the nineteenth century. The later period (by which time the Old Belief had developed into a large, well-defined, and often prosperous movement) interested only a few ethnographers. A few articles described Old Believer traditions, but a journal devoted to ethnographic studies lamented that scientific work on late nineteenth-century Old Belief was very weak.[13]

After the reforms of 1905, Old Believers published their own version of the schism's history. In their interpretation of events, of course, the Russian Orthodox church (always noted in quotation marks as the "Orthodox" church) had fallen into schism—even heresy—by leaving the

path of the ancient piety. Old Believer ideology thus oriented itself historically: V. G. Senatov's *Philosophy of the History of the Old Ritual
(Filosofiia istorii staroobriadchestva)*, for example, traced the development
of Christianity as seen through an Old Believer lens.[14]

The 1917 revolution muted both Russian Orthodox and Old Believer
voices. Until the 1960s, Soviet historians spent relatively little time studying the Old Believers. V. D. Bonch-Bruevich, who became V. I. Lenin's
secretary after the 1917 revolution, published a valuable seven-volume
set of sources on Old Believer history just before 1917 and remained par-
tially involved in Old Believer study after the revolution.[15] Some ethnographic work was done among the Old Believers, including well-known
studies on the Siberian Old Believers, and the Soviets did continue to
publish source material.[16]

Soviet historians and ethnographers renewed their interest in the subject in the 1960s and since then have published excellent work. Although
some of these scholars, such as V. F. Milovidov, maintained the traditional Soviet perspective on religion (Old Belief as a backward remnant
of pre-Marxist Russia),[17] fresh insights, scholarly analysis, and much raw
source material have been generated through the auspices of the univer-
sities of Novosibirsk, Moscow, and Ekaterinburg.[18] Under the leadership
of Academician N. N. Pokrovskii, scholars in Siberia have produced a
constant stream of work, including an excellent monograph series, entitled Archeography and Source Studies of Siberia *(Arkheografiia i is-
tochnikovedenie sibiri)*, that focuses on the Old Belief. Pokrovskii's own
publications can hardly be overestimated. Moscow State University and
Ekaterinburg State University scholars have pursued the collection and
analysis of Old Believer books and published distinguished scholarship
on Old Believer book culture.[19] These centers of study have now begun
to analyze the twentieth-century Old Believer experience.[20]

Until recently, the Old Belief aroused little interest among scholars in
the West. In the nineteenth century, virtually no western scholar wrote
about this facet of Russian Orthodoxy, which itself remained largely a
mystery.[21] The beginning of the twentieth century saw some activity
among German ethnographers on Masurian Old Believers.[22] The first
American book on the schism derived completely from secondary
sources.[23] J. S. Curtiss's study of the Russian Orthodox church from 1900
to 1917, however, pioneered the historical study of Russian religion and
included material on the Old Believers. For many years, the works of
Curtiss and Pierre Pascal remained the only good western-language
treatments of the Old Believers.[24]

The post–World War II period, with its new emphasis on Slavic studies, produced nuggets of good scholarship on the Old Believers.[25] These
studies uniformly addressed the Old Belief in the period from 1666 to
1850.[26] In general, the American academy has changed little since the

1960s, when Michael Cherniavsky noted that historians treated the schism as "the expression of Muscovite traditionalism, [with] attention to form rather than substance, ignorance, inertia—the antithesis to the Western Reformation and its search for change."[27] A few specialized works, such as Cherniavsky's 1966 article and Robert O. Crummey's groundbreaking *Old Believers and the World of Antichrist,* have offered cogent analyses of Old Believer history in western languages. Cherniavsky, whose interests lay in cultural history, argued persuasively that, although the Old Believer reaction to the state began well before Peter I, it gained strength during his reign. He concluded that, while the Old Believers were holding to the ancient piety, a "new religion" combining state and secular interests would take the place of traditional Orthodoxy for Russian culture. Crummey has shown how the Old Belief developed from a movement relying on charisma and apocalypticism to become a relatively stable, industrious, and, at times, highly successful subculture within the Russian empire.

Given the more recent opportunity to travel and collaborate with Russian scholars, westerners have begun to produce significant new studies of the Old Belief. As a result, the early years of the schism are now being portrayed with greater variation and nuance. Scholars in Germany, Canada, and the United States are using newly accessible archival material to analyze Old Believer historical and religious development from the seventeenth century to the present.[28] Ethnographers, historians, and sociologists are also analyzing Old Believer communities in the American diaspora.[29]

New Methods for Studying the Old Believers

Scholarly interest in the Old Believers has begun to mesh with advances in social science theory, particularly in cultural anthropology. Inasmuch as Old Believers define themselves on the basis of their rituals and symbols, cultural anthropology can be especially useful for analyzing the Old Belief. Because symbols and rituals are *experienced* by the faithful, not simply understood in an intellectual way, scholars need to break down the distinction between symbolic and concrete structures, between the "signs" of the old ritual and the "real" issues at stake in the Old Belief. In other words, there must be an effort to integrate the rituals binding the Old Believers with the social or economic life that grew out of their shared experiences.[30]

This task is not easy. It would be simplest to follow Emile Durkheim's model and say that old ritualist symbols reduced conflict, reinforced consensus, and produced harmony in society. Yet Durkheim's theory seems incomplete, almost glib, when analyzing Old Believers, especially once the movement had become established. Why did Old Believers not accept the new Nikonian symbols, thereby lessening conflict with the rest of their Orthodox brethren? Adoption of the new symbols might have helped to reduce strife and to reinforce conformity among Old Believers. The new symbols, however, seemed to be interpreted at a level deeper than simply that of social control.[31]

In addition, Durkheim's model of religious ritual, widely accepted by western anthropologists, has made interpretation of the old ritual more difficult. Almost a century ago, Durkheim claimed that

> Religious phenomena are naturally arranged in two fundamental categories: beliefs and rites. The first are states of opinion and consistent in representations; the second are determined modes of action. Between these two classes of facts there is all the difference which separates thought from action.[32]

If Durkheim's model were to be used to study Old Believers, scholars would misunderstand the kernel of old ritualist interaction with symbols and rituals. For the faithful, pre-Nikonian rituals *realized* rather than *represented* heaven on earth. Orthodox literature is replete with references to this process of realization, which is less well developed in the Christian West.

Nevertheless, many scholars still claim that ritualized religious experience is somehow less developed than a cerebral view of religious symbols. Studies have often sought to show that "primitive" groups retained external ritual religion while more "developed" societies internalized or intellectualized their religious belief. This paradigm has had the dire effect of marginalizing old Russian piety in scholarly dialogue, because old ritualism apparently did little but reinforce Russia's "backwardness." Once declared primitive, old ritualism could safely be disregarded in the sweep of Russian modernization.[33] A mainline Russian history textbook, for example, claims that the Old Believers' "religious position could hardly maintain itself against that of intelligent people."[34]

Instead of social cohesion or dogmatic representation, Old Believers hoped that their symbols and rituals could actually transform them into better Christians. Following ancient eastern Christian traditions, Old Believers accepted the proposition that ritual life could help them to achieve "the final goal at which every Christian must aim: to become god, to attain *theosis*, 'deification' or 'divinization.' For Orthodoxy, man's salvation and redemption mean his deification."[35] Accordingly, the Old Believers worried that ritual change could undermine the possibility of deification. For them, the church schism of the seventeenth century not only broke tradition, but also subverted the chance for salvation.

Yet what exactly was the relationship between Old Believers and their symbols? Did old ritualists love the two-fingered sign of the cross because of its antiquity, or did they somehow experience Christianity in a unique way because of this sign? An elderly Old Believer might go to sleep making the two-fingered sign of the cross, so that, if death came, rigor mortis would harden her fingers into that sign. This was arguably not a symbolic gesture but an experiential one, a commitment to the sign of the cross as a path toward salvation. In another context, a contemporary scholar has written:

> Commitment to a proposition of any kind entails a relationship between symbol and person that can transcend language. Commitment is both more and less than a semantic process, for the symbol to which one is committed does not only represent. In the relation of commitment, the symbol blends with experience. It is more likely to appear as a feeling that can be described than as a content that can be deciphered. It is a relation of meaningfulness, not only of meaning.[36]

Consequently, we can understand the Old Belief as an ongoing relationship between the symbols of pre-Nikonian Orthodoxy and the lives of the old ritualist faithful. This method intrinsically relates symbolic structures to social activity, and later chapters will employ this approach when investigating the liturgical, architectural, and artistic output of Old Believers in the late imperial period. Understanding the interplay between Old Believers and their symbols can yield a better analysis of how the forces of tradition interacted with the power of change in the post-1905 period. Old Believer church buildings, for example, sprang up across Russia. How did the design of those buildings comment on the activities going on inside of them? Did architecture provide a path to accept, resist, or respond to forces of modernism? Such questions can best be answered by serious study of architecture as symbol.

Another useful term in the language of Old Believer symbols is the "iconic principle," introduced by anthropologist David Z. Scheffel. Defined as the "insistence on regarding major symbols of orthodoxy as faithful copies of divine prototypes," the iconic principle helps to explain the relationship of symbol to believer in the old ritual.[37] If Old Believers were meant to strive for divinization, to recreate the image and likeness of God, their symbolic life provided the icon, or path, toward that goal.

Many of these ideas, from *theosis* to the iconic principle, might also be used to describe non–Old Believer forms of Eastern Orthodoxy. All Orthodox, for example, conceived of icons as conduits of grace, as divine prototypes. How then was the Old Belief at variance from the dominant Russian Orthodox church? Perhaps the difference was not so much in kind as in degree. Theologians have long claimed that the Orthodox refused to distinguish symbol from dogma (thus the Creed was known more accurately as the "Symbol of Faith"), while that distinction became crucial to the western Christian experience.[38] Old Believers, however, incorporated this traditional view of symbols on a scale markedly higher than did other Orthodox. The physical care and maintenance of icons (as described in chapter 5), for example, held for Old Believers a religious importance that had been lost upon other Russian Orthodox believers.[39]

Assuming that the Old Belief (like other cultural systems) worked "not . . . through the mind alone, but through the body as well,"[40] one can find linkages between physical actions and religious symbols, on the one hand, and the social or political milieu within which Old Believers interacted, on the other. As Scheffel has noted: "Old Believers insist on demonstrating the faith through the medium of the body, and that's a long way from practicing a 'ritual method of living' out of blind traditionalism."[41] Recalling the elderly Old Believer making the two-fingered sign while sleeping, it is apparent that the names Old Believer and Old Ritualist can indeed be interchanged. Because ritual and belief fused to provide a distinctive religious and social experience, both names are equally appropriate descriptors.

Moreover, the history of the Old Belief has been a constant struggle between outside forces (such as church, state, or secular society) and the old ritual itself in the construction of Old Believer identity and life. Studying the symbols and rituals of the Old Belief as they differed from post-Nikonian Russian Orthodoxy in fin de siècle Russia can therefore illuminate the "fused communication"[42] that propelled Old Believers into a unique Russian subculture.

The Community

During the late imperial period, the community question—that is, the debate over defining the Old Believer subculture—proved to be an enduring issue. The edicts on toleration and on Old Believer communities in 1905 and 1906, respectively, accepted the existence of Old Believer communitarian principles. The state assumed that old ritualists naturally organized themselves into coherent, independent communities, and it based its legal recognition of Old Believers on this concept. Although widely accepted, the concept of community engendered debate among Old Believers about the definition, boundaries, and rights associated with the community. This debate will be considered in chapter 7.

For scholars of the Old Belief, the community question lies at the core of understanding Old Believer social organization and religious activity. This book demonstrates the importance of community cohesion to Old Believer life. Old Believer autonomy and local control of religious and social affairs, as this study argues, aided Old Believers in their interaction with a modernizing Russian Empire.

In developing language with which to analyze the Old Belief, scholars have had little luck in defining (or even describing) the community phenomenon. Many sources attest that Old Believer communities were strikingly different from their Russian Orthodox counterparts. Churchmen and ethnographers alike ascribed standards of wealth, cleanliness, sobriety, order, and a sense of self-reliance among Old Believers that were not seen in the typical Russian peasant village. The existence of Old Believer communities as identifiable entities is thus not in serious doubt; the definition of what constituted a community, however, remains obscure.[43]

In some ways, it would be attractive to lump Old Believer communities into a "premodern" framework, to see them as small, rural, family-oriented, self-governing units characterized by close personal bonds.[44] In fact, Old Believers did tend to live on the outskirts of the Russian empire (in the far north of European Russia, in Siberia, along the Don River, and even in Poland). Many also maintained clan ties through intermarriage, mutual aid, and the communal responsibility for decision making. The traditional view of Old Believers living in remote Russian villages, however, underestimates the variety of Old Believer groups. Many Old ritualists lived in cities and frequently established multiple communities that interacted with one another while still having separate identities. In the wider context, urban settings and lack of geographical boundaries defy the definition of Old Believer communities as remote.

Analysis of the life of Old Believers within their communities must therefore be based on factors other than geography. How might the Old Believer community be defined broadly enough to recognize its variety but narrowly enough to make it meaningful? Although theories such as network building, marriage analysis, and gossip pattern analysis might shed light on communication links among contemporary Old Believers, these theories give little solace to historians working with scant written data.

Another indicator of community structure (and one perhaps more accessible to historians) is the mental state of Old Believers themselves. Victor Turner has argued that communities contain a kernel of mental "communitas" that appears in the absence of other social structures. Communitas is egalitarian, democratic, and "emerges where social structure is not. . . . Community is the being no longer side by side (and, one might add, above and below) but with another of a multitude of persons."[45] In other words, community organization precludes forms of hierarchy. Turner claims that community spirit appears most strongly among marginalized groups, specifically mentioning Christian holy fools and Tolstoian peasants as examples, and he describes an apocalyptic mood that often fuels communitas. Turner could well include Old Believers in this list because of their status as "others," their forebears' initial certitude concerning the last days of the world, and their creation of independent structures.

According to Turner, an apocalyptic mood—such as that which accompanied Old Believer self-immolation—rarely sustains itself for an extended period. Instead, the energy infusing early communities moves past the existential or spontaneous communitas to a more normative form that organizes the movement into a viable social system. Such a process in the Vyg community has been ably described by Robert Crummey.

Once the community has transformed itself from a spontaneous social group to a more stable one, Turner maintains, "ideological communitas" codifies and preserves the energy and spirit that made like-minded individuals group together in the first place.[46] According to this model, Old Believers at the end of the imperial period existed in a state of ideological communitas because they had developed a stable, visible, and self-perpetuating system of social organization that remained separate from other parts of Russian society.

Turner's model does have an aura of utopianism about it, which makes it less useful for the study of Old Believers. In addition, it would be exceedingly difficult to corroborate his claims with historical data. After all, it is difficult to analyze the "withness" of the "above and below" nature of communities in any historical way. Although Turner's theory can help to define a path taken by historical communities, it proves to be less enlightening for analysis of Old Believer historical phenomena.

Turner does imply, however, that communities (Old Believer or otherwise) are based on interaction among individuals and on continuing communication among members of the group. In applying Turner's idea, historians may find language to be a glue for the community. Indeed, linguists have long studied the old ritualists to identify peculiar ways of speech and vocabulary. For example, Old Believers know immediately that they are talking with co-religionists when they speak of their hero Avvakum; the faithful tend to stress the middle syllable of the name, while most contemporary Russian speakers stress the last!

A system of communication, what has been called communicative action, provides the building block for communitarian organization through shared sets of assumptions and trust among the membership.[47] Robert Crummey has argued that Old Believer book culture helped to create a "textual community" that connected Old Believers through mutual adherence to pre-Nikonian Russian religious rites. The printed word thus helped to combat disintegration during persecution and to link Old Believers with one another.[48]

For the historian, however, the communication issue can move beyond written and spoken language to that of symbols and rituals—the language of the Old Belief. In the late imperial period, Old Believers began an open and public conversation about their religious rituals and symbols, ranging from the construction of new chapels and the publication of liturgical works to the debate over the relationship between old ritualists and nonbelievers. This conversation was not so much a matter of religious fanaticism or revolutionary zeal. It was, instead, a search to retain links among Old Believers while not getting lost among the new ideas and structures of fin de siècle Russia. Although it is impossible to determine the fate of Bolshevism had there been a Russia of Old Believers, it is clear that the old ritualists tried to use their religious and cultural communication to strengthen a social system decidedly different from that of their neighbors at the turn of the century.

Profile *of the* Old Belief

I believe in one God, always to the end. This is the
faith of Christ. This is the apostolic faith. This is the
faith quickly spread from one end of the earth to the
other, universal. It is the faith of the writings of the
holy God-bearing fathers and affirmed by the ecu-
menical teachers, with the works of the confessors,
and adorned with the blood of the martyrs. It is such
and we believe and confess it with the holy fathers.
And those who do not believe we curse, and they
will be damned, thrice. And they that believed, and
of other writings and words thus taught, those the
present Orthodox Catholic Church confesses. Eternal
memory to them, thrice.
—*The Book of Faith (Kniga o vere)*

Here lies the essential difference between Russian
Raskol and German Protestantism: the one is sec-
tional, narrow-minded, bigoted, jealous, and pharisaic; the other is universal, whole-souled, liberal,
generous, and tolerant.
—*Albert F. Heard, The Russian Church
and Russian Dissent*

 Questions of social science theory aside, most
western scholars know little about even the
most rudimentary history of the Old Belief. Before considering a more nuanced interpretation
of how the Old Believers created their own
view of the modern world, here is a profile of
the Old Belief at the beginning of the twentieth
century. The legal status, demography, and religious-social organization
of the Old Believers in the late imperial period all contributed to their interaction with a rapidly changing world.

The term Old Believers includes a number of groups that arose as a result of Russian church reforms initiated between 1654 and 1666. Old Believers desired to maintain the traditions, rites, and prerogatives of Rus-

sian Orthodoxy, while Nikon, patriarch of the Russian church, wanted to make Russian practices conform to the practices of the Russians' contemporary Greek counterparts. Nikon's opponents, conscious of both a departure from tradition and an encroachment of central control over local autonomy, refused to change practices.

Much of this early history is still poorly understood. Recent scholarship has shown that the Old Belief did not coalesce into a "movement" until perhaps a generation after the schism. Because local concerns tended to override any broader organization of Old Believers, the leadership of the Old Belief probably had only limited authority over a small core of supporters.[1]

Thanks to support from the tsar, Nikon embarked on a series of persecutions that lasted, in varying degree, right up until the Act of Toleration of 1905, with its more open-minded attitude toward religious belief. Legal persecution of the Old Belief waxed and waned depending on the threat perceived by the dominant church and state. Concrete policy, however, rarely translated into actual practice. Since the number and distribution of Old Believers remained virtually unknown, no measure (either repressive or liberating) produced quantifiable results, although most government and church officials did agree that the Old Belief became dramatically stronger in the last seventy-five years of the empire.

For the Old Believers, the possible loss of sacramental life splintered the movement shortly after the 1666 schism. Since no bishops consecrated new hierarchs according to the old ritual, Old Believers quickly found themselves bereft of canonical clergy. The decision on how to deal with that absence increasingly defined the stripe of any particular Old Believer.

Differences within the Old Believer communities solidified into a number of *soglasiia*, a word best translated as "concords." Because they were dogmatically Orthodox, the Old Believers could not be called independent "churches" or "faiths." The differences amongst the concords lay not so much in doctrinal issues as in sacramental procedures and interaction with the state. To describe Old Believer groups as "sects" would also cause confusion. It seems that their own term, concord, suits the voluntary associative characteristics of the differing Old Believer groups and is the best English word to translate the Russian idea.[2]

Old Believer Legal Status

Reaction against Old Believers emanated from both the Russian Orthodox church and the secular state. In pushing through his ritual and textual changes, Patriarch Nikon relied heavily on his relationship with Tsar Alexei Mikhailovich to suppress popular opposition. Although Nikon's desire to create a theocratic state in Muscovy never bore fruit, his actions resulted in the development of close ties between church and state on matters regarding the Old Belief.

The history of the Old Belief's early years tells of numerous confrontations between agents of the state and Old Believers. Those who retained the old ways of Russian piety could be subjected to terrible corporal punishment, such as having a tongue cut out, being burnt at the stake, or, in the most horrible instance, being smoked alive "like bacon."[3] Sometimes, however, death came at the hands of Old Believers themselves. In a twist on the Russian tradition of "passion-bearing" (Boris and Gleb were the first saints canonized for accepting death without active resistance), Old Believers burnt themselves alive in their churches rather than accept the ritual changes of the revised Russian Orthodox church.[4] Although this was the most extreme form of resistance and did not happen often, it did provide an effective and surprisingly frequent deterrent to state seizure of Old Believer groups. Self-immolation continued even into the period of Peter I, a whole generation after the first Nikonian reforms.

Peter I's position toward the Old Believers was typical of his own early brand of realpolitik. Old Believers were not tolerated as political opponents of the state, especially of Peter's western-looking reforms. He implemented a double poll tax on Old Believers, based on a census they viewed as anti-Christian since it was perceived to be enrollment in the books of Antichrist. Peter even taxed the beards that Old Believers refused to shave, as well as the traditional clothing that they would not change for western European dress.

In matters advantageous to the state, however, Peter I allowed Old Believers to live as they wished. He also encouraged religious toleration for Lutherans and Catholics, at the same time obliging them to help develop Russian technology. Likewise, he refused to persecute Old Believers (in the Vyg community, for example) while they were producing ore for his war machine.[5] The apparent contradiction within Petrine policy meant that both religious persecution and religious tolerance were acceptable so long as they met Peter's political needs.

During this time, the Old Belief, while allowed to exist as a religious entity, still suffered under separate laws and governmental decrees, some of which were secret and therefore not published in the Complete Collection of Laws of the Russian Empire (*Polnoe sobranie zakonov Rossiiskoi imperii*).[6] The situation of the Old Believers improved dramatically, however, during the reign of Peter III when a period of general acceptance of the Old Belief was inaugurated by the Russian imperial government. Although not considered Orthodox, Old Believers did receive the right to congregate in prayer. During the rule of Catherine II, the great Old Believer centers of Preobrazhenskoe and Rogozhskoe were founded. In these centers, curiously known only as "cemeteries," Old Believers created large complexes of chapels, churches, bell towers, and charitable institutions such as hospitals and almshouses. Preobrazhenskoe and Rogozhskoe became the focus of Old Believer merchant and industrial development for succeeding generations.

In 1819, Tsar Alexander I created a secret committee to study possibilities for rapprochement between moderate Old Believers and the state. Initially, Alexander desired an end to animosity with the Old Belief as part of his "spiritual mobilization" of Russia. Although the committee originally hoped to frame a dialog with the Old Believers, by the end of Alexander's reign it had begun to promote the use of restrictive measures on Old Believer groups across the empire.[7]

Alexander I's ukase of 26 March 1822 recognized the right of Old Believers to exist and to congregate, and it even accepted the flight of priests from the Russian Orthodox church to serve Old Believers. In providing this legal basis for Old Believer communities, imperial policy guaranteed them the breathing room to expand their numbers and, especially, their economic strength as merchants and industrialists. Large Old Believer centers could afford to lend money to their members for little or no interest, sure that this money would find its way back to the communal treasury at the borrower's death. Some Old Believers even bought co-religionists out of serf bondage and brought them to work at Old Believer factories.[8]

Meanwhile, the church itself had softened its attitude about the Old Ritual. In 1800, it created the *edinoverie,* a special arm of the official church that continued to use the old rite. Although initially successful, the edinoverie never swayed the majority of priestly Old Believers and even fewer of the priestless Old Believers who had become convinced that priesthood would be lost until the Second Coming of Christ.[9]

In the wake of the controversial succession of Nicholas I to the Russian throne, Old Believers once more found their legal status eroded. Even by the end of Alexander's reign, the state had already begun again to refer to Old Believers as *raskol'niki* (schismatics). This name had earlier been dropped as too judgmental. As Nicholas worked out a new relationship between church and state, he began to close the Old Believers' places of worship, seize their property, and harrass the faithful. By 1834, the gains made by Old Believers before 1822 had been completely lost.

The policy of the next tsar, Alexander II, toward Old Believers proved much more liberal than that of his father. The era of Great Reforms in jurisprudence and society included a long-standing debate over the old ritualist question, but no substantial policy changes resulted. More significant than legal changes in this period was the laissez-faire attitude of the state toward the Old Believers. Although laws from the Nikolaevan period curtailing Old Believer freedom stayed on the books, the state generally stopped enforcing them. Old Believers again flourished both in Moscow and in the far reaches of the empire. The Russian Orthodox

church remained an adamant opponent of the schism but began to pur-
sue expanded missionary activity to the Old Belief rather than direct persecution.

Alexander II's death and the succession of Alexander III further revised the Old Believers legal status. Study of the old ritualist question increased during the early years of Alexander III's administration and cul-
minated in the law on Old Believers of May 1883.[10] This new law served
as the capstone to imperial policy on the Old Belief until the revolutionary changes of 1905.

Historians have shown mixed reactions to the law and its legacy. Old
Believers made substantial gains in their legal position. They could
legally hold passports and register themselves as Old Believers, though
under a grandfather clause in which persons were classified as Old Believers only if their forebears had been Old Believers. This precluded the
vast majority of old ritualist faithful from registering. One expert claims
that the law "contained a substantial package of measures designed to
ameliorate the very difficult situation under which the Old Believers had
lived."[11] Other historians maintain that the law actually tightened restrictions on Old Believers, since many laws aimed against them previously
had been ignored. Certainly the Old Believers were unable to appreciate
Alexander III as a reformist tsar. Furthermore, his policies, as carried out
by the general procurator of the Holy Synod, C. P. Pobedonostsev,
seemed to limit the rights of the Old Believers whenever possible.[12]

State policy toward religious communities remained generally static
through the early reign of Nicholas II but reversed itself during the revolution of 1905. At that time, against the wishes of the Russian Orthodox
church, the emperor granted full toleration of all religious groups
through his edict of 17 April 1905.[13] In the late imperial period, this date
would be celebrated by Old Believers as the beginning of a silver age of
growth and wide public acceptance.[14]

In the ensuing debate over the exact nature of Old Believer rights (better defined by the act of 17 October 1906 on Old Believer and sectarian
communities),[15] the Russian Orthodox church used its substantial influence to sway legislative opinion in the State Council away from laws that
would further erode the church's position vis-à-vis the Old Believers. In
the end, the legislation debated by the Duma and State Council to solidify the edicts of 1905 and 1906 never became law. Instead, it died a slow
and ignominious death in committee, to the chagrin of Old Believers and
to the delight of conservative forces in the established church.[16]

Although the changes that swept over Russia between 1905 and 1907
managed to redefine the state's attitude toward Old Believers, the conservative backlash (especially after 1909) served to remind them that
their brand of Russian Orthodoxy would never be accepted on the same
level as that of the established, state-sponsored church. While the acts

freeing the Old Belief were not rescinded, adherents of the old ritual did experience a significant erosion of their political position. Even as Minister of Internal Affairs P. A. Stolypin championed freedom of conscience (including freedom for secular marriages and intermarriage), the drive to regularize such matters declined with his loss of influence. On the marriage issue, as on many other issues, secular and sacred matters intertwined and Russian Orthodox church leaders demanded that the government keep out of what they believed to be religious questions.

A group of wealthy industrialists, headed by P. P. Riabushinskii, led the short-lived Old Believer foray into national politics. The Riabushinskii circle actively pursued a liberal political agenda that sought to marry the entrepreneurial spirit of Old Believer industrialists with the Old Believer traditions of self-governance and reliance on Russian tradition. The circle (also known ironically as Neo-Old Believers) hoped that it could forge a different kind of Russian society, based on pre-Petrine religious and social traditions, while also participating in the new roles necessary for twentieth-century modernization.

Riabushinskii backed the passage of the ill-fated Old Believer bill and, with his co-religionist industrialists in Moscow, supported liberal (especially "Progressive") politicians in the Duma. Specifically, Riabushinskii used his daily newspaper *Morning of Russia (Utro Rossii)* to urge "its readership to unify their efforts, and to join the political battle on the side of moderate forces in order to save Russia from the 'Reds,' who invited anarchy, and the 'Blacks,' who wished to restore the old order."[17] This was an extreme example of Old Believer political consciousness—the vast number of Old Believer groups did not take an active part in Duma affairs.

Population of the Old Believers

No one knows how many Old Believers lived in Russia. The first census of the empire, called for by Peter I, convinced Old Believers that to be counted was tantamount to being enrolled in the books of Antichrist.[18] On a more down-to-earth level, Old Believers realized that being counted made them subject to the double poll tax. Thus, Old Believers rarely cooperated with imperial authorities during census enumerations. The Old Believers could easily hide from the authorities simply by calling themselves members of the Russian Orthodox church, especially if they had bribed the local priest to enroll them on parish registers.

By the middle of the nineteenth century, it had become clear that the census system did not nearly approximate the true number of Old Believers, and officials began to worry that the Old Belief was experiencing rapid growth. Both governmental and scholarly interest then turned to counting Old Believers in Russia. The central problem was to discover

what proportion of the true adherents of the old faith were actually registered with the government and what proportion remained more or less
secretly affiliated with the old rite.

P. Mel'nikov's article in the *Russian Messenger (Russkii vestnik)* provided a major contribution to this topic.[19] Beginning with the first census
of Old Believers, Mel'nikov traced the history of Old Believer enumeration into the reign of Nicholas I. Mel'nikov pointed out that official estimates of Old Believers, made annually between 1826 and 1864, ranged
from approximately 800,000 to 1,000,000 souls but showed no significant
increase over successive generations.[20] Mel'nikov demonstrated, to the
contrary, that the Old Belief had in fact strengthened rather than stag-
nated.

A number of independent statistical expeditions during the mid-nineteenth century corroborated the opinion that Old Believers existed in
much larger numbers than those appearing in official documents. Although the expeditions only studied the population of a few provinces,
their findings could hardly have been more dramatic. Whenever independent researchers took a rough census, thousands of peasants and
townspeople declared themselves Old Believers. In Nizhnii Novgorod
the expeditions found the highest discrepancy between official and independent censuses. Official censuses had counted 20,246 Old Believers of
both genders; the independent expedition put the number at about
172,500. Other expeditions reported somewhat less mammoth differences, but all the independently done censuses resulted in higher
figures.[21] Most important, these expeditions concluded that a far higher
percentage of the total population held to the Old Belief than was ever
imagined by imperial authorities.

Mel'nikov based his article on a number of published reports from
this period, the best being A. von Bushen's *Statistical Tables of the Russian
Empire (Statisticheskiie tablitsy Rossiiskoi imperii)*. Although von Bushen included the state's counting of Old Believers in his tables, he also explained the impossibility of the official system's reckoning the numerical
strength of the Old Belief.[22] Tax codes made counting Old Believers even
more difficult. Simple economics dictated that Old Believers would regularly discount the number of men in a community during a census, because the male head of household had to pay the double poll tax. Female
Old Believers did not incur this levy and thus did not have to be hidden
from official counting to such an extent.[23] The question of numerical
strength in relation to gender remains sketchy at best.[24]

Given the paucity of reliable empirical data, scholars had to use other
methods to estimate the number of Old Believers in the empire. The most
promising new technique surveyed records of the established Orthodox
church. Many Old Believers, after bribing clergymen, or through some
other means, managed to place themselves on parish birth registers.

Scholars argued, however, that such Old Believers would never participate in the Eucharist of the established church. Von Bushen, for example,
added together three categories of religionists: (1) known Old Believers,
(2) registered Orthodox who confessed their sins but did not take communion (an irregular practice among Orthodox), (3) registered Orthodox
who had not confessed their sins. Von Bushen claimed that the sum of
these three groups represented the number of probable Old Believers
and showed that this came to 10 percent of the empire's total population,
or roughly one-sixth of all Orthodox![25] An exceedingly rough estimate
that did not take into account other factors (such as lay dissatisfaction
with the church), this assessment did correspond far better to the figures
gathered by statistical expeditions than to those yielded by official censuses.[26] Notwithstanding its questionable methodology, von Bushen's estimate has survived as the best guess, and the figure of 10 percent of the
total population has been regarded as authoritative up to the present
time.

Perhaps more important than any objective enumeration, however,
was the belief by bureaucrats, Russian Orthodox church officials, and regional administrators that the Old Belief had grown dramatically from
the mid-nineteenth century onward. In response to the pressure of independent statistical studies and the climate of the Great Reforms, official
census numbers of Old Believers rose rapidly during Alexander II's reign
and later. What remains unclear is whether the actual number of Old Believers grew or if counting techniques advanced. The relaxation of Old
Believer laws in 1883 and the creation of more modern counting methods
probably helped to make the 1897 census the most accurate ever taken of
Old Believers up to that date, but its Old Believer total of less than 2 percent of the population remained unconvincingly low.[27]

Although they debated the exact number of Old Believers and their
perceived influence in Russian society, scholars agreed that the geographic centers of the Old Belief gravitated to the outskirts of the empire.
These centers seemed to grow up as far away as possible from state and
ecclesiastical authority—except in Moscow, where Old Believers retained
large and prosperous communities. The Vyg monastic complex exemplified this geographical phenomenon, providing spiritual leadership from
the most remote part of European Russia, far in the north country. As
early as 1863, von Bushen noted that in most, if not all, of the empire's
border provinces the population was approximately 10 percent Old Believer. His estimate was at least ten times that of official data of the period.[28]

While lacking numerical data, impressionistic evidence concurs with
von Bushen's assessment of Old Believer strength in the borderlands.
One missionary priest, D. Alexandrov, claimed that "all of Siberia is in
the hands of the [priestly Old Believers] and the Baptists."[29] An article in

the Orthodox religious journal *The Wanderer (Strannik)* described three areas of particular Old Believer strength. These formed a band of provinces along the eastern border of European Russia, spreading from Nizhnii Novgorod and Viatka in the north, then circling south and through the Urals and west into the Don oblast'. (Apparently the far north—Olonets, Arkhangelsk, and Vologda—was not considered statistically important because it was so little populated.) The article noted areas of Siberia with a particularly high Old Believer population, especially Tomsk, Tobolsk, and Irkutsk.[30] Other sources claimed an even more dramatic influence of the Old Belief in these provinces. The 1890–1891 report of the general procurator of the Holy Synod claimed, for example, that up to two-thirds of the Perm diocese was Old Believer. Less than a decade later, however, the official census enumerated only 7.17 percent of Perm residents as registered Old Believers.[31]

The band of border areas stretching along the eastern edge of European Russia was much less populous than were other parts of the empire. In the far northern provinces and in the Urals there dwelt fewer than five people per square verst—one square verst equals approximately one square kilometer—rising to ten to nineteen people per square verst in the Don oblast'. Siberia, even more remote, had a population density of just .53 persons per square verst and was inhabited by 1 million Old Believers living in almost total independence from outside society. By comparison, some western parts of the empire had a population density of as much as 125–130 persons per square verst.[32]

The question remained whether a specific geographic area had created an environment wherein the Old Belief could thrive or whether the faithful had sought such far-flung locales in order to live better the life of the Old Belief. A nineteenth-century European commentator on the Old Believer phenomenon clearly threw in his lot with the former idea:

> Outward surroundings have great influence, and the predominance of Old Believers in the most distant and less populous districts is not accidental, but is a natural result of the condition of the people who are thus isolated; they have little intercourse with one another, and still less with the outer world; they remain more primitive in their habits, and cling more persistently to ancient customs.[33]

This argument was based primarily on evidence from the priestless Old Believer experience. In areas that rarely saw a clergy member even before the schism, the typical liturgical life was one in which the faithful themselves performed "reader services"—those services that did not need clergy. Accordingly, Old Believers felt predisposed by the very nature of their history to accept an Old Belief without a church hierarchy. As the quotation shows, however, the argument also concluded that rural believers seemed by nature "primitive" compared to their more urbane counterparts.

Old Believers also showed a remarkable inclination for flight and emigration *toward* the borderlands. Not all northern and Siberian peasants inherently loved the Old Belief; rather, Old Believers moved to far-flung provinces and acted as outposts of Russian tradition in areas where the Old Belief could best survive. As one missionary priest put it, "The schism of the old ritual, which caught fire in the center of Rus', reached to its borders."[34]

Even in the post-1905 period, evidence suggested that the emigration of Old Believers remained strong. One magazine noted, for example, that many co-religionists were moving away from the Siberian province of Tomsk to

> the very backwoods of the forest . . . [where] they are concerned with farming, cattle-breeding, hunting and nut production. In the past year up to three thousand have migrated from various parts of Tomsk province. The motive for migration is a higher standard of morals.[35]

This article brought up yet another reason for Old Believer out-migration: distrust of the moral climate in urbanized Russia. Indeed, many Old Believers apparently were not fleeing persecution by the state so much as the climate of permissiveness, disorder, and lack of religious piety that they encountered in densely populated areas.

Old Believers emigrated not only to remote districts but also to more populous areas where the Russian Orthodox church held little influence. Some old ritualists followed the partitions of Poland westward, settling in the rural provinces of Suwałki and Masuria, and, in another direction, as far away as Turkey and Austria. While the repatriation of such emigré Old Believers became a topic of discussion after 1905,[36] it seems that flight from the centers of the empire never stopped completely. Not only did the farthest reaches of Siberia receive Old Believers but so did the United States and Canada, giving credence to the theory that many Old Believers really preferred to move away from central Russia. Emigration also led to the popular conception of Old Believers as pioneers of the Russian wilderness.[37]

Differences of opinion clearly arose between Old Believers from remote areas and those living in more populous parts of Russia. In general, Old Believers from both the far northern Russia and Siberia struggled, in the late imperial period, to maintain a more monastic and segregated posture than that of their central or western counterparts. According to some observers, Siberian Old Believers acted in such a fanatic manner that they were considered members of an "extremist religion."[38]

Such comments, while giving an impression of Old Believer attitudes, shed little light on the intricacy and variation to be found among Old Believer communities in various geographic areas. The geographical aspect of the Old Belief must remain a constant part of the discussion of the religious characteristics of this society. As Old Believers themselves wrestled to define the ancient piety, the more cosmopolitan faithful tended to accept interaction with forces of modernity, while the rural Old Believers tended to view innovation as an encroachment on the ancient piety.

Old Believer Organizational Structures

Although the history of various Old Believer groups has received substantial treatment by nineteenth- and twentieth-century scholars, there exists little or no analysis of how Old Believer groups defined themselves and their relation to the world in the final years of the last Russian dynasty. After the revolutionary year of 1905, each group had to decide how to respond to its new status as a completely legal entity. For the first time, the imperial government was not engaging in persecution of the old ritualists. How did the faithful respond?

Old Believers maintained a dizzying variation of opinion, including a whole spectrum of views on the sacraments (fig. 1). Half-schismatics (polu-raskol'niki), for example, accepted some Russian Orthodox sacramental life but prayed regularly only with other half-Old Believers. Typically, such half-Old Believers received baptism and marriage in the Russian Orthodox church yet declined regular attendance there. Instead, they held their own services according to the old ritual and buried their dead with the prayers of the community, led by lay men and women. Such old ritualists believed that accepting Russian Orthodox sacraments constituted a necessary evil but felt that a believer should die within the bosom of the old rite.

One little-known concord, for example, was the Chashnye (Cellarers), who received sacraments from the Russian Orthodox church, but then celebrated abbreviated services elsewhere, usually in the cellar of someone's home.[39] Many such half-Old Believers never openly aligned themselves with any specific concord but instead maintained a secret allegiance to the Old Belief. Although scores of small, locally formed groups sprang up, they tended to wither and die, leaving few traces of their history. There were literally scores of concords.

Next came the priestly Old Believers (popovtsy). All of them, at some point in their history, accepted clergy from new-rite sources. These priestly Old Believers included the Belokrinitsy and the beglopopovtsy (fugitive-priestly), who accepted clergy consecrated in the state-sponsored church.

Furthest from the church were the priestless old ritualists—the Pomortsy, Fedoseevtsy, Filippovtsy, and Spasovtsy—all of whom firmly

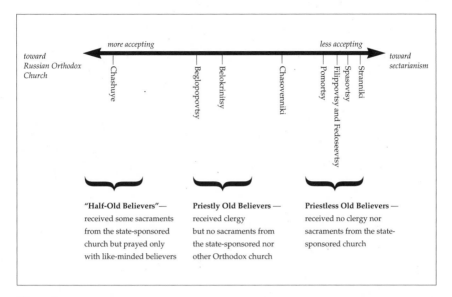

Figure 1 Acceptance of Russian Orthodox Church Sacramental Life by Old Believers

believed that the sacramental life had been taken up into heaven, just as Elijah had ridden his fiery chariot away from a sinful world only to return in the last days. These Old Believers, at the most extreme end of the scale, tended to reject accommodation with the state and with other forces of modernity, while Old Believers most willing to accept Orthodoxy's Holy Mysteries had a tendency to interact with outside society and to tolerate prospects for change. This tendency, however, should not be overrated. Many priestless Old Believers, for example, were able to meet with local Russian society more easily than were some of their priestly brethren.

Local Initiative, Local Organization

In broad terms, Old Believer communities on the local level were organized according to similar patterns, regardless of concord. Contrasting themselves with the centralized model of parish life found in the Russian Orthodox church, old ritualists prided themselves on their local and autonomous system of governance. Clergy (priests, preceptors, and abbots) usually came from within the community, or from one nearby, and all members of the concord elected the group's clerical leadership.[40] Likewise, the community as a whole discussed and voted on major questions of religious importance.

Democratic management of religious affairs found precedent in both

the autonomous organization of pre-Nikonian parishes and in the
monastic rule maintained at the Solovetskii monastery in Russia's extreme north. This monastery, a dramatic holdout against the Russian Orthodox church, saw its continued expression in the Vyg and Leksa
monastic settlements that, in turn, established the Pomortsy concord.
One American historian has claimed that Vyg was

> anti-Western, anti-militarist, and anti-expansionist. It provided communal
> ownership of property, collective labor, and mutual aid in a religious sur-
> rounding, far from the center of state power. . . . It was also hierarchical
> and regimented: discipline, obedience, loyalty, and chastity were required
> (though the last did not always hold up).[41]

Vyg regarded itself as a conservator of the Solovetskii tradition rather
than as an heir to a northern Russian peasant democratic or communitarian tendency, a view put forth by Russian populist historians.[42] In the
context of lay participation, however, the result was the same. Old Believer history provided a model for organization that paired staunch ritual traditionalism with loose and sometimes fluid organizational structure. The core of Vyg lay in the spiritual leadership of an old ritualist
priest, preceptor, or abbot and included a council of community elders as
well as regular participation by all community members.[43] Rather than
being an innovative form of community organization, these Old Believers claimed that their way most nearly reproduced the parish structure
of pre-Petrine Russia.[44]

Localized organization of religious life made the Old Belief an increasingly attractive alternative to the centralized and often ponderous structure of the Russian Orthodox church in the late imperial period. The
"community structure of management in religious matters," complained
one Russian Orthodox church bishop, "in which every member of the
community holds the rightful voice in discussion of religious activities"
provided a cornerstone of Old Believer appeal.[45] The bishop also noted
the accessibility of Old Believer clergy to their flocks. Within such communities, lay members could find an engaged religious life, much to the
chagrin of Russian Orthodox church authorities.[46]

Old Believer communities also provided an active role for women,
compared to lay parishes in the Russian Orthodox church. Women
played a particularly strong part in the maintenance and expansion of
the Old Belief. Although final authority rested with the leader of the
men's monastery, the Leksa women's monastery (sister to Vyg) often
provided much more of the wealth and a far larger number of monastics
than did its male counterpart.[47] The historian P. S. Smirnov claimed that
women in Old Believer lay communities retained influence that would

have been lost to them in other segments of Russian society and that they not only helped to keep alive the pre-Petrine way of life *(byt)* but also to proselytize for the Old Belief. Women, according to Smirnov, provided the driving force behind the Old Belief.[48]

Old Believer communities also helped to maintain the physical well-being of their members. Albert F. Heard, an English observer of the Russian church, mentioned that Old Believers were "liberal and charitable, and many of them dispense their wealth freely and generously."[49] The wealth of Old Believer merchants and industrialists has been noted many times, but even the most modest Old Believer communities usually made provisions for mutual aid, rendering their settlements more prosperous-looking than other Russian villages.[50] Old Believers were known for long-standing and distinguished traditions of alms giving and financial support for co-religionists.[51] One report from the Orthodox church sniffed that "unquestionably the most attractive, tempting side of schism consists of the material mutual aid among schismatics."[52] Russian Orthodox episcopal authorities even claimed that the Old Believers used material goods to lure poor adherents of the established church, including impoverished pastors, into the arms of the schism. The 1913 general procurator's report illustrated both the practice of Old Believer self-help and the suspicious reaction of the church:

> Thanks to the support of the wealthy . . . and the strong development of old ritualist mutual aid, [Old Believers] live, in material terms, incomparably better than the Orthodox. "In mixed villages, for example," observes the bishop of Pskov in his report, "without much difficulty it is possible to distinguish the homes where old ritualists live and where the Orthodox [live]. This material support, from which the old ritualists profit through the wealth of their co-religionists, compels them, although without an interior sympathy which is sometimes highly remarkable, to hold on to their error. Their mutual assistance provides not a small temptation, and for the poor Orthodox who, seeing that all old ritualists live well and in prosperity, automatically arrive at the thought that the very old ritualist faith itself must be true, if the Lord helps the old ritualists to live well and without poverty.[53]

The long-standing Old Believer commitment to mutual aid thus provided a way to trumpet the superiority of the Old Believer community over the Russian Orthodox parish.

Old Believer industrialists were also widely reported to give preferential treatment, good benefits, and high pay for co-religionists working at their factories. Russian Orthodox officials attributed such employment practices not to selfless aid but to the crafty manipulation of workers.

They were undoubtedly right in some instances—the mammoth Ri-abushinskii and Morozov industrial firms sought out Old Believers they could trust to create a loyal work force.

Among some Old Believers in the late imperial period, concern gradu-ally arose over new, voguish forms that mutual aid might take. Charity began to move beyond the borders of the local community as Old Be-liever magazines appealed for aid to impoverished brothers and sisters both in Russia and in the diaspora.[54] In response, some Old Believers be-gan to change their attitudes about mutual aid. These people believed that increasing urbanization and the breakdown of closely knit rural vil-lages mandated new types of mutual aid, especially the creation of for-mal mutual-aid societies.[55] Such societies would follow the model of credit-seeking financial cooperatives (already in place for years at the Moscow Old Believer centers) and would augment more traditional methods of mutual aid. Some even envisioned a nationwide network of Old Believer self-help organizations.[56] New forms of philanthropy also enabled cosmopolitan Old Believers to interact with other social groups toward a general social revival. While interest in philanthropy and coop-erative ventures abounded in all facets of the populace during this pe-riod, Old Believers distinguished themselves by their highly developed sense of mutual aid, strengthened by years of necessity under imperial repression.

Other Old Believers worried that national organizations would ruin the personal nature of their mutual aid. Charity toward co-religionists bonded believers, they argued. Large organizations would break apart this relationship. Charity did not develop from pride or haughtiness on the part of the giver but was personal and direct. "The gospel's idea of charity," wrote one author, was "as a donation, coming from the heart, imbued by love for those who are nearby, or for the good of the charita-ble act [itself]."[57] Thus, Old Believers risked losing the very foundations and strengths of their mutual aid through the growth of impersonal charitable functions and organizations. These new arrangements also en-dangered the faithful by attempting to mix charity with merrymaking, for Old Believers had begun to "create public events, balls, dancing evenings, lotteries, outdoor parties, etc., with charitable goals. Who then takes the liberty to designate all of this as Christian good work?"[58] Adding pleasure seeking to philanthropy, the author believed, led Old Believers away from communal prayer in search of secular gatherings. Rather than a novel way to do good, such activities threatened the fabric of communitarian life. It was better to help fellow Old Believers within one's own community, quietly and humbly.[59]

As shown in the mutual-aid issue, there was some tension between lo-cal and centralizing forces in the Old Believer concords. Old Believers had convened irregularly in periods of lax state persecution.[60] After the Act of

Toleration of 1905, however, all Old Believer groups gathered regularly and openly. There was, in fact, an explosion of local, regional, and national Old Believer conferences, the vast number of which have yet to be studied. At the highest level, Old Believers maintained the tradition of these national meetings *(s"ezdy)* and spiritual councils *(sobory)* that had been lost in the Russian Orthodox church through much of the synodal period.[61] These conferences will be discussed in the context of each concord.

Priestly Old Believers *(Popovtsy)*: The Beglopopovtsy and Belokrinitsy

The Old Believer movement began very early to suffer the consequences of losing its old ritualist priesthood. One group decided that the only way to preserve a sacramental life was to invite fugitive priests, already consecrated by the Russian Orthodox church. The Old Believers would anoint them and welcome them back to the old rite. This group, known as the beglopopovtsy (fugitive-priestly) Old Believers, tried to balance the prospect of having to consort with Russian Orthodoxy against the likelihood of losing clergy.[62]

The fugitive-priestly concord provided a link between the Russian Orthodox church and the Old Believers. This concord tended to differentiate between the concepts of ritual and dogma more than other Old Believer groups did because it accepted the *dogmatic* canonicity of the Russian Orthodox church while rejecting its *ritual* formations. Fugitive-priestly Old Believers claimed that false teachings by Nikonian Russian Orthodoxy did not undermine the church's status as Orthodox. They realized, however, that the Russian Orthodox church was an imperfect system and refused to receive a full hierarchy from it, accepting none over the rank of priest.[63]

For its first 150 years, the fugitive-priestly group was a dominant force among Old Believers. Though less popular in the hinterlands of far northern Russia and Siberia, fugitive-priestly Old Believers commanded a large following in central Russia, where the faithful desired a complete sacramental life and where they could find a constant stream of refugee priests from the dominant church. For the beglopopovtsy, the need to celebrate the Holy Mysteries overpowered any lingering suspicions of the Russian Orthodox church.[64]

Early in the nineteenth century, a number of events overwhelmed the fugitive-priestly movement. In 1800 came the creation by the Russian Orthodox church of the institution of *edinoverie* (unified faith) to lure Old Believers back to the fold.[65] The *edinovertsy* (those who practiced the unified faith) were to celebrate the old ritual under the auspices of the Russian Orthodox church. They were thus united to the Nikonian church and made subservient to the Holy Synod created by Peter I. While tacitly accepting the old ritual through the edinoverie, the Russian Orthodox

church itself nevertheless retained a policy of anathema toward followers of the old rite. Even so, edinoverie tempted many priestly old ritualists back to the church by approximating the Old Belief and granting the
legal rights associated with membership in the Russian Orthodox
church.

About forty years after the creation of edinoverie, the fugitive-priestly
faithful suffered another setback. A policy of generally lenient treatment,
from Paul I through Alexander I, was followed by renewed persecution
of Old Believers under Nicholas I. Previously, priests had feared little
reprisal for abandoning the Orthodox church, but during Nicholas's
reign, pressure from both state and church increased, practically stop-
ping the flow of clergy to the Old Belief.

By the end of the imperial period, fugitive-priestly Old Believers
found themselves depleted both in numbers and influence. Their theological proximity to the edinovertsy also made them a target for missionaries. Since the fugitive-priestly concords received priests from the Russian Orthodox church, the edinovertsy asked them why they could not
simply rejoin the church. The fugitive-priestly countered with three arguments: (1) Old Believers could never accept the synodal arrangement
of the Russian church; (2) the Russian Orthodox church *as a whole* had
broken with the old rite (and continued to maintain a policy of anathema
toward them); and (3) fugitive-priestly groups wanted to receive only the
lowest-ranking priests, not those who had begun to rise within an apostate synod. Finally, the beglopopovtsy reminded the edinovertsy that, far
from embracing the old rite, many edinovertsy churches had compromised themselves by deviating from that rite.[66]

Fugitive-priestly groups, like all Old Believer organizations, took advantage of the Act of Toleration of 1905 to convene many conferences.
Although they did not have strong representation in Siberia,[67] their conferences—held in cities stretching from the Don River all the way to
Nizhnii Novgorod—showed that the movement still commanded the allegiance of Old Believers located across European Russia. Some fugitive-
priestly Old Believers had emigrated as far as Turkey; 800 of them returned to Russia between 1910 and 1912.[68]

These Old Believers understood that their religious way of life was
imperiled. Conferences had met even before 1905, and the leadership
hoped to avoid the chaotic nature of those previous events.[69] As more
than 200 delegates attended the group's first all-Russian conference in
1908, members candidly admitted the problems facing their concord.[70]
Specifically, the 1908 conference hoped to resolve questions on "the life
and death of our church," the consolidation of Christians into legal communities, the creation of an all-Russian fugitive-priestly brotherhood,
and the search for a Russian bishop.

The search for a hierarchy consumed most of the energy of the confer-

ees. In both their 1908 and 1912 meetings, some delegates declared that
the fugitive-priestly should receive a bishop only from within the Russian church. Other delegates thought that the beglopopovtsy should wait
until God gave them a hierarchy and that the current moment—notwithstanding the new freedoms—was perhaps not the correct time. Many beglopopovtsy hoped that a Russian old ritualist hierarchy could someday
unite all Old Believers.[71] When the beglopopovtsy met again in 1912,
they continued to debate the possibility of alignment with other Old Believers.

. . .

Development of the Belokrinitsa Old Believer hierarchy dealt the
hardest blow to the fugitive-priestly movement. In creating a church
complete with full episcopal hierarchy and complete sacramental life, the
Belokrinitsy allowed Old Believers to retain their ideology and identity
without obligation to the Synodal church. Known also as the Austrian
Hierarchy, the Belokrinitsy dated from 1846 when the Bosnian bishop
Amvrosii agreed to lead an Old Ritualist diocese at the fugitive-priestly
monastery of Belaia Krinitsa, Bukovina, in the Austrian Empire. With a
bishop in place, the Belokrinitsy (as they became known) consecrated
priests and no longer needed fugitive clergy.

Questions inevitably arose about the canonicity and acceptability of
the Belokrinitsa hierarchy, especially Amvrosii's unassisted consecration
of other bishops. This practice broke the canon law that called for two
bishops to bless a third. Although the Belokrinitsy pointed out the emer-
gency nature of the practice, other Old Believers decided to continue taking fugitive priests rather than invest their souls in questionable canonical practices. Bishop Amvrosii's background as a deposed (but not
defrocked) hierarch of a non-Russian church made him suspect in the
minds of many old ritualists, who only trusted in the sanctity of the Russian tradition. With the help of the large priestly Rogozhskoe center in
Moscow and the aid of wealthy Old Believer industrialists, the Belokrinitsy, nevertheless, became the single largest organization among
Old Believers.[72] They spread throughout the empire, creating dioceses all
the way from the western provinces to the Russian Far East.[73]

Having established a hierarchy, the Belokrinitsy needed to decide
how much independent authority to accord the laity at the local level
and how much to reserve for a central hierarchy. Such a decision was
necessary because the wording of the Act of Toleration of 1905 specified
that communities themselves should select their own pastors. The matter
of selecting a pastor lay at the heart of a major difference between the
Old Believers and the Russian Orthodox church. The issue related both
to the election of and to the removal of priests from a community, whenever such an action became necessary.[74]

The Belokrinitsa hierarchy had earlier split over another matter. On

one side, the *okruzhniki*—named after the "Okruzhnoe Poslanie"
eparchial letter of 1862—rejected the idea that Antichrist reigned in Russia. The okruzhniki, led by the Brotherhood of the Honorable Cross in
Moscow, had become the most numerous Belokrinitsy by 1905. Not only
did they desire a major role for the laity in church matters, they also ap-
proved of ties between Old Believers and society. The more conservative
Belokrinitsy were called *protivookruzhniki*—those against the circular-
ists.[75] Although a minority, the protivookruzhniki maintained a
formidable presence, having at least two bishops in their midst. One of
their conferences included more than 100 delegates and many monks.
They resisted any attempts to lure them back to the larger okruzhnik
group.[76]

The Belokrinitsa conferences of okruzhniki, dating from the turn of
the century, became the best known of Old Believer gatherings. By the
time the emperor decreed the act of toleration, the Belokrinitsy had already begun meeting in annual all-Russian conferences.[77] These conferences, in tandem with regional eparchial meetings, covered matters of
political, financial, educational, and spiritual concerns. In the period between all-Russian conferences, a spiritual council met regularly to pass
judgment on interim measures. The council consisted of an equal number of clergy and lay members.

Recent Priestless Old Believers: The Chasovenniki

Chasovenniki existed somewhere between the poles of priestly and
priestless Old Belief. They did not celebrate a full sacramental life but
differentiated themselves from priestless groups in their view of the
clergy. While most priestless Old Believers claimed the apostolic succession (the laying of hands begun by Christ and passed through the apostles to all bishops) had been cut off forever, the Chasovenniki believed
that clergy were simply not accessible to them. This led them to a constant search for a hierarchy, a task that other priestless Old Believers
thought useless.

Chasovennik historiography, like that of other Old Believer concords,
has been colored by the folklore of the group itself. During the period of
tolerance in the eighteenth and early nineteenth centuries, Old Believers
who later became Chasovenniki remained part of the fugitive-priestly
mainstream, accepting priests from the dominant church. According to
Chasovennik oral tradition, it was not the crackdown under Nicholas I
that caused the loss of their priests. Instead, it was the distrust felt by the
Chasovenniki toward the orthodoxy of priests who had fallen under
western influence. Without a source of clergy, the Chasovennik concord
became a de facto priestless Old Believer group.[78] The loss of priesthood
occurred over a long period of years and across a wide geographical

area, concentrated in Siberia and the region of the Ural Mountains.

Observers from the established church scoffed at the Chasovennik idea of a "lost" old ritualist hierarchy, and they tended to popularize bizarre legends attributed to these Old Believers. One such story recounted the existence of a certain "Miletius . . . patriarch of Africa, America and Terra-firma, and of Paraguay, and of Zelli-Khil, and of Magellan's land, on Patagonia, and of Brazil and Abasnia."[79] Another claimed that Meletius was instead "patriarch of Slavo-Belovodskii, Ost-Indeiskii, Fest-Indeiskii, Iust-Indeiskii i Anglo-Indeiskii and the Japanese islands."[80] Although they sounded outrageous, such legends seemed plausible to the Old Believers who themselves lived on the distant fringes of the empire.[81] Even if these fanciful reports contained only a grain of the Chasovennik legend, they showed how much the faithful desired an untainted hierarchy.

Chasovennik Old Believers created a rather loose confederation after the Act of Toleration of 1905. Their uncertain past—neither priestly nor priestless—had provided little chance for their communities to bond through shared ideology and world view. Chasovenniki distrusted clergy, sacraments, the Antichrist, and relations with the outside world. The shared traditions, viewpoints, and assumptions that unified other Old Believer groups were thus rather weak among Chasovenniki. In one regional conference, for example, a delegate claimed that it was necessary

> through baptism to refute Satan, even if the baptism is performed by a layman; [that] the church must exist on earth until Judgement Day, and that the priesthood in the church of Christ must be eternal, because without the clergy there can be no Christianity, and, in conclusion . . . [that] the last antichrist has not arrived and does not rule.[82]

Another delegate doubted the earlier speaker's optimistic theory: "If the antichrist does not now rule," he replied, "then in all of our beliefs we were mistaken up to this time."[83] The dispute over Antichrist led to other splits as well. In one locale, some people taught that the rule of Antichrist precluded any sacraments, and they began to baptize themselves. Others from the same group decided that Antichrist had not yet arrived and tried to find fugitive priests or to subside on "spare gifts"—elements of the Eucharist that had been passed on and watered down for generations.[84]

While most Chasovenniki were hoping for a new priesthood to celebrate the sacraments, others went out and actively looked for it. Some Chasovenniki maintained a close dialogue with the Belokrinitsa hierarchy; certain brothers Serebennikov were even "caught in the net of the devil" and taught their community that salvation was impossible without a sanctified priesthood.[85] One Russian Orthodox church missionary said that ten thousand Chasovenniki had prepared to become edinovertsy in 1912, but a leading figure among the Chasovenniki disputed any such claim.[86]

During the late imperial period, the Chasovenniki went through the same debate that priestless Old Believers had argued two hundred years before. While priestless concords had used the intervening centuries to create a stable ideology and world view, the Chasovenniki still faced the task of defining their place as priestly, priestless, or, perhaps, neither of the two. The process of self-definition among the Chasovenniki took place, however, in an atmosphere quite different from that of earlier Old Believer development. Schism and state persecution had been fresh in the minds of the older priestless groups. The Chasovenniki, on the contrary, lost their clergy long after the original schism, in a period of less persecution but more secular pressure. To their advantage, after 1905 the Chasovenniki had legal freedom of religion and assembly in which to develop their own tenets. Such freedoms, coupled with advances in communication, allowed communities of Chasovenniki to interact more easily than ever before. In the most basic sense, the years from 1905 to 1917 gave the Chasovenniki a chance to cement bonds of community that had been tenuous during their first generation.

Local organization of Chasovenniki in Siberia followed the pattern already described. Lack of intercommunication over vast distances complicated an already muddled theological and ideological situation, so communities among the Chasovenniki became far more independent than did those among other Old Believer groups. In their other stronghold— the Ural Mountains—Chasovennik faithful tended to organize themselves around the industrial works that employed them. Their journal *Ural Old Believer (Ural'skii staroobriadets)* regularly published articles about Old Believer activity at many of the Ural factories.[87]

The Chasovenniki convened conferences to discuss the same themes deliberated by other priestless groups. On a national scale, the single all-Russian Chasovennik congress in Ekaterinburg put religious, not political, affairs at the top of the agenda. Conferees talked about how to find a unity "in the spirit of the faith" among Chasovenniki as well as how to find some common agreement on the sacraments, especially baptism, marriage, and communion.[88]

Priestless Old Believers (Bespopovtsy)
The Pomortsy, Filippovtsy, Fedoseevtsy, Spasovtsy, and Others

When Old Believers realized at the end of the seventeenth century that they had no consecrated hierarchy, many faithful concluded that they were doomed to live in a sacramental desert. For those who became priestless Old Believers, the only rational decision following the death of priests was to forgo the Holy Mysteries. On the most mundane level, priestless Old Believers often lived in or had fled to the very outskirts of the Russian empire. (Rural believers had only rarely seen a priest even before the schism.) Furthermore, priestless Old Believers considered the Russian church tainted by Nikon's reforms and by its damnation of the old ritual. In addition, the church's hands were stained with the blood of Old Believer martyrs. From such hands, who could accept the Body and Blood of Christ?

Largest and most historically significant of the priestless concords, the Pomortsy (Those Along the Sea) may have been the prototypical priestless Old Believers. They traced their roots to the Vyg monastic community, and their name recalled the area around the lakes of the Russian Far North, especially Saro Ozero (Lake Saro).[89] The Vyg monastic community's predominance among priestless Old Believer settlements and monasteries stemmed both from the teachings of Vyg leaders and from the success of the Vyg community during the eighteenth and nineteenth centuries. As part of the priestless segment of Old Believers, the Pomortsy believed that the apostolic succession had been jeopardized through the apostasy of the Russian Orthodox church after the schism of 1654–1666. The Pomortsy concluded that the priesthood was lost not only among Old Believers but also within the Orthodox church.

As monastics, early fathers and mothers of the Vyg community taught that marriage was no longer advisable for Old Believers after the schism. The Vyg position on marriage, however, was never as adamant as that of other Old Believer leaders, and during the course of the nineteenth century a quasi-canonical marriage ceremony developed among the Pomortsy.[90] This gave them a real advantage over the priestless groups that adamantly proscribed marriage and it led to the Pomortsy's predominance by the twentieth century. In fact, within one generation of the acceptance of marriage, enough lore had already sprung up about the history of the marriage institution that some Pomortsy claimed it had always been acceptable.[91]

The Pomortsy followed the general model of Old Believer organization outlined above. With freedom of religion and association granted in 1905, the Pomortsy began to build a centralized structure to handle problems between communities; to maintain discipline over preceptors and abbots; and to take up issues of general religious importance, including the education of Old Believers throughout the empire. Pomortsy met occasionally during the nineteenth century and began to convene regional conferences as early as 1905. The first Pomortsy all-Russian congress of 1909 established a national organization.[92] Although participation in this congress and its ruling council was voluntary, the aim was to centralize Pomortsy into a single body. The congress *(sobor)* created another eighteen-member body, namely the spiritual commission and court, to handle discipline and protocol, as well as an eleven-member education commission to consider issues pertaining to Old Believer schools and their curriculum.[93] The eighteen-member council took up important matters in the period between congresses.

Throughout their history the Pomortsy walked a fine line between consorting with antichristian powers, manifested by the state and the Russian Orthodox church, and living within the world dominated by those powers. The problem of prayers for the tsar epitomized the Pomortsy's plight: could one pray for an emperor who drew his lineage from anti-Christian sources such as Peter I? The tension between a desire to cut themselves off from the world while still needing to interact with it provided a catalyst for reoccurring schisms and debates among the Pomortsy. By the late imperial period, the political issue of "giving Caesar his due" through prayers for the emperor had been largely decided: prayers for the tsar were deemed neither heretical nor sinful. Such a posture on the part of the Pomortsy did not translate into general acceptance of the non-Old Believer world. Interaction with the rest of society, while sometimes unavoidable, was fraught with dangers for these priestless Old Believers, who so easily could be led astray from the true faith.

While the Pomortsy accepted diversity of opinion on many issues, some of its members went too far, incurring censure from the congress. A group called *sredniki* (who had appeared in Tambov during the previous century) taught that the Resurrection of Christ had occurred on a Wednesday. This the Pomortsy congress condemned. It also disapproved the recent falsities of one Gregory Tokarev, who was teaching a new sort of iconoclasm. In addition, the sobor disavowed those who venerated only plain crosses (not crucifixes) as well as those who asked elderly women to baptize children.[94] The Pomortsy were adamant: any teaching that compromised traditions of Russian Orthodoxy (as they conceived it) had no part in their concord. The Pomortsy claimed that only *their* twin paths of ritual and belief remained pure. Sectarians who appeared on the local Old Believer scene were treated as deviations from what the Pomortsy believed to be the true faith. The lack of a strong educational system, however, and the decentralized organizational structure of the Pomortsy provided fertile earth for such seeds of dissent. Leaders of the Pomortsy concord hoped to stamp out such heresies through their central congress and through a widespread network of Old Believer schools.[95]

. . .

Both the Filippovtsy and Fedoseevtsy traced their roots to the Pomortsy concord but occupied more radical places on the spectrum of Old Believer ideology. In the early nineteenth century, when the leaders of Vyg acquiesced to the demand of prayers for the emperor, a number of the more extreme faithful (led by a certain monk Filipp) left the Pomortsy. Thus the Filippovtsy resembled the Pomortsy in all ways except in the adamant belief that the state was the handmaiden of Antichrist. While Pomortsy maintained this belief in theory, the Filippovtsy in practice were much more severe. Pomortsy considered the Filippovtsy to be a *tolk* (a "persuasion") rather than a full-blown concord and viewed them as the closest brethren to the Pomortsy themselves. By the turn of the century, Filippovtsy had lost their numerical influence and largely reintigrated themselves into Pomortsy life. They did, however, serve as the guardians of radical priestless views by continuing to reject the influence of both the state and the dominant church.

Like the Filippovtsy, the Fedoseevtsy concord was named after its first important leader, Feodosii Vasil'ev. In the eighteenth century, Vasil'ev, although never breaking completely with Vyg, called for a ritual distance between Old Believers and the world, a break that not even the strictest Vyg leaders had counselled. The Fedoseevtsy and Pomortsy also disagreed on the best representation of the crucifix and other points of liturgical symbolism.[96] Because Vasil'ev and his followers lived geographically separated from Vyg, they eventually grew apart from the Pomortsy.

Views on marriage precipitated the final break between the Fedoseevtsy and the Pomortsy. Although early Fedoseevtsy had actually proposed a more lenient standard for marriage than did their counterparts at Vyg, by the mid-nineteenth century Fedoseevtsy had become quite exacting in the matter of conjugal relationships. Fedoseevtsy leaders "quixotically attempted to force their increasingly secularized parishioners to live as monks."[97] The Fedoseevtsy also strove to maintain a higher degree of psychological and physical separation from the world around them than did their Pomortsy counterparts. The Fedoseevtsy believed that Antichrist ruled the world beyond the Old Belief, leaving all society and its products ritually unclean. For this reason, Fedoseevtsy held a more uncompromising position than did the Pomortsy regarding interaction with society through eating, drinking, carrying passports, and serving in the military.[98]

Nineteenth- and twentieth-century Fedoseevtsy disagreed over the need to compromise their positions regarding marriage, Antichrist, and ritual apartheid. Imperial authorities were shocked when extremist reformers "took over" the movement in 1819 and advocated the complete abrogation of imperial law.[99] Throughout the imperial period, however, the Filippovtsy and Fedoseevtsy agreed in principle on both continued abstinence from marriage and distrust of anti-Christian society. Leaders of the Pomortsy felt the need to explain their own practice to hard-line priestless Old Believers, and they published a lengthy defense in the Pomortsy journal *Shield of Faith (Shchit very)*.[100]

At this point, the situation became confused. Although the Pomortsy and Filippovtsy both had roots at Vyg, it was the Fedoseevtsy (related but independent of Vyg) who decided in the late imperial period to call themselves *Staro-pomortsy* (Old Pomortsy). In apparent answer to this, the Pomortsy then called themselves *zakonobrachnyi*, translated as the "legal-marriage" Pomortsy.[101]

The Fedoseevtsy's greatest contributions to the development of the Old Belief lie in two related areas: the growth of the Preobrazhenskoe cemetery (founded during the reign of Catherine II) and the industrial and financial wealth engendered by its members. Preobrazhenskoe's golden years began with the leadership of I. A. Kovylin, a "very adroit and able manager"[102] as well as a pious interpreter of the Old Belief. Kovylin's work helped all Old Believer concords to win better treatment from the imperial authorities. Through Kovylin's efforts and those of his successors, the Preobrazhenskoe complex became the focal point for Fedoseevtsy everywhere and one of the most well-known Old Believer communities in Russia.

Although the Fedoseevtsy gave one Preobrazhenskoe chapel to the Pomortsy, the cemetery retained its reputation as a Fedoseevtsy center. The Preobrazhenskoe compound and the Fedoseevtsy community in Moscow were, as a whole, tremendously wealthy throughout the late imperial period, due to the tradition of Fedoseevtsy industrialists willing their assets to Preobrazhenskoe after death. The cemetery often gave low-interest loans to Fedoseevtsy, who then built up their own capital, later returning it manyfold to Preobrazhenskoe. In 1912, for example, Preobrazhenskoe held a conference to discuss building on its grounds a 70,000-ruble hospital for Old Believers.[103] Along with chapels and a cemetery, the Fedoseevtsy maintained a printing press, an almshouse, and other institutions for Old Believers.[104]

The Fedoseevtsy gathered in Moscow for a major conference in 1907.[105] Like the Pomortsy, they created a council of representatives comprised of members from the larger congress.[106] The Fedoseevtsy deliberated their relationship with the Pomortsy and asked the latter to do the same. Meetings between the concords occurred throughout the post-1905 period although, notably, they were not called "discussions," considered a codeword for polemical debates. Instead, participants called their talks "conferences," to show the close relationship between Pomortsy and Fedoseevtsy.[107]

Legal toleration gained national recognition for previously obscure Old Believer groups. The Spasovtsy,[108] for example, became known for their complete refusal to accept outside influences and their adamant disapproval of all clerical sacramental life. The group traced its lineage to the late seventeenth century, but its extremist positions and geographical remoteness (especially in Siberia) had left it out of the Old Believer mainstream. The Spasovtsy claimed that all Orthodoxy after Patriarch Nikon was heretical; that the only "Great Pastor Archbishop" was Jesus Christ, whose episcopacy was eternal; and that believers should shun interaction with those of other faiths.[109] Editors of mainstream Old Believer magazines even had to explain the Spasovtsy to their readers, since the group was so little known outside Siberia. Some Old Believers accepted Spasovtsy as their own and publicized the Spasovtsy's fight against coerced burial in Russian Orthodox cemeteries.[110]

Conclusion: Facing a New Era

Patterns of organization created in localized Old Believer communities often duplicated themselves on a national scale. Although Old Believers made every attempt to convene during the nineteenth century, national meetings did not begin to take place regularly until the first all-Russian conference of (Belokrinitsa) old ritualists in 1898. Leaders of that conference disregarded its illegality and correctly believed that the authorities would not intervene since the meeting coincided with an important merchant fair in Nizhnii Novgorod, where many Old Believers would be present.[111] By 1900 the Belokrinitsy felt bold enough to print (by hectograph) official proceedings of their sessions. The conference-and-council structure became the national organizational model for the majority of Old Believers, both priestly and priestless.[112] While the pattern of organization predated the 1905 reforms, the group's new legal status guaranteed the wide participation and interest of countless Old Believers in issues that transcended local or regional problems.

Although Old Believers had become adept at circumventing secular law, they were also willing to take advantage of it when it became possible to do so.[113] After the legal revolution of 1905, Old Believers of all persuasions began to meet openly and frequently. Their conferences—sometimes regional in scope, sometimes national—generally consisted of both lay believers and clergy from a single old ritualist group.[114] Even the Belokrinitsy, who had their own complete hierarchy, invited lay leaders to participate in decision-making bodies. A regional Belokrinitsa conference in August 1913, for example, included twelve bishops, fifty-seven priests, and sixty lay leaders.[115] The conferences of priestless Old Believers had to rely even more heavily on lay participation because they had no canonical priests or bishops. The largest priestless conferences occurred in 1909 and 1912 when hundreds of Pomortsy from throughout the empire gathered in Moscow.[116] The administration of priestless Old Believer concords, however, maintained its voluntary nature. Inasmuch as the priestless organization had no hierarchy, it relied on individual pastors to follow recommendations at the community level.

Conference agendas illustrated the needs of various concords. National Belokrinitsa conferences, for example, regularly revolved around a number of large themes, including the "old ritualist question" before the State Duma, financial concerns of the hierarchy, and the creation of educational possibilities for Old Believers. Priestless Old Believer congresses, to the contrary, focused on the question of ritual, the role of preceptors, and the relations among various priestless groups. The decentralized character of priestless Old Believer organizations necessitated little need for central financial accounting. Finally, as interest in political matters bloomed among the Belokrinitsy leadership, various priestless Old Believer groups remained aloof from interaction with the state.[117]

Regional conferences debated issues that did not appear on the national docket. While national congresses often included erudite representatives of the Old Belief, local conferences gave common believers a chance to speak their minds. For that reason, many of the quasi-religious questions not discussed at the national level heard rancorous debate in regional meetings. These questions included issues such as technological innovation or proper Old Believer clothing. Finally, regional conferences revealed the differing points of view adopted by believers of the same concord who lived in diverse geographic areas. Cossack Pomortsy in southern Russia, for instance, diverged from their Muscovite brethren on community organization and interaction with the state. Indeed, geography sometimes linked the Old Believers of one region more closely with one another than with their co-religionists in distant areas. The Pomortsy and Chasovenniki in Siberia, for example, resembled each other more than they did members of their own concords who lived in European Russia.

Chapter Three

Liturgy *and* Community

Without liturgy there is no Christianity.
—*Old Believer Bishop Mikhail*

 Rituals and symbols of the Old Belief served as important agents of transformation, as they provided an iconic principle to influence the organization and world view of the faithful. The desire of Old Believers to maintain ritual orthodoxy resulted in a unique fusion of religious and social experience. This chapter focuses on the liturgical life of the Old Belief and explains how its system of ritual and symbol (especially the pattern prevailing in the early twentieth century) sought to mold its believers into Christians quite different from their Russian Orthodox counterparts. The chapter will analyze Old Believer traditions, points of view, and assumptions about the relationship between tsar, clergy, and community, as set forth in liturgical life, contrasting the ways of the Old Belief with those of Russian Orthodoxy.

The analysis will not interpret each difference in liturgics between the old and new rites,[1] for missionaries and theologians of the nineteenth century published volumes on this subject.[2] Nor will the chapter note every textual or grammatical change between ancient and reformed texts. Old Believer polemicists of the early schism made it clear that even the reformed books were riddled with inconsistencies and mistakes, just as Nikon had described the pre-1654 texts. Since variation in practice did not become completely enshrined in religious texts of the post-Nikonian period, leaving no standard text, judgments about some specific changes must remain conjecture.

Following the historic reforms of 1905, Old Believers gained an important tool with which to affirm their identity in Russia. For the first time they could legally edit and print their own liturgical texts. Old Believers used this opportunity to publish scores of books—receptacles of the ancient piety—to reaffirm the old rite. Every liturgical work carried the statement that the texts within it were "in all agreement with those [used] during the patriarchate of Joseph, Patriarch of Moscow and all

Russia" (i.e., before Nikon's reforms). This statement proved to the reader that the liturgical language had not been changed and underscored the Old Believers' faith that the liturgy they celebrated had crystallized before the Nikon period. Finally, it demonstrated that the prayers contained in the text had not been recently composed.[3] All prayers published after 1905, however, were not actively used by all Old Believers. Although liturgical texts from the pre-Nikonian period continued to be recopied and reprinted,[4] differences between priestly and priestless religious practices remained.

The Liturgical Imperative

Old Believers took advantage of the Act of Toleration of 1905 to argue that only *their* liturgical life provided an unshakable rudder in a sea of change, revolution, and modernity. One writer explained the need for a consistent liturgical ritual in this way:

> As for ancient Israel, when fire, storms and lightning served as signs for the presence of God on Sinai, so the ritual serves for people—always and everywhere—as a symbol and witness of the reality of the presence and influence of God on people. The Orthodox church believes that every ritual performed in its name has, therefore, some other sanctifying, renewing, and fortifying meaning.[5]

Changes that had occurred in symbol and ritual could not be taken lightly since they represented revisions in the faith itself. The established Orthodox church, according to Old Believers, had lost its birthright by altering the ancient symbols. Polemicists claimed that the Russian Orthodox church continued to denigrate liturgical ritual and symbol, changing them at whim. Old Believers maintained that the twentieth-century Russian church had lost its defense against those who desired to introduce increasingly modern and foreign notions into the faith.[6] Old Believers chastised Russian Orthodoxy for bowing to western-style intellectual or philosophical theology and chided the church for accepting a voguish religion devoid of liturgical rigor.[7] At the same time, old ritualists, too, sometimes fell prey to philosophical questioning:

> At every cross-road [people] shout loudly to the youth about various abstract systematic philosophies, about the freedom of the spirit, free religion, etc. Indeed, it is difficult here for the young old ritualist . . . to think about the rituals—not only to think about, but to perform those [rituals] which are quite difficult. . . . The ritual seems to be smaller, petty, and not of much importance in comparison with various philosophical systems and free religions.[8]

Although buffeted by revolutionary winds, Old Believer leaders taught that the ritual itself provided the method and the path to truth and salvation. Ritual necessitated disciplined behavior that would bond believers into community and save them from individualistic philosophies. Ritual and its rigorous implementation, not some imported philosophy, could instruct Old Believers about political and social interaction.[9] Socially conservative and religiously traditional, old ritualist teachers believed that the repetition, sequence, and discipline of following the old ritual liturgical life would shape a Christian outlook. One writer likened the performer of liturgical ritual to an engineer: the first time he constructs something, he does not know the correct sequence or system to make everything run smoothly; then he finds a system—a ritual—with which to finish his work efficiently and correctly.[10]

The Faithful and the State

The Act of Toleration of 1905 called for some response from Old Believer communities. While the edict neither radicalized nor reconciled these communities to the established regime or church, some change did permeate Old Believer rituals in relation to the state. The Pomortsy, for example, had tried throughout their history to find a balance between interaction with or damnation of the Russian state. By the late imperial period, the Pomortsy had decided that giving Caesar his due through prayers for the emperor was neither sinful nor heretical. This period provided the Pomortsy an opportunity to standardize their liturgical views on the tsar. In 1906 a Pomortsy council confirmed that prayers could be said to recognize the tsar's generosity and to ask for his health. In 1909 the council published an acceptable prayer for the emperor: "Lord save and have mercy on our sovereign tsar."[11] While this form of prayer had historical precedent and the Pomortsy accepted the tsar as temporal ruler, they confined themselves to using *only* these lines, presumably because the tsar needed God's mercy for following the apostasy of Russian Orthodoxy. The congress concluded that a service might be celebrated for the Honorable Cross, following the prayer for the emperor. Although this service contained no explicit reference to temporal authorities, it was a traditional supplication for strength, apparently for the tsar. Even those Pomortsy who subsequently condemned the tsar's edicts recognized an "imperial gift in the exercise of divine services."[12] During World War I, the Pomortsy celebrated a public supplicatory service *(moleben)* for both tsar and people. While this stretched the Pomortsy attitude regarding prayers for the sovereign to a new limit, at no time did the Pomortsy acknowledge imperial power in their regular liturgical services.[13]

Priestly Old Believers retained a rich heritage of prayers for the tsar, but these supplications, like those of the priestless, conferred only minor importance on any outside authority. Both the quantity and the significance of priestly prayers for temporal authorities paled in comparison with those of the Russian Orthodox church. In both Old Belief and Orthodox Great Vespers, for example, all priests and deacons made their way to the west end of the church to chant the *litiia,* a solemn yet flexible set of prayers that contained special requests and memorials, including invocations of important saints as well as prayers for the salvation of both tsar and people. The Old Believer litiia differed from that of the Russian Orthodox church. In the former, the priest prayed for the health, victory, and peace of the tsar, the subjugation of his enemies, and the "mercy and remission of his sins";[14] the Orthodox ceremony, however, made no mention of imperial sin. In this way the old ritual rendered the tsar a human, fallible leader while the Russian Orthodox church portrayed him as a more infallible one. The old ritual litiia remembered only the tsar and did not include prayers for the empress, the emperor's mother, son, or household, as did that of the established church. Old Believers demonstrated a marked lack of interest in the imperial family and the political influence it wielded, and they did not pray for "all Christ-loving armed forces" either, as did the Russian Orthodox church. Finally, the old rite ended the first section of litiia by proclaiming, "We pray for all brothers and all Christians, for health and salvation." Russian Orthodox texts deleted this, effectively leaving the community of believers out of the prayers. The liturgy of the Old Belief thus minimized the importance of secular authority, while Russian Orthodox services reinforced its importance at the expense of the community.

Nor did old ritualists pray for the entire royal household during the litanies of the Eucharistic service.[15] Like the litiia, litanies could be modified to fit specific circumstances. For example, in a 1913 old rite book of the liturgy *(sluzhebnik),* the fourth supplication of the Great Litany read

> For the lord tsar kept by God, the grand prince ___, and for all boyars, and for his troops, let us pray to the Lord.[16]

The same prayer in the established church, however, included the entire imperial household:

> For our pious, autocratic, great lord emperor Nikolai Aleksandrovich of all Russia; for his spouse, the pious lady Aleksandra Feodorovna; for his mother, the pious lady empress Maria Feodorovna, let us pray to the Lord.
>
> For his heir, the pious lord tsarevich and grand prince Alexei Nikolaevich, and all of the tsarist household; for all his Chambers and his military, let us pray to the Lord.[17]

The symbolic importance of the state clearly contrasted with that of the lay believer in the prayers of the Russian Orthodox church. By contrast, Old Believers also retained the use of "lord tsar" and "grand prince" instead of the more exalted "emperor." These were wholesale distinctions, not simply textual deviations.

Liturgically even more important than the litiia, the Great Entry demonstrated the same differentiation between state and people shown in the vesperal service. The Great Entry was a focal point of the liturgy, occurring shortly before communion itself, and for the priestly Old Believers it best defined the relationship between God and his people.[18] In this part of the service, all priests and deacons gathered around the altar while holding the implements of the Eucharist. They then came out of the altar to stand in front of the Royal Doors and faced the congregation. In the old rite, deacon and priest repeated the following prayers, each twice:

> May the Lord God remember all of you in His Kingdom always, now and ever, and unto the ages of ages.
> All of you may the Lord God remember in His Kingdom always, now and ever, and unto the ages of ages.
> May the Lord God remember all of you in His Kingdom always, now and ever, and unto the ages of ages.[19]

In the rite of the Russian Orthodox church these prayers were deleted. Instead, the priest chanted the following:

> May the Lord God remember in His Kingdom our pious, autocratic, great lord of all Russia Emperor Nikolai Aleksandrovich, always, now and ever and unto the ages of ages.
> May the Lord God remember in His kingdom his spouse, the pious Empress Aleksandra Feodorovna, and his mother, the pious lady Empress Maria Feodorovna, always, now and ever and unto the ages of ages.
> May the Lord God remember in His Kingdom the lord tsarevitch and grand prince Aleksei Nikolaevich, and all the tsarist household, always, now and ever, and unto the ages of ages.
> May the Lord God remember in His Kingdom the holy governing synod, and our lord over-priest ___, Metropolitan ___, Archbishop ___, Bishop ___, always, now and ever, and unto the ages of ages.
> All of you Orthodox Christians may the Lord God remember in His Kingdom, always, now and ever and unto the ages of ages.[20]

Rather than being the focus of six prayers, here the faithful were relegated to last place, after the imperial family and the church hierarchy.

During the liturgy of St. Basil, performed only during the Great Lent and on particularly high holidays, the same comparison could be made. The old ritual emphasized the relationship between God and his community, the state-sponsored church elevated external political and spiritual authority over the community.[21]

The symbolism of liturgical change was lost neither on the Old Believers nor on the officials of Russian Orthodoxy. Reporting on a edinoverie conference, an Old Believer journal claimed that "Representatives of the edinoverie complained that as the liturgy was being said among them during the Great Entry, 'it turned out' that instead of 'May the Lord God remember all of you,' edinoverie priests had begun to remember the 'Tsarist House.' The council of edinoverie resolved to reaffirm the old text."[22] The article continued its discussion of the Great Entry by noting that, in 1799, Old Believers had asked the emperor Paul to legalize the Old Believers' acceptance of fugitive priests from the Russian Orthodox church. The metropolitan of Kazan, Amvrosii, seemed willing to agree with this request on condition that the Great Entry be changed. The Old Believers declined.

The Faithful and the Clergy

While Old Believer books and practices left little room for the state in liturgical observance, they did provide for a lively interaction between clergy and faithful during the liturgical cycle. The symbolic "conversation" between segments of the community further provided a paradigm for relations between clergy and laypeople, a practice that had been lost to Russian Orthodoxy by the early twentieth century. Among the Old Believers, for example, priests maintained a symbolic interaction with their congregation through the order of forgiveness (proshchenie). Three times in the regular liturgical cycle—at the end of Compline, Midnight Service, and Hours—the priest of the old rite bowed to his congregation and said:

> Bless me, holy fathers, brothers, and sisters, and forgive me, a sinner, for whatever sins I have committed in all the days of my life, in soul and body, in words and deeds and thoughts, and by all my senses.

The congregation replied, "May God forgive and have mercy on thee." At one point the congregation bowed back to the priest and asked,

> Forgive me, holy father, and bless me, for whatever sins I have committed in all the days of my life. I have sinned immeasurably in soul and body, in sleep and idleness, by demonic darkness, by impure thoughts, by forgetfulness, and by judging. I have sinned in my heart and by all my senses, by hearing and sight, voluntarily and involuntarily; and there is no sin which

I have not committed. But I repent of all of these; forgive me, holy father, and bless me, and pray for me a sinner.[23]

While the prayer for forgiveness of the congregation's sins was longer than for those of the celebrant, the celebrant was first to ask forgiveness from his flock. The placement of the prayer intimated that he, like Christ before him, acted as both servant and judge. One Old Believer writer explained that the priest himself "appeals to all present in the temple with the request to forgive him, who is himself a sinful man."[24] Most important, the order of forgiveness was to be read at significant breaks in the service, either when the community left the church in the evening "as if for death"[25] or when it began the culminating service of the cycle, the liturgy itself. The theory of divine services called for a "general reconciliation with everyone"[26] at these points. One commentator claimed that the order of forgiveness was not a prayer at all, but a mutual act of forgiveness between clergy and laity. When a priest served without any laity present, he asked forgiveness from the holy fathers of the church.[27]

The formal order of forgiveness was lost to priestless Old Believers who, in its stead, often repeated their opening prayers twice—first as an informal order of forgiveness and then actually to start the services.[28] If a member of the community arrived once prayers had begun, the preceptor *(nastavnik)* was sometimes called to repeat the forgiveness bows with the tardy parishioner who was waiting at the back of the chapel.[29] For his part, the preceptor (as well as each member of the community) bowed to the congregation when entering the chapel for divine services.[30] Although unable to maintain the forgiveness ritual performed by a priest, the bespopovtsy realized and approximated it with lay language.

By the late imperial period, the order of forgiveness as it existed among the Old Believers had been lost by the Russian Orthodox. The evolution of instructional material illustrates this loss. Old rite Books of Hours *(Chasovniki)* printed by both priestly and priestless Old Believers prescribed that "the priest says the dismissal *(otpust)* and the order of forgiveness *(proshchenie)*."[31] A prayer manual beloved by the Old Believers, the *Son of the Church (Syn tserkovnyi)*, also detailed the correct celebration of the order of forgiveness.[32] Revised liturgical books of the Russian Orthodox church gradually deleted the order of forgiveness, reflecting the death of this liturgical tradition. One clue to its demise came in a Russian Orthodox church Book of Hours *(Chasoslov)* of 1848, which mentioned "the dismissal and the *customary* forgiveness."[33] Concurrently published with the old ritualist books mentioned above, another Russian Orthodox Book of Hours noted "the dismissal. And we receive *(priemlem)* the customary forgiveness."[34] During the course of the nineteenth and early twentieth century, therefore, the idea of mutual forgiveness in the Russian Orthodox church evolved into the laity's "reception of the customary forgiveness."

In the Old Belief, bowing for forgiveness was a central part of clerical interaction with the community. In priestless services (and perhaps less frequently in the priestly tradition) a reader first asked the priest or preceptor for a personal blessing, crossed himself or herself while opening the holy book, and read an appointed passage. When the preceptor moved to the front of the chapel to proclaim the gospel, he turned and bowed twice—to the men and women of the faithful assembled—asking for blessing from the entire congregation. Such blessings were rarely done by priests of the Russian church, and their absence highlighted the separation between clergy and community prevalent in Russian Orthodox parishes.[35]

As part of the pastoral liturgical duties, the clergy moved about the altar and nave with a censer, blessing the icons and the congregation. In the Old Believer tradition, the censer specifically made the sign of the cross in front of the faithful (sometimes in groups, at other times individually), bestowing the blessing of the Holy Spirit directly on each member of the community.[36] In response, the Old Believers held out their hands as if "in an evening sacrifice" to receive the blessing. (In the priestless tradition those who had not previously participated in the order of forgiveness could not accept the blessing, but rather bowed as the censer passed by.)[37] The blessing held both religious and social importance—members of the community who persistently altered their physical appearance (men by cutting their beards, women by wearing unseemly cosmetics or cutting their hair) did not open their arms to receive this most physical blessing.[38] In contrast, clerics in the Russian Orthodox church did not cense the congregation with the sign of the cross, nor did the faithful accept the blessing with open arms. Again a significant tradition was changed in the Orthodox church as interaction between the clergy and people waned during the numerous censing events that were a part of divine services.

The importance placed on the relationship between clergy and faithful among the Old Believers exemplified the attitude of the Old Belief about the life of the community itself. The system of prayers, bows, and blessings repeated regularly throughout the liturgical cycle provided an icon of clerical roles: pastor of the community, member of the community, and servant of the community. The system also provided a model that stressed the importance of both lay believer and clergy within the liturgical cycle, placing the burden of repentance and forgiveness on the entire congregation of believers.[39] The Old Belief's system of ritual and symbol, especially as it differed from what had developed in the Orthodox church by the late imperial years, sought to create a different type of Orthodox Christian—one who had a collegial relationship with clergy and took active part in liturgical ritual.

The Faithful Community

Old Believers not only resisted the expansion of the role of secular authorities in their liturgical life, they also maintained texts that clearly helped to bond believers into a communal voice of prayer "in one thought, and accord, and love of union."[40] In addition to the spoken word, physically rigorous worship, uniformity, and discipline in ritual activity all created an atmosphere that promoted communal unity in prayer. The act of bowing, for example, was so important as a ritual action that an Old Believer archimandrite called it a primary example of the old rite itself.[41] Making bows simultaneously, both to the waist and prostrate to the floor, maintained ancient religious traditions synonymous with Old Believer identity. Unlike the more private devotions of the Russian Orthodox church of this period, Old Believers signaled their desire for communal worship by beginning and ending their divine services with simultaneous "entrance bows" that were made whenever one entered the church to stand in prayer, then again at the end of the service.[42] In the priestless tradition, the congregation made the entrance bows twice, first as an order of forgiveness and then again to begin liturgical services. These bows also marked the passage from secular to sacred space and time, from concerns of the world to those divine. Only if a person had recently been involved with the outside world was it necessary to perform the forgiveness bows. If a person arrived too late for the congregational bows, he or she was not allowed to receive the blessing of the censer.[43] In this way, the priestless groups liturgically replicated their views regarding the correct relationship of the faithful to the non-Old Believer world.[44] Bows were also often used as public penance, especially for untoward interaction with the outside world.[45]

The question of bowing, especially its timing and method, preceded the reforms of 1654–1666. Some parts of the Russian church had eliminated bows during the seventeenth century, including the prostrations traditionally made during Great Lent. Psalters reprinted by the Old Believers recounted the struggle between zealots and those who preferred change:

> Since these prostrations are spurned at the present through the enmity of our ancient foe and adversary, the devil, by certain priests who have not the fear of God within themselves, many do not do the prostrations . . . whether out of laziness or carelessness, or out of brazenness or disregard for the dread future judgment and eternal torment.[46]

In reverence for the tradition of bowing, Old Believers sought to regulate the act itself. Prostrations were to be completed simultaneously and in a specified manner. This contrasted with the Russian Orthodox rite, where prostrations were often deleted or made only when the spirit moved an individual.[47] The *Son of the Church* explained that:

> When thou art to make prostrations, do not beat the ground with thy head and do not knock it on the floor of the church or house. Simply bend thy knees, and bow thy head low, but do not strike the ground with it. Move both hands together from thy heart and place them gently on the ground; do not stick them out like axes. When thou bendest down or gettest up, do not shuffle or stamp thy feet; likewise, bend and straighten both knees together. Watch and learn this from experienced and educated people.[48]

While the Russian Orthodox still prescribed bows at specific points in the service, by the turn of the nineteenth century this rule was rarely followed. Worried that leniency in bowing might invade their own ritual, one Pomortsy writer claimed that:

> one may find in the holy writings references to bows to the waist. But bowing one's head—this is only for the joy of the demons and it is better not to make bows at all than to twist the laws and just nod in front of the holy icons.[49]

Conversely, in the desire to maintain discipline and communal prayer, the old rite did not condone making *extra* bows during the divine service. Such actions smacked of pride, a pharisaic display of piety, and served only to disrupt the communal harmony of divine services. While physical condition or the directives of a father confessor might govern the number of bows done by a Christian at home, in the temple a believer could only bow with the rest of the congregation:

> Other bows than these prescribed we dare not do lest we cause scandal among the people; rather, we stand with fear and trembling. . . . Some people make bows and prostrations other than those ordered by the service book [Typicon] during the Holy Liturgy and other services, but they do it not according to the tradition of the holy fathers nor unto their salvation, but rather unto sin. For it behooves Christians at church services in common to keep the appointed order handed down by the holy fathers.[50]

In the desire to mold all into a single instrument of praise, Old Believers discouraged actions that distracted the congregation from prayer. Robert Crummey has shown that "in the tradition of earlier reformers within the Russian church, [priestless Old Believer leaders] took severe measures to guard against frivolity, disrespect, and carelessness" during divine service even in the early days of the schism.[51] Old Believer protocol called for, among other practices, standing through long services with little movement, usually with arms crossed over the chest. Believers maintained orderly rows, leaving room for prostrations in between. Although Old Believers did occasionally leave the nave (especially to rest during a long service), in general practice they continued to stand through long services. The *Son of the Church,* for example, instructed: "Do not change thy place except in case of great necessity or crowding or to honor some other person. Stand resolutely at thy place; do not move thy feet and do not lean against a wall or column."[52] Another old ritualist publication stressed that believers should "take part in the general words of prayer and not read them as if praying one's own prayer."[53] Old Believers blessed themselves only at specified points in the divine services, for example, to mark the beginning of important prayers. Movement was forbidden during these prayers. Such practices contrasted starkly with those of the Russian Orthodox church at the turn of the century, where the faithful walked about freely, venerating icons, lighting candles, and changing places. Orthodox members rarely stood in lines since they only infrequently bowed to the floor. Churchgoers made the sign of the cross at will, personally commemorating particularly beautiful prayers and only rarely blessing themselves simultaneously. In despair, one Old Believer exclaimed: "What priests there are now! . . . They do not pray in a Christian manner, they do not know how to baptize. They make bows as they see fit, not as we do in one bow."[54]

Old Believers became widely known by their reliance on the ladder *(lestovka)*—a small prayer-rope common in pre-Nikonian Russia. Revered as a badge of honor by Old Believers, it accompanied them during private devotions and public prayers. In formal photographs or portraits, Old Believers nearly always carried this ladder. The prayer-rope, akin to the rosary, well illustrated both the old rite's love for bowing and the desire that abstract faith be connected to physical reality. The ladder's leaves (usually made of leather), counters, stitching, and adornments all symbolized important facets of Christianity. The prophets of the Messiah, Christ's birth by the Theotokos, his years preaching on earth (which itself had a special symbol), the evangelists, the Gospel, and the Holy Mysteries of the church all appeared symbolically. Thus an Old Believer carried with him or her a shorthand account of God's new testament with humanity. The counter beads reminded each Old Believer of both an important article of faith and the number of bows to be made. Total counters numbered 110, and the faithful might be given one or more lestovka of bows as penance after confession or to be made when one could not attend the liturgical cycle. The *Old Ritual Pormorian Magazine (Staroobriadcheskii pomorskii zhurnal)* deemed the *lestovka* (also known as the *vervitsa,* or branch) important enough to include the long legend of its use in the journal's premier issue.[55] Another Old Believer writer explained that

> The holy ancient-Orthodox Russian church generally determined and introduced the custom of Christians praying with the lestovka. . . . Not to carry out this custom of the holy fathers is to promote temptation among believers and to give a bad example to the young. The Lord Himself said that those who tempt such "small ones" condemn themselves to bitter suicide.[56]

Conclusion

The Old Believer practices of bows and prayerful discipline provided models—icons—for the behavior of the faithful. All prayers, activities, and thoughts were to be made communally, and the believers' voices were to meld into one voice greater than the sum of its parts. Liturgical life was thus a comment on the social organization preferred by the Old Believers.

For the theologian, such a liturgical life has significance only in humanity's relationship with God. For the layperson or pastor, rite creates a stable, organized form of worship, one to be handed down from generation to generation. For the historian, studying variations in liturgical life reveals perceptions of community and government as well as of communion with God. Participation in rites gives believers a common ground, a common set of assumptions about the world and its relationship to the divine. A language of symbol thus develops within the congregation itself. By the end of the imperial period, the symbols of the old rite had become much more communitarian than those of their Russian Orthodox church counterparts. It was this community, hoped the faithful, that would guide them through a changing world.

An Architecture
of Change

The nature of Old Believer religious ideology placed particular importance on the physical building as a symbol and focus of ritual life. Liturgical spaces commented symbolically on both the religious and social activities that occurred in them, especially on the social organization of the community. This study has already shown the primary importance placed on communal liturgical prayer in Old Belief and how liturgy related to the faithful's interaction with the state, clergy, and society. Yet, if communal prayer were truly to effect a change in the believer, then a suitable space needed to exist. In the post-1905 period, Old Believers were able to explore for the first time how liturgical spaces could fit both the needs of traditional religion and the possibilities of a modern age.

Emerging from their previous shadowy legality, Old Believers sought to integrate their own views with the emerging modern society, culture, and politics of the period. The attempt at integration was realized in the construction of many Old Believer religious buildings between 1905 and 1917. The history of these liturgical spaces illustrates the paradoxical nature of the Old Belief in the early twentieth century.[1] This chapter will analyze the Old Believer relationship to its sacred spaces by studying the effect of legalization on the construction and use of liturgical space and by investigating the symbolism of liturgical space as the nexus of religious ideology, social interaction, and modern influence.

Analysis of Russian architecture has just recently begun to include Old Believer contributions. Previous architectural texts either did not mention Old Believers at all or placed them only in the context of northern Russia, associating them with ancient wooden building forms indigenous to that region. Old Believers have received credit for maintaining traditional Russian building practices in the face of increasing western influence. Although one standard history of Russian architecture does not include Old Believer buildings at all, another study claimed that "the style of wooden architecture did not change over the centuries and later examples, particularly in the north where many conservative Old Believers settled after the schism in the 1650s, are based on ancient models."[2] A recent work, written by a noted restorer of the Kizhi complex of wooden churches, invests Old Believers with immense responsibility: "It was the Old Believers who defended and preserved the traditional way of life, the art and above all the churches of medieval Russia. They were the only effective resistance to the formidably overwhelming power of the state."[3] This analysis, although exaggerated, correctly links Old Believer architecture with the group's political situation.

Scholarly preoccupation with north Russian conservatism presents a chicken-and-egg problem for the study of Old Believer liturgical spaces. While Old Believers in the north did enjoy a measure of freedom to maintain the old ways, the region's conservatism both produced and was influenced by the Old Belief. The Vyg community, for example, provided a focus for cultural as well as religious life to the sparsely populated northlands. To claim, however, that "the demise of the Old Believer movement spelt the end of wooden church construction"[4] because of the destruction of Vyg in 1864 misjudges the death of the Old Belief and of Russian traditional architecture. Instead, the happy union of social conservatism with Old Belief combined to keep traditional church design and symbolism intact throughout the imperial period and beyond. Indeed, the history of the Vyg community and the cultural development of the north intertwined. An independent northern peasantry, "stable, industrious, and often isolated from the outside world,"[5] complemented the culture of the Old Belief. The architectural influence of the Old Belief has long endured: "Soviet scholars have uncovered literary and artistic treasures, lovingly preserved by the inhabitants of remote northern villages whose cultural life still preserves traces of the influence of Vyg and its offshoots."[6] Vyg's influence on architecture, however, was an anomaly, not the rule. In other parts of the empire the Old Believers had to build more circumspectly than in the autonomous north.

Sacred Building and State Authority

Both the imperial government and the Russian Orthodox church, understanding the importance of a place of worship, at first outlawed Old Believer buildings outright. Failing that, authorities endeavored to license and restrict temple design and construction. Then, when Catherine II ascended the throne, she granted Old Believers relative freedom of worship and association, including the right to build temples. Paul and Alexander I also treated the Old Believers liberally on this issue. Under Nicholas I, the building or restoration of chapels was forbidden once again, leaving many structures to disintegrate or be sealed shut.

The reign of Alexander II brought an amelioration of the Old Believer plight. An edict of 16 August 1864 gave Old Believers the right to repair decrepit chapels and other structures, so long as the outside view did not resemble a Russian Orthodox church.[7] Alexander III's ukase of 3 May 1883, however, ended the more laissez-faire attitude of the state and forbade any open show of Old Believer religion.[8] By curtailing the building or renovation of chapels and churches, the government again hoped to keep Old Believers from luring members of the dominant church into schism. Under the terms of the 1883 law, no renovation, construction, or public display of the old ritual was acceptable without express permission from the Ministry of the Interior and the Holy Synod. These two bodies fought bitterly about the Old Believers as well as about other issues.

Bureaucracy made legal religious building and restoration next to impossible for most Old Believers. Those who petitioned the government on this issue preceding the reforms of 1905–1906 often received approval from the Ministry of the Internal Affairs, only to be denied by the Russian Orthodox consistory. Local consistories argued that plenty of Old Believer chapels already existed or that no special reason existed for chapels to be built.[9] The burden of proof for the necessity of building or repairing a liturgical space inevitably fell on the Old Believers, thus insuring the consistory could always veto the plan. Proposals appealed as far up as the general procurator were almost always denied too.[10] The Minister of Internal Affairs questioned the church's attitudes on this issue:

> Only in rare cases do the religious authorities recognize as proper the petitions of the schismatics for permission to open new prayer houses, on the grounds that each new house of prayer not only helps to strengthen the Schism, but also makes missionary preaching more difficult. . . . The protests of the bishops against the opening of prayer houses proceed generally from the view that this is dangerous for Orthodoxy and produces disaffection among the believing—but if such protests are recognized to the extent of refusing the petitions of schismatics, then nowhere and never can new prayer houses be opened. . . .[11]

Despite these problems, some Old Believer communities did build or restore their places of worship. Taking advantage of bureaucratic infighting, industrial centers in the Urals sometimes managed to construct Old Believer chapels on their grounds, although often kept in poor repair. Although Moscow industrialists were able to build such chapels too,[12] Old Believers in distant provinces had considerably better luck than did their Moscow counterparts when constructing prayer houses.[13]

The Act of Toleration of 1905 transformed the legal situation regarding church construction, freeing Old Believers to open their own temples. Some local officials tried to undercut the new situation. In Kazan in 1906 a missionary priest purportedly told Old Believers, "Your life and death are in my hands. I may want to allow [renovation of your church], I may not want to."[14] The priest's attitude, as reported in an Old Believer magazine, did not reflect the new thinking about the reconstruction of liturgical buildings. It did, however, hint at the importance placed on such projects by the Old Believers themselves. The priest understood that corporate worship—the life and death of an Old Believer community—was strengthened by a suitable space. In retrospect, it seems natural that the old regime would guard its prerogatives, but this attitude infuriated zealous Old Believers. With respect to the Act of 1905, one Old Believer complained: "And this, after 17 April!"[15]

Old Believers themselves were sometimes slow to understand the significance of the 1905 edict. In the Moscow region, Old Believers continued until late 1906 to petition the Ministry of the Interior for permission to build chapels. Ministry officials duly passed on these requests to the consistory. On 3 June 1906, after refusing comment on a number of these appeals, a consistory official replied that the law of 1905 gave Old Believers complete freedom to build temples as they saw fit. The officer, however, noted that the consistory did not agree with the statute.[16] Later petitions, even those that included statements from local Russian Orthodox priests, were filed without receiving comment and even without a consistory seal.[17]

Despite being hindered in early efforts to restore churches and prayer houses, Old Believers approached the task with gusto. In previous generations the faithful often had to pray in a makeshift chapel—usually one room of a peasant house. Now they looked forward to building a more concrete focal point for their liturgical life. Community organization aided the building of church structures, because an established group of Old Believers often existed before a liturgical space could be built. The Spiritual Consistory records show that Old Believers had been trying for years to construct temples. In other words, Old Believers already had membership, leadership, and financial structures in place while waiting for the chance to build a place of prayer. When the legal situation changed in 1905, they exploited their new status and began to build temples almost immediately.[18]

As leaders of the Russian Orthodox church suspected, the 1905 act provided a means for Old Believers to propagate their faith. Although the substantial Pokrovskii Cathedral in Moscow held the seat of the Belokrinitsa metropolitan, the Belokrinitsy continued to build in the city, including one church costing more than 200,000 rubles.[19] The Pomortsy convened their 1909 all-Russian conference in a newly constructed Moscow temple—the first one in the city built specifically by Pomortsy. The expansion of the Belokrinitsy and the presence of a major new Pomortsy temple in the old capital illustrated the Old Believers' growing visibility as a legitimate form of Orthodox worship. In all, at least fifteen Old Believer liturgical buildings were constructed in Moscow between 1905 and 1917, not counting private devotional chapels.[20] The Russian Orthodox church, ever jealous of its position, observed the Old Believer building boom even in small towns and villages and worried that many new structures were "magnificent and grand."[21] Russian Orthodox leaders even sought to curb Old Believer influence by restricting use of the word "church" (*tserkov'*), arguing that such a term should only be used by the Russian Orthodox. The government noted, however, that Old Believers usually used the word "temple" (*khram*), instead of "church," thus providing a reasonable differentiation between the structures of the two rival groups.[22]

Interest in construction and design was reflected in the Old Believer press, often through short articles from regional correspondents. Magazines also fanned excitement over building projects by producing long descriptions, pictures, and photographs of structures all across Russia. Such articles could be seen in almost every issue of Old Believer journals. Some of these articles included designs and cost figures described in great detail, as aids to building for other communities. The construction boom continued well into the second decade of the twentieth century. On the eve of World War I, for example, Old Believers were still opening large and ornate temples.[23] The Old Believers prided themselves on their new liturgical buildings, whose construction proved the Old Belief's vitality.[24] Old Believer writers, moreover, began to see the opening of liturgical buildings as a civil right and defended the freedom from having temples closed "by caprice," as they had been during previous generations.[25] One magazine succinctly connected the church building to the life of the old ritual by calling the opening of a new temple in Arkhangelsk "The Celebration of the Old Belief."[26]

Tradition, Innovation, and Design

During those periods before 1905 when Old Believers had a chance to build as they wished (as during the reign of Catherine the Great), some remarkable temple facades resulted. At Preobrazhenskoe, a major center of priestless religious life, they constructed in 1805 a "gothic chapel" (fig. 2), following the somewhat more traditional, yet also highly adorned, Nikol'skaia Chapel of 1784 (fig. 3), but earlier than the Krestovozdvizhenskii Chapel of 1811 (fig. 4). These structures, designed by F. K. Sokolov, were all built during the period of toleration that coincided with the creation of the Preobrazhenskoe community. Their exteriors exemplified the variation that appeared among Old Believers when no official persecution was present.[27]

The Rogozhskoe cemetery cathedral, built by the Belokrinitsa

Figure 2 The "Gothic Chapel" (1805) at Preobrazhenskoe Cemetery was built during a period of lax state persecution. It has elaborate and nontraditional decoration. Courtesy of the Center for Traditional Russian Culture.

Figure 3 The Nikol'skaia Chapel (1784), also at Preobrazhenskoe Cemetery, predates the "Gothic Chapel" and shows less elaborate exterior decoration.

Figure 4 The Krestovozdvizhenskii Chapel (1811) returns to more traditional motives and provides yet another variation of exterior design at the Preobrazhenskoe Cemetery.

popovtsy congregation in Moscow, provided another significant pre-1905 exception to the plain exterior legislated by imperial authorities. The Cathedral of the Pokrov Mother of God (fig. 5), center of the Belokrinitsa hierarchy, enclosed a traditional interior with classical pilasters and columns. The foreign-inspired exterior of the Pokrov Cathedral was complemented after 1905 by a highly traditional Russian bell tower church situated next to it. In short, the necessity to conform to the society of the day influenced Old Believer design to the point of employing gothic and classical motives. Old Believers after 1905 thus found themselves without a clear external design tradition.

In legislating the appearance of the exterior of an Old Believer temple while ignoring the interior, previous centuries of imperial law fostered a dichotomous relationship between the outside of Old Believer structures and their inside design. This phenomenon in turn created a curiosity of Old Believer building style. While tradition mandated a strict interpretation of liturgical space indoors, the outside of Old Believer buildings varied in light of legal problems, local conditions, and regional aesthetic. Old Believers struggled under the constraints of these legal issues until 1905, as their liturgical spaces were forced to conform to standards administered by those unsympathetic to the religious ideology of the Old Belief. To make matters worse, legislation often prohibited any outward signs of Orthodoxy on Old Believer buildings (bell towers, crosses, and the like). This prohibition forced Old Believers to blend into the style prevalent in a given geographic area. In some ways, the situation symbolized the Old Belief itself—while maintaining tradition within their own community (as in the largely unchanged interior design), the faithful often needed to fit their lives into the fabric of local society, as echoed in the unobtrusive exterior of their temples. For the half-Old Believers, moreover, the plain exterior of Old Believer temples harmonized with an outward indifference to the old ritual that masked interior belief.

At the time of the 1905 reforms, therefore, traditions of exterior church design had to be self-consciously recalled and revived. By this stage in their history, Old Believers had largely accepted the idea that a building's exterior did not have to mirror its interior traditions, a concept that freed designers of post-1905 edifices to combine traditional architecture with the building materials and aesthetic of the art moderne style. In a very real way, after 1905 "everything old was new again." Old Believer use of medieval forms was heralded as innovation in architectural design. Simplicity of line and lack of ornament tied the Old Believer's previous legal situation to a modern aesthetic sensibility. Additionally, exposure in the press created renewed public interest in the Old Belief. Architectural magazines commented positively on the designs of Old Believer churches, helping to fuel a fin de siècle renaissance in traditional

Figure 5 The most boldly nontraditional exterior of its period, the Pokrov Cathedral (1792) at Rogozhskoe Cemetery employs classical pilasters, pediments, and windows—clear deviations from medieval Russian themes. Courtesy of the Rogozhskoe Cemetery.

building design. As a prominent architectural historian has said, "much that is innovative in Russian church architecture at the beginning of the twentieth century can be attributed to Old Believer communities."[28] Another author noted that

> It was certainly not [the Old Believers'] intention to return to the Orthodox forms of the State religion, and for this reason their architects attempted to suggest in their churches not only the Orthodox character of the Old Believers' faith and its relation to Byzantine and Russian history, but also their long exile in the north.[29]

It seemed a paradox that the Old Belief—an ultratraditional form of Orthodoxy—seemed better able to make itself relevant to the new cultural age than did the more "modernized" Russian Orthodox church. After years of persecution, the new freedom that transformed the localized organization of Old Believer communities created an atmosphere of great vitality in the Old Belief, a vitality that was missing in the established church. This liveliness found its outlet in both the sheer number and the design of Old Believer liturgical buildings constructed between 1905 and 1917.

The Pomortsy temple of the Resurrection, constructed in Moscow in 1909, exemplified this link between traditional Russian symbols and a

Figure 6   The simple lines of the Voskresenie Temple (Pomortsy concord, 1909) in Moscow combine the aesthetics of medieval and modern Russian architecture. Although using traditional components, the mass and geometric design of the temple are strikingly forward-looking. Courtesy of Penguin Books.

Figure 7 The Pomortsy temple in St. Petersburg shows medieval design themes in one of the most important buildings for that concord. Courtesy of University of California Press.

modern aesthetic (fig. 6). Its "beautiful external appearance and the richness of its internal finishing make it among the most remarkable church structures in the city of Moscow," claimed *Zlatostrui*.[30] One could easily identify typical elements of ancient Russian style—pitched roof, front bell tower, and onion domes—but the construction technique and simplified lines of the chapel gave it an appearance that straddled tradition and modernity. The design by I. Bondarenko concretely illustrated the situation facing Pomortsy after the Act of Toleration. Although their historical strength and leadership came from far northern Russia, where they promoted a life detached from the rest of society, the Pomortsy lived throughout the empire. In a more cosmopolitan environment, the faithful began to break down the walls of apartheid between themselves and the outside world. The new Pomortsy temple in Moscow thereby symbolized the group's need to fit its religious sensibility into modern conditions while retaining the traditions of its elders. In building its St. Petersburg temple, the Pomortsy returned to more established forms, including a Novgorod-style bell tower, roof, and dome design (fig. 7).

Old Believer temples enveloped a highly traditional worship space with dramatically new design and building techniques. Although the

Pomortsy temple was constructed with modern materials, the building's interior design and furnishings retained traditional motives.[31] Such a mixture confirmed Old Believer willingness to interpret ancient building exteriors in light of contemporary conditions while at the same time keeping the conventional interior elements. The new bell tower at the Pokrovskii Cathedral recalled early Muscovite themes as well. These themes, like other symbols of Old Believer life, declared not only that Old Believers were genuine Russian Christians but that the Old Believers—not the Russian Orthodox—were the true heirs to the Russian religious birthright. In their use of established design elements, the Old Believers attempted to "rework traditional forms in the spirit of a new age"[32] and to proclaim themselves the only vital, true Russian Orthodox.

Izba, Temple, and the Communal Life

As architectural historians have noted, Old Believer buildings in northern Russia and Siberia never had to bifurcate exterior and interior design, due to the autonomy granted the old ritual in such sparsely populated regions. In these geographic areas, Old Believers followed architectural traditions and guaranteed themselves a reputation as conservators of ancient styles and techniques. Somewhat insulated from political and social influences, Old Believers held to simple, traditional styles handed down through generations, and their buildings provided examples for architectural design across the empire after 1905.

Old Believer temples in far northern Russia and Siberia made their most basic point of reference the traditional hut *(izba)* structure of the Russian peasantry. Elements of this design had informed Russian church architecture from the baptism of Rus' onward. Although most prevalent in the wooden churches of the north (notably some of those now preserved in the Kizhi complex), *izba* influence was seen in stone churches as well. A nineteenth-century analyst recognized that the ancient form of wooden church architecture in Russia resembled a "simple *izba*." He claimed that "this form of church diffused north-west of Moscow and reached to the Olonets province [in the north] and the Ural Mountains [in the south], and hence moved through all of the area of the Novgorod colonization."[33] Another interpreter explained that "just as the tripartite plan of the *izba* is repeated in the palaces of the Russian aristocracy, so it dominates the design of the [ancient] Orthodox church, whose liturgical function also called for three different areas."[34]

The hut, almost always constructed of wood, consisted of a series of rectangular cells placed end to end. Although the central cell *(klet)* contained the main, heated living area—also called the *izba*—another storage room and passageway were sometimes added. The underlying structure of three rectangular cells arranged linearly could be enlarged or subtracted as necessary. Atop the cells lay a wooden roof, either of pitched or tent construction.

This living arrangement, while hardly a sophisticated design, provided a number of benefits. The cells could be easily and quickly constructed from roughhewn timbers and modified for specific purposes. In addition, the *izba* enveloped the myriad activities taken on by the family. Like other premodern people, Russian folk spent their indoor life mostly in one large room, rather than in a number of small chambers (as would have been the case in bourgeois culture). Privacy was inconsistent with the *izba,* which encouraged a communal life for its inhabitants. All the family lived together, regardless of age or place in the family structure.

Northern Russian Old Believer structures can be stylistically compared to the Lazarii Muromski Church (fig. 8), believed to be the oldest extant example of Russian wooden architecture and now located in the Kizhi complex on Lake Onega. Churches like Lazarii Muromskii provided the basis for later Old Believer design. In northern Russia, as one

Figure 8 Preserved at Kizhi, the Church of Lazar Muromskii illustrates the prototypical *izba* design with three separate cells. Courtesy of Harry N. Abrams.

Russian scholar has explained, the religious space was often built with just two cells, creating a chapel instead of a sanctified church.[35] Priestless Old Believers (the dominant group in the north) borrowed freely from chapels of this design that

> were to be found in hamlets and, like memorial crosses, in places with a special spiritual significance, where a pious Christian might want to make the sign of the cross. . . . The main difference [between them] was that a church had an iconostasis but a chapel had neither iconostasis nor sanctuary, and its interior was modest and simple.[36]

An ethnographic study of Old Believers in Tomsk province, published in 1930, claims that priestless chapels built there and in Kazakhstan were nothing more than *izby* with added bell towers and that these chapels resembled wooden churches of the Russian north, thousands of miles away.[37] Siberian Old Believer bell-tower design apparently recalled structures built of stone in Pskov and Novgorod.

Izba design harmonizes with Old Believer symbolism of the temple, transforming a group of individuals into a cohesive whole—an Old Believer community. The need for communal prayer, added to the fact that Old Believers often had to pray in a converted room of a home, created the linkage between *izba* as home and *izba* as prayer house. As can be seen in its design, the temple was an integral part of Old Believer life, a true house of prayer for the community: the Old Believer temple literally "housed" the community. A related analysis of Old Believers has also shown that the home could be seen as a chapel, just as the chapel could be seen as a home:

> Despite its ordinary appearance, the home is considered a place of elevated ritual status. If one sees a genuine church as a reflection of heaven, and the local chapel as the reflection of a church, then the home may well be understood as a reflection of the chapel. It is the lowest link in the chain connecting God with His followers and the past with the present.[38]

Thus the relationship between home and chapel—between *izba* design and temple design—was explicit for the Old Believers. In the temple, as in the home, the communal needs of the faithful weighed more heavily than the desires of any one individual. In 1909, for instance, leaders of the Pomortsy self-consciously refused to dictate the exterior design of a temple, saying that both old-Russian church style and the style of a "simple house" were acceptable.[39]

The imperative for communal prayer made the temple a central symbol of Old Believer spirituality. Early in the Old Believer experience, for example, the Vyg community began to place its chapels (one for men and one for women) in the geographic center of the community, as spiritual and architectural foci for the hermitage (fig. 9).[40] After 1905, Old Believers constructed throughout the empire buildings that attempted to disseminate the proper view of prayerful life. The organizational theme of the Old Believer community radiated from the temple, which enclosed the community at prayer. One Old Believer monk explained it this way:

> The temple must be, for Christians, a visible, real means of unification among themselves—a symbol of unity. In them [i.e., the temples] must flow together thoughts of all people in one general anthem of prayer and unbroken brotherly union, never hostile, spiteful, wrathful, envious, hateful, or disdainful. As one . . . all must be encircled with peace, accord, unity of spirit, and love.[41]

In other words, the symbolism of liturgical space reinforced the communal relationship among Old Believers and reminded them that, in the process of prayer, all Old Believers were spiritually joined together, regardless of social position.[42]

The traditional interior of Old Believer temples, which changed little

Figure 9 The chapel provided a visual and religious focus for the Vyg Pustyn'; it was the community's most impressive structure and even had a clock in its belltower—unique among Old Believer churches. Courtesy of Russkaia Kniga.

over the centuries, followed the interior floor plan of the *izba* church: a series of squares or rectangles oriented west to east. At the west end of the structure stood the vestibule (fig. 10, no. 1), known in Russian as the *trapeza* and identified in western European churches with the narthex. This part of the structure might be compared to the porch room of the *izba* and served some of the same functions—entryway and social meeting area. In bespopovtsy chapels, especially, the vestibule also functioned as a type of buffer between the profane and the holy, sometimes even between men and women. Visitors might stand in the vestibule.[43] It might be used as an overflow area for the nave or for those performing a penance, who might stand there during the service or make low bows to ask community forgiveness. By the late imperial period, the narthex had been generally lost in Russian Orthodox church design but was revived in Old Believer buildings of the period.

The plan of Old Believer religious space made sense in relation to its religious function: priestless Old Believers, for example, said the old ritual "entrance prayers" twice—first to cleanse themselves after contact with the outside world and then again to begin liturgical services.[44] If, however, someone arrived when prayers had already begun, he or she did not join the congregation in the nave until after having recited the prayers at the narthex. In this way, the back of the building acted as a filter between the profane and the sacred and marked the passage from secular to sacred space and time, from concerns of the world to those divine.[45] Even in homes used as chapels, the same differentiation might take place.[46]

Sometimes temples were built as one large cell, thus transforming the vestibule into simply the western portion of the building. The trapeza could therefore be integrated into the nave as a congregation grew or as a separate porch or meeting area was built. This arrangement left but one large room demarcated by railings or steps instead of walls. While commingling the sacred and profane areas, even single-room chapels did not forsake the basic dynamic of internal design: churchgoers entered the west end of the building and blessed themselves when crossing into the nave itself (fig. 10, no. 2).

The combination of vestibule and nave into a single large room, more or less undifferentiated, provided one adaptation of traditional *izba* design. It symbolized a blurring between sacred and profane areas, between the unclean outside world and the ritually cleansed Old Believer community, a process that began to happen increasingly in the late imperial period.[47] That is, while remaining true to a distinction between the community and the outside society, some Old Believers seemed willing to accept a liturgical building that lacked the differentiation between the community of believers and the external world.

The next cell eastward from the vestibule lay the nave, the temple's

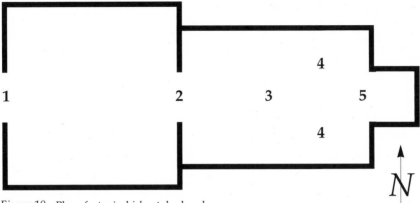

Figure 10   Plan of a typical *izba*-style church.

body (fig. 10, no. 3). Here, where the walls held icons or biblical inscriptions, the congregation celebrated services. Traditional form called for the room to be divided in half, west to east, with women standing on the north side and men on the south. Wooden benches either hugged the outside walls of the chapel or stood in rows across the nave.[48] A few chapels hid the sexes from each other's view by drawing a curtain down the center. This occurred especially in Old Believer monasteries, where the segregation of gender held special importance.[49] The practice had many variations. In Wojonowo, Poland, for example, there was no separation by gender,[50] whereas in Pogorzelec, Poland, in the early twentieth century, the oldest men stood in the front of the chapel and the oldest women stood in the back, while in varying degrees younger men and women stood closer to the middle of the nave.[51] (A close modification of this pattern remains today in Oregon and Alaska bespopovtsy chapels, where men tend to cluster in the front and women gravitate toward the rear; women there are only called to help celebrate the divine service during a shortage of men.) Such patterns may have reflected the size of a community. Small groups were probably more lenient in this regard than were large ones. Differences also illustrated variations in custom by geographic region. In the upper Kama river region, the literate stood at the front of the nave, the illiterate behind them.[52]

   In the front of the nave, sometimes divided by a small screen, railing, or step (but still clearly a part of the central cell), stood the choir *(kliros)*, as in the tradition of ancient Russian Orthodox churches (fig. 10, no. 4).[53] A choir area physically connected to the altar and the nave helped to integrate the congregation into a communal liturgical experience. This front-and-sides position in wooden churches has been described by nineteenth-century architectural historians. It had already occurred even in

seventeenth-century monumental structures—the Cathedral of the Trinity in Sergiev-Posad is a pertinent example.[54] The Russian Orthodox
church later changed this design, however, and began to move the choir
behind and above the nave; thus a western-style choir loft separated the
kliros from the rest of the church. Such a physical repositioning of the
singers served to make the choir an independent part of the sacred service, no longer on the same plane as the rest of the congregation. In the
late imperial years, the Old Believers in their building boom revived the
older design on a large scale.

Russian Orthodoxy had also come to embrace polyphonic singing, es-
chewed by the Old Believers. Polyphony, while liturgically acceptable,
helped to defeat the theory of communal worship central to the Old Believer experience. First, it undercut the symbolism of singing in mon-
ody—one sound as if from one voice. As polyphonic singing became
ever more intricate and westernized, it reinforced the physical separation
of the choir from the congregation in the nave because it required specialized musical training. (By the late imperial period even the great Russian symphonic composers—Tchaikovsky, Rimskii-Korsakov, and others—wrote for Russian Orthodox choirs.) The Russian Orthodox church
choir thereby became increasingly professional and remote from the rest
of the congregation. Compared to the Old Belief, with its choir linked to
monodic chant by signs *(znamennyi raspev)* and stationed in the nave itself, polyphony came to symbolize the loss of the ideal of communal
worship.[55]

Beyond the kliros, the design of priestly and priestless temples diverged. For the priestly Old Believers, an iconostasis (usually of carved
wood) stood in front of the choir area, much as in any Orthodox church.
In a priestless chapel, however, Old Believers tended to use the east wall
as a sort of wall-iconostasis instead of employing a free-standing structure. According to Orthodox tradition, the iconostasis screened the sanctuary from the nave, but in a priestless church there could be no consecrated altar. As a result, the bespopovtsy built chapels without
sanctuaries, transforming the east wall into the iconostasis, in accord
with the design of ancient Russian wayside chapels. Even so, the iconos-
tasis-front wall preserved standard organization: an icon of Christ en-
throned stood in the middle, flanked by icons of saints and the holy family. Underneath, there was usually a row of great holiday icons, then
icons of all-saints, lesser holidays, and others. Some chapels even had
royal and deacons doors, albeit without an altar behind them.[56]

Some analyses of Russian church architecture have noted that priestless Old Believers refused to hang icons on the wall—an accepted Orthodox fashion—saying that such practice blasphemed holy images. Instead,
priestless Old Believers built shelves and stood their icons upon them.
Not all sources support this claim, but interior views of priestless build-

ings often show such an arrangement. Quite possibly, the tradition of placing icons on shelves grew out of the transitory nature of Old Believer parishes in the early schism. Ancient icons, so revered by Old Believers, would have been lost to the persecuting forces of church and state had they been permanently affixed to a wall. Standing on a shelf, icons could be easily removed for hiding or taken with the faithful on their flight from persecution. The tradition lived on even after the legalization of the Old Belief, recalling (like the plain exterior of many Old Believer temples) the inconstant nature of the Old Belief in Russia before 1905. In some wealthy post-1905 buildings, however, traditional iconostases were built of wood and placed along the east wall of the chapel. They proclaimed a permanency previously only rarely seen among Old Believer buildings.[57]

If priestless temples must be understood as an extension of the ever-malleable *izba* design, then the easternmost cell made not only theological but also architectural sense. A sanctuary, after all, contained the altar consecrated by a priest and signifying the tomb of Christ wherein transformation of bread and wine took place. Without a priesthood there could be no altar and thus no sanctuary.[58] In place of the consecrated altar, a table holding a cross and gospel stood in the front-center of a priestless chapel, always in the main cell but sometimes raised up a step (fig. 10, no. 5). This gospel table imaginatively performed a service combining the elements of lectern and altar table.[59]

To understand the gospel table's function, some explanation of Orthodox worship is in order. The full Orthodox liturgy—lost to the priestless—consisted of two sections: the Liturgy of the Word and the Liturgy of the Gifts. The crowning point of the Liturgy of the Word came at the Little Entry, when the clergy brought the gospel from the altar, round about in front of the royal doors, and presented it to the congregation. At this point a deacon or priest read the appointed gospel selection of the day, setting the book on a moveable lectern.[60]

Since the Liturgy of the Gifts was theologically impossible for priestless Old Believers, their cycle had to end with the reading of the gospel. Thus, instead of a portable lectern that no longer needed to be moved for the Great Entry, the gospel table took on the permanence traditionally allowed the altar table itself. This surrogate altar provided the focus in much the same way as an altar inside the sanctuary of a priestly church. In the priestless tradition, the gospel table became a permanent fixture at the east end of the nave, in the same relative position as the reading lectern. Here, before the gospel, the preceptor would bow to the assembled community to ask forgiveness and would then proclaim the Word of God.

Much might be made of the creation of a substitute altar used for the gospels instead of for the Eucharist. Indeed, Old Believers had earned a reputation as lovers of holy books, especially those books that predated the Nikonian reforms. Old Believers read, touched, and collected books with adoration and were widely believed to be more literate than the average Russian.[61] The love for books and the high literacy rate (among other factors) have led scholars to claim that the development of the Old Belief was analogous to the Protestant Reformation in western Europe. According to this theory, the preeminence of the written word in priestless temples could be construed as the symbolic elevation of the gospels above the Holy Mysteries. Creation of a permanent gospel table instead of the altar table might then be seen as a way of replacing the Body and Blood of Christ with the Word of God, much as in the Protestant tradition.[62]

The argument, although faulty, does reveal some facets of Old Belief, such as Old Believer bibliophilia. Unlike the Protestants, who held up the Bible as the single source of divine exposition, Old Believers revered books *themselves* as vessels of tradition and thus keys to salvation. A common priestless attitude (present even in the late twentieth century) held that religious questions were not open for debate: "You have Holy Books—you open the books and there is your answer."[63] More often than not, liturgical and polemical texts received the same adoration by Old Believers as did the gospels, a clear differentiation from the teaching of Martin Luther.

Rather than representing a move toward Protestantism, the existence of a permanent gospel table in the place of a sanctified altar symbolized the incomplete nature of priestless Orthodoxy. Old Believers did not try to create a new religion, or even a new religious sensibility. Instead, they believed that they were maintaining, as fully as possible, the traditions of Russian Orthodoxy as it developed in premodern Russia. In the spiritual desert that resulted from the loss of the priesthood, the bespopovtsy needed to provide a central focus for their chapels and to establish that the reading of the gospel was the culminating liturgical act available to them. In light of this realization, the written Word provided not innovation but rather the means to transmit the piety of Old Rus' to succeeding generations.

The interior space of Old Believer liturgical buildings emphasized the unity of the membership (fig. 11). Priestly Old Believers continued to use a floor plan traditional to Russian churches. This design included an integrated choir and the retention of a single physical level for all worshipers. Priestless groups even more clearly stated the unity of members in their design. For them, both the spiritual father and the altar had to be moved into the nave of the building since the altar area did not exist anymore. While the design was done for theological reasons, the organization of Old Believer communities also saw its realization every time they gathered to pray. For, in Old Believer buildings, the preceptor (*nastavnik*) acted as a lay leader of the congregation and so stood within it.

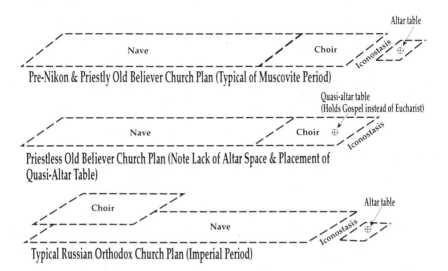

Figure 11   Typical use of liturgical spaces in Old Believer and Russian Orthodox buildings. Some variations occurred because of geography and period.

Many priestless Old Believers placed special significance on the eastern end of the chapel, especially the area between the gospel table and the front wall, which followed the tradition of a sacred altar space found in priestly churches. An ethnographic study of Masurian Old Believers described this phenomenon among some contemporary faithful, but the tradition existed at the turn of the century too:

> A certain nostalgia for the sanctuary appears in terms used to describe their chapel by those people deprived of the Eucharist. Thus the wall which carries the icons is called by them the "iconostasis," and the space between it and the stands to which only those who celebrate the religious ceremony have access is, always according to their terminology, the "holy of holies." In the absence of an altar the two designations are obviously improper.[64]

The "obvious" impropriety of this nomenclature makes sense, however, in terms of the priestless Old Believers' desire to retain all facets of Orthodoxy available to them. Much as in joining the functions of lectern and altar, Old Believers needed to make some areas in their buildings foci for communal worship—many communities even retained the term "altar." Not all locales maintained these language distinctions. Some, for example, believed that certain areas were particularly sacred but did not use the terminology described above. The distinction between more- and less-holy areas, however, provided legitimation of priestless chapels as true houses of worship and as links to the piety of old Rus', whose traditions the Old Believers struggled to maintain.

In this as in other facets of their sacred design, the Old Believers demonstrated that they were an integral and vital part of Russian culture, not a deviation from it. The Old Believers' vision of themselves as heirs to the Russian tradition was confirmed by the magnitude of the construction they embarked on after 1905. Their temples, while recalling the most traditional Russian designs, were set within modern conditions and illustrated the Old Belief neither as a radical departure from Orthodoxy nor as a Protestant statement against it but rather as a living and vital remnant of traditional Christianity. At the same time, the basic plan of Old Believer liturgical spaces reinforced the central role for a community of believers in the life of the church. Old ritualist structures emphasized that identity and salvation were not to be found through faith in a personal savior but, rather, in communitarian songs of repentance and praise.

Representing *the* Old Belief

But this is what is done in our time: the image of our
Savior Emmanuel is painted with a puffy face, red
lips, curly hair, thick hands and arms, swollen fingers, fat thighs, and the whole of him paunchy and
fat like a German; nothing lacking but a sword at his
hip! All this is painted from carnal notions, for the
grossness of the flesh is dear to heretics and they
have repudiated higher things.
—*Archpriest Avvakum*

While liturgy and architecture clearly illustrate
the communal imperatives present in Old Believer symbolic and ritual life, the pictorial representation of the Old Belief in iconography
and secular art further illustrates how the Old
Believer system of symbols interacted with the
Russian public at large. One of the most obvious of these symbols was the holy icon itself.
While Old Believers had revered icons through-
out their history, the relationship between the old ritualists and their religious art after 1905 took on meanings specific to the late imperial era.
Consequently, the interaction of Old Believers with their most important
iconic forms represented also the reaction of the Old Belief to a changing
Russian culture. More specifically, the Old Belief's artistic expressions
served to illustrate both shared symbols and diversity among Old Believers in this period. The art of the Old Believers delineated their relationship to the established Russian Orthodox church, indicated their views of
westernization and technical modernization in Russia, and commented
on artistic expressions that competed with iconography.

The imperial government had until 1905 banned the public use of
icons—processions and the like—by Old Believers, realizing the influence of these images over the faithful. Much like the new legal attitude
toward Old Believer sacred buildings, however, the Act of Toleration of
1905 opened the way for public use of icons. The Rogozhskoe community received legal permission to hold seven processions in 1905 and

1906, both inside and outside the cemetery compound, and then pro-
ceeded to hold three more without consent of the authorities. This gave
pause to police observers who were not yet comfortable with open Old
Believer liturgical activities.[1] Moscow police also kept particular tabs on
icon processions in these years because socialist political rallies were
sometimes timed to coincide with them.[2] In the provinces, however, Old
Believers came under somewhat more active persecution in this regard
even after 1905. Provincial officials did not always uphold the 1905 Act
of Toleration, and some even actively forbade Old Believer processions,
showing "the characteristic views of our provincial administrators on
'the freedom of conscience.'"[3]

Old Believer publications also responded quickly to the newly found
freedom and began to instruct readers in the intricate symbolism, technique, history, and theology of iconography. Such attention tapped a
reservoir of popular interest in icons. In the Old Believer journals, authors sought to propagate and reaffirm the importance the Old Belief
placed on iconography. The *Church (Tserkov')*, for example, published in
1911 a lengthy description of the icon for the Transfiguration of Christ.
An explanation of the symbols and texts depicted on the icon accompanied a description and photographs. The article also outlined the historical development of that particular representation, provided the provenance of specific icons in the Pokrovskii Cathedral collection, and
compared Russian styles to other examples in the Greek tradition.[4] A
similar article examined early Russian carved icons, pointing out their
historical and theological significance and explaining the development of
the technique.[5] In general, these articles conveyed two implicit messages:
first, that iconography held intrinsic importance for the Old Believers, all
of whom should have been able to understand and interact with the
iconographic symbols; and, second, that Old Believer icons were inextri-
cably linked to the Russian past, even to ancient Greek Orthodox traditions. Thus, the icons legitimized the Old Belief, showing it to be a more
"pure" Russian Orthodoxy than that of the established church. In the
same vein, Old Believers condemned the influence of the Renaissance-inspired Italianate realism that had become popular in the iconography of
the Orthodox church from the eighteenth century. The archpriest Avvakum noted the beginning of this trend (see epigram that opens this
chapter), but Old Believers had subsequently been gagged in their objec-
tions to it. The question of the iconography of the ancient piety versus
that of the Italianate style became a source of considerable tension between Old Believers and the Russian Orthodox church.

As in other Orthodox churches, icons lined the walls and iconostases
of Old Believer churches and chapels. They even adorned the ceilings.
The Pokrovskii Cathedral of the Belokrinitsa in Moscow had one of the
most important collections of ancient icons in Russia.[6] In every Old Believer home (as in the homes of other Orthodox), icons held a place of

special prominence. Although they might commemorate any saint or holiday, Old Believer icons (like other icons in Russia) generally portrayed Christ, Mary, major holidays, and name-day saints. For a more exotic example, the Pokrovskii Cathedral, in its substantial collection, owned an iconographic map of the seventeenth-century Moscow Kremlin.[7]

The Old Believers' treatment of icons exemplified some of the old ritualists' basic ideas about their own religious experience. The icon played a much larger part in the religious life of the Old Belief than simply that of a didactic device. In keeping with their sense of symbol, Old Believers preserved more than other Orthodox did the idea that icons provided a conduit for grace by being perfect images of the prototypes depicted on them. Thus, icons that reflected the ancient piety became symbolic of Old Believer religious identity itself. The veneration of iconographic styles that predated the reforms of 1654–1666 (including icons painted later but in the corresponding style) showed allegiance to the old ritual religious practices painted thereon. Old-style icons illustrated the preferred clerical dress of Old Believers (somewhat changed by the post-Nikonian rite), the method of prostrating oneself in reverence before God, and other particulars of Old Believer tradition. In an atmosphere that had been charged with the fear of persecution, and in which the traditional hierarchy had been lost, Old Believers had turned to icons as proof of their link in the chain of Russian spirituality. Without the support of the government or the state-established church, icons provided evidence that (quite literally) "God is with us; know, all ye nations and bow down, for God is with us."[8]

Moreover, since the ancient styles of iconography were believed to be earthly forms of heavenly prototypes, the details of ritual practice shown on the icons proved the veracity of Old Believer ritual life. For example, Old Believers only kept icons that showed a two-fingered sign of the cross (fig. 12), never the Russian Orthodox church's three-fingered variation (fig. 13). Holding one's hands out as if in "evening sacrifice" (fig. 14) was acceptable by Old Believer iconographic standards, but Christ's blessing could not be made in three-fingered form or in the Greek-derived sign made to represent the words "Jesus Christ" (fig. 13, left side).[9]

In contrast to such strict interpretations of some iconographic characteristics, Old Believers of the late imperial period did realize that diversity existed in the style and production of icons and crucifixes. A council of priestless Old Believers in 1909 took up just this question, showing remarkable temperance in their interpretation of the crucifix's correct style:

> *Question:* Is it possible to worship a cross with a depiction of the Holy Trinity and the title INTsI [Jesus Nazarene King of the Jews]?
> *Answer:* Crosses, both metal ones and those on wood, in the eight-edged view with the attached Image Not Made by Human Hands, the sun, the

moon, and the archangels, and the words *"Is Khr Tsr Slavy Syn Bozhii"* [Jesus Christ King of Glory Son of God] are accepted for reverence in the church. Other crosses were not seen in the ancient church. Pilate himself wrote the title of INTsI [Jesus Nazarene King of the Jews], as is said in the Gospel words of Pilate. So do not take enmity with brothers of the faith who by ancient custom make crosses with the title and the depiction of God the Father and the Holy Spirit.[10]

Figure 12   The symbols of the Old Belief, as portrayed by an Old Believer artist. Note the two-fingered sign of the cross, three-bar cross, and older-style chalice, bishop's crown, and scepter. The circle at the top shows the old ritual method of preparing the bread for communion. Courtesy of Russkaia Kniga.

Figure 13 The symbols of the Russian Orthodox Church, as portrayed by an Old Believer artist. Note the differences in hand position, use of Greek crosses, and western-style bishop's crown. Courtesy of Russkaia Kniga.

The council differentiated here between two variations in crucifix design. In the first place, it specifically defined which crosses were "seen in the ancient church" and so were acceptable for the Old Believer faithful. In doing so, however, the council did not condemn crosses made in variant styles so long as they were held dear by "brothers of the faith." Chasovenniki and the priestly Old Believers (as well as the Russian Orthodox church) all used Pilate's inscription on their crucifixes, and the

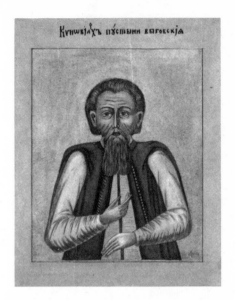

Figure 14 A late nineteenth-century picture of Old Believer hero Daniil Vikulov. The figure holds out his hands rather than making the sign of the cross. Courtesy of Russkaia Kniga.

Pomortsy council's refusal to condemn these crucifixes illustrates a broadening of attitude from earlier discussions on the subject. Closer to home for the Pomortsy, however, was the problem of the Fedoseevtsy, who attacked the Pomortsy specifically on the question of crucifix inscription.[11] Nonetheless, the council's liberal interpretation of an important symbol illustrated in itself an attempt to reach out to other Old Believer concords. This attempt was clearly not a position of increased fanaticism, as representatives of the Russian church claimed.

The occasion for Old Believers to meet in councils and to publish journals also provided the opportunity to define the attitude of the Old Belief toward Russian Orthodoxy on the issue of iconography. Old Believers of all concords roundly condemned the use of "heretical" Russian Orthodox church icons: "It is possible to live in the world and in friendship with [people who keep new style icons]," claimed one Old Believer publication, "but it is not possible to forgo one's religious convictions for this friendship, for this is servility to man and a sin before God."[12] Russian Orthodox church icons often portrayed saints canonized after the church schism and were therefore doubly unacceptable to those who believed the Russian Orthodox church to be in apostasy (or heresy). No Old Believers could accept such icons, and leaders prohibited their use in prayer.[13] More conservative Old Believers, especially in the countryside, sometimes prayed only with cast metal icons, probably because they believed that these were the least likely to have been adulterated or changed from traditional designs.[14]

In the most extreme manifestations, some Old Believers even forbade veneration of their icons by members of the Russian Orthodox church. The *Otchet* (Review) of General Procurator Pobedonostsev reported that some priestless Old Believers

> have reached the point in their fanaticism where, if an Orthodox were to enter any of their homes and, seeing an icon, make the sign of the cross, if that icon were not covered with linen, [the Old Believers] reckon it to be defiled, and then scrape [the image away] with a knife. But if by chance it is during a meal, then all situated at the table eating and drinking leap from the table to the floor as if [the table] were defiled.[15]

While this report represented a view calculated to portray Old Believer extremism, it probably included a grain of truth. In a less dramatic example of the same phenomenon, many Old Believers kept their icons in cabinets or behind glass, so as to insulate the pictures themselves from being sullied by the presence of the heterodox. Old Believers even condemned the wearing of rubber boots that had crosses molded on their bottoms— "four-edged crosses which they tread under their feet."[16] Those who wore such footwear trampled on the sign of the cross and followed in the footsteps of the patriarch Nikon, who reportedly had eight-edged crosses sown into the soles of his shoes. These actions—insulating the physical icon behind glass and prohibiting some brands of galoshes—portrayed the Old Believers' refusal to differentiate between religious symbol and an internal belief structure. Old Believers thus considered an offense toward a symbol to be an affront to holiness and to God himself. These behaviors also tended to bring religion to the everyday level; Old Believers lived in a world inhabited by the physical reality of their religious life. In fact, the relationship of cross-shapes on boots to the Holy Cross is a particularly clear example of interactive symbolism. Old Believers, who certainly knew that it was not *the* Cross on the bottom of a boot, nonetheless refused to tread upon something that remotely suggested the symbolic center of their faith.

Russian Orthodox missionaries usually had little quarrel with Old Believers on the matter of iconography. While journals such as *Missionary Review (Missionerskoe obozrenie)* published scores of articles on iconography, most of these writings defended traditional views in response to the ideas of the iconoclastic sectarians. Since Old Believers retained a valuable part of Russian spiritual heritage in their iconography, the Russian Orthodox church made only passing criticism on this topic. Moreover, on a basic level, missionary literature on iconography was apologetic; by leaving the polemical attacks to the Old Believers and concentrating instead on defending its own practices, the Russian Orthodox church tacitly acknowledged the old rite's Orthodox legitimacy on this issue. One missionary article, for example, produced archaeological evidence proving that four-edged crosses already existed in the pre-Nikonian Russian church.[17] Old Believers were rarely swayed by such arguments. For them, showing historical precedent for four-edged crosses provided no ipso facto impetus for acceptance of new rite iconography. In fact, the opposite extreme sometimes occurred: one Old Believer polemicist claimed that the state's continuing use of the term schismatic in relation to Old Believer icons amounted to nothing less than a "new iconoclasm."[18]

The Old Believers' insistence on the integrity of ancient iconographic styles heralded an increasing differentiation between their icons and those of the Russian Orthodox church. In the seventeenth century, Patriarch Nikon, in a rare moment of agreement with Old Believers, had hoped to purge western influences from iconography. In a typically severe manner, Nikon reacted to what he considered to be improper icons: he had them burned in pyres outside the churches of Moscow.[19] His reaction embodied the last gasp against a steadily westernizing aesthetic. With Peter I's opening of Russia to western Europe, iconography of the Italianate style began to dominate the icons of the Russian Orthodox church.[20] This style, as its name implies, replaced traditional Russian sacred art with the aesthetic of Renaissance Italy. By the turn of the nineteenth century, the difference in iconography between Old Belief and the Russian Orthodox church had increased dramatically.

In the face of changing styles, Old Believers characteristically held fast to old Russian traditions and roundly denounced western influences.[21] In stark contrast to the increasingly humanist style of Russian Orthodox church iconography, traditional style maintained that icons should portray another world, not of this earth. The artistic device utilized in Old Believer icons to portray various points of view (instead of the use of a western-style perspective based on the vanishing point) and the presence in these icons of more than one source of light (rather than a single source as found in Renaissance-inspired iconography) emphasized the theology of the icon, not the humanist, historicized representation. Old Believers maintained that iconographic portraits and scenes were never meant to be naturalistic portrayals of their themes. Instead, according to them, icons were to abstract the subject into a transfigured state, removed from the humdrum of perspective and a single-point light source. "The icon," said one Old Believer article, "is not so much the bodily *image* of the saint as it is his *spirit*, zealous for God. In [Old Believer] icons this victory of the spirit over the flesh is immediately apparent. . . . The appearance of the [saint] here reveals the difficulty of the path leading to the Kingdom of Heaven, and imperceptibly but clearly a person's thoughts fly from earth to heaven."[22]

To illustrate the difference between Old Believer images—through which the believer might transcend carnal life—and the humanistic, flesh-inspired, westernized, Russian Orthodox church icons, Old Believers in this period popularized a number of "before and after" interior views of churches. These views clearly showed the westernization of religious art in the Russian Orthodox church. In the "before" picture, the faithful stood and prostrated themselves in front of traditional icons; in the "after" illustration, the iconostasis was chock-full of western artistic techniques—vanishing-point perspective and naturalistic surroundings being the most obvious.

For Old Believers, crucifixes were as important as painted icons. Both were painted on wood and molded from brass, and "the most important thing was for the crosses to be *'vosmikonechnyi'* (eight-edged), that is, to have three cross-bars and inscriptions with contents the same as those used in the Muscovite state up to the middle of the seventeenth century."[23] A single-bar cross became known to the Old Believers as the "shadow of the true cross," or the "sign of the cross," and could be used only as a stylistic device to enclose the correct eight-edged cross. Although Old Believers accepted that the "heretical" four-edged cross also represented the crucifixion of Christ, they claimed that the ancient church believed the Savior was in fact crucified on an eight-edged cross.[24] To them, the four-edged cross symbolized the Russian Orthodox church's accommodation to Western Christianity with its perceived laxity on issues of traditional piety. Did not the shadow of the "True Cross" represent but the shadow of true Christianity?

While they continued to deplore new-rite iconography, Old Believers did not cut off all contact with the Russian Orthodox church. The attitude toward non–Old Believer icons, however, varied somewhat by concord. On the most conservative end of the spectrum stood the Pomortsy and Fedoseevtsy communities. Among these Old Believers the desire to insulate themselves remained especially strong, even though they considered the issue of icons a disputable area. When asked if it were possible to buy religious vessels and icons from the Russian Orthodox church, a 1909 Pomortsy council argued that

> It is not necessary to take icons and crosses from the heterodox, and also it is possible to buy metal icons from the Fedoseevtsy [instead of the Russian Orthodox church]; in the absence of your own craftsmen, it is justifiable to buy utensils, oil, and palms of the foreigners.[25]

The answer was ambiguous. This statement did not forbid the trade in icons and utensils; rather, it said that such trade was not "necessary," leaving open the possibility in time of need. The council also decided that a seal of approval might accompany ancient icons and that a storehouse in Moscow might distribute these old icons to the Pomortsy faithful in the provinces.[26] Such decisions revealed the desirability of maintaining traditional icons while realizing the necessity of interaction with members of other concords and the Russian Orthodox church.

Other sources portrayed an even more conservative attitude toward the procurement of icons than that outlined above. In the nineteenth century, the St. Petersburg Fedoseevtsy fathers taught that the faithful should not receive icons from excommunicated believers or from master iconographers outside of their concord.[27] A later manuscript (from about 1890) claimed that the Fedoseevtsy should take icons only from "Christians" and not from "foreigners," or "non-believers."[28] This extreme view illustrated the relationship between piety and art, as portrayed in icons. If the iconographer was not "right-believing," or did not live an exemplary life, his art was spiritually inferior and thus inappropriate for veneration by Old Believers. The artist, the icon, and the faithful all had to work together in the process.

Among the Belokrinitsy the icon problem was treated rather more liberally than it was by the priestless Old Believers. The Belokrinitsa journals the *Church (Tserkov')* and *Old Believer Messenger (Staroobriadcheskii vestnik)*, for example, carried advertisements for professional iconographers. One advertiser was the Sergei Tikhonovich Bolshakov firm,[29] another the Vasilii Pavlovich Gug'lnov iconographic and restoration company. While the former seemed to cater mostly to Old Believer and edinovertsy liturgical needs, the latter did not appeal specifically to Old Believers and claimed to produce icons in the "Byzantine, Greek, Novgorod, Moscow, Stroganov, and Friazhskii styles." The notice trumpeted the firm's medals at Russian iconographic festivals and proclaimed its place as official iconographer to members of the imperial family, who were anything but Old Believers. While some styles advertised by the firms would have been traditional enough for the Old Believers, the "friazhskii," a westernized style, could not have been. The regular appearance of the advertisement, however, suggests that the priestly Old Believers found it acceptable and the firm viewed it as profitable. The Riabushinskii and other wealthy priestly Old Believer families actively collected old icons regardless of their provenance, and the Belokrinitsy apparently took a similar stance on newly painted examples.

The love for ancient icons provided a rare point of religious rapprochement between the Old Believers and the Russian Orthodox church during the late imperial period. *Tserkov'* proved willing to publish reports on archeological finds in Russian Orthodox churches, such as the discovery of a particularly beautiful "Nativity of Mary" in the Moscow Savior-Transfiguration monastery.[30] Old Believers, expressly forbidden to pray with "heretics" or "outsiders" (which included members of the Russian Orthodox church), often desired to venerate wonder-working icons housed in such churches. The Pomortsy conference, otherwise strict on matters of faith and heresy, admitted that "it is not objectionable to worship and kiss the powerful and wonder-working icons, which are accepted by the [Old Belief], in a heretical church."[31] Not only could the Pomortsy go to see these wonder-working icons, but they were also given leave to venerate and to kiss them! The council thus stretched the definition of acceptable interaction with the Russian Orthodox church, a phenomenon otherwise strictly limited.[32] The priestly Old Believers also published the names of Russian Orthodox church buildings that housed particularly good collections of icons, so that the faithful could find spiritual strength even among the Nikonians.[33] Through these decisions, various Old Believer concords accepted that some interaction with the Russian church was, if not desirable, at least necessary. In fact, some Old Believers taught that the dissemination of old rite icons to "heretics" could provide both financial and spiritual benefit to Old Believer iconographers, since these icons might help to convert nonbelievers back to the fold of the old rite.[34]

In response to the easing of tension, Russian Orthodox churches sometimes undertook a persuasive approach to luring Old Believers into their buildings. One village, for example, simply "replaced catholic [!] icons of the eighteenth century in the parish church with icons of the Byzantine style."[35] The 1904 diocese report for the village concluded that "it is necessary to consider the comforting phenomenon that schismatics . . . come to our church, celebrate in its prayers, kiss holy icons, stand before them, and receive the blessing of the priest."[36] A report by the provincial governor of Saratov on his meeting with the local Belokrinitsa Old Believer hierarch in 1911 specifically noted that the governor was free to venerate the prereform-style cross offered by the bishop.[37]

For Old Believers, the changing relationship with the official church raised the larger question of piety within the new rite—what was the connection between wonder-working icons, relics, and other symbols of the ancient piety that had been co-opted by Nikonians?[38] Vessels of piety surely did not lose their importance and yet were continually sullied by the Russian Orthodox church. For example, the Belokrinitsa hierarchy welcomed the famous wonder-working icon of the Kazan Mother of God to a church in Vladimir province, yet the revered icon had been housed since the schism in a Russian Orthodox church.[39] The Old Believers also needed to answer the missionary assertion that piety existed wherever there were holy icons and relics, regardless of rite. Some Old Believers responded with the argument that (as in the plight of the church under the Tatar yoke) icons and relics maintained their spiritual efficacy independent of the apostasy or foreign domination of the church.[40] Beyond the question of polemics, these issues illustrated again that the Old

Believers had developed a sophisticated attitude about the meaning and power of religious symbols. The Old Believer arguments did not come from mindless fanatics, a view popularized by some Russian Orthodox polemicists, but revealed a self-conscious analysis of religious symbols and their importance. Moreover, as Old Believers came to recognize that sacred objects did exist in Russian Orthodox churches, so also they accepted a link between the established church and the traditional piety of the Old Belief. Such a stance, taken even by the more conservative wing of Old Believers, hinted at an intersection of Old Believer interests with those of the Russian Orthodox church.

Icons as Sacraments

Icons demanded special care as the crossroads where the divine met a sinful world. The regard shown for the physical icon illustrates particularly well the interactive nature of Old Believer symbols. Ethnographers chronicling Old Believer religious practices often commented on the extraordinary adoration given to icons. This included the loving, time-consuming, and sometimes costly rituals that Old Believers maintained with regard to their holy pictures. A priestless Old Believer conference in 1909, for example, clarified its position on the oil-burning lamps that by tradition stood or hung before each icon. One of the faithful asked if it was acceptable to use inexpensive lamp oil instead of olive oil. "It is not pleasing [to God to burn lamp oil]," came the reply, "for it is necessary for a sacrifice to be clean, and not as a sacrifice of Cain."[41] Likewise, only pure beeswax candles were acceptable as sacrifices, not inexpensive paraffin ones.

Unlike the priestly Old Believers (who showed somewhat less institutional interest in the question), priestless groups used their post-1905 freedom of association and religion to define the exact teachings of the old rite in regard to icons and other physical relics of the faith. Priestless national conference proceedings often included discussion of such matters, while the priestly Old Believers took up these issues through the informal system of "Answers from the Editors" in Old Believer magazines. In general, the priestless Old Believers placed greater emphasis on the physical icon itself and the ritual concerning holy pictures.

How to interact with an icon had great significance for the Old Believers. Decisions regarding icons were published in the priestless Old Believer conference proceedings alongside advice on prayers for the tsar, the need for penance, and debates on excommunication, showing the equal weight given to each subject. In their love for correct icon care, priestless Old Believers expressed a desire to maintain the open conduit of grace that they perceived in icons. While the painted image was not literally God, the faithful hoped that their interaction with a concrete symbol could help them achieve a unity with the prototype before whom they bowed. Sacrifice to an icon needed to be pure because the image itself was a pure expression of a divine prototype. In like fashion, Old Believers often informally called icons *"Bozhe"* or *"Bog,"* variations of the word "God."[42] This terminology reinforced the view that icons were more than mere portraits or teaching devices.

In icon care, as in other areas of faith, Old Believers did not differentiate between the form of religion (i.e., the ritual care for icons) and an abstract belief system. Instead, the Old Belief maintained a unified approach to the subject of piety, claiming that form provided the vessel for meaning. In the same way that a gas or liquid might take the form of its container, old ritualists believed that faith took on its comprehensible, iconic form in symbol and ritual. By maintaining purity and veracity in ritual matters such as icon lighting or cleaning, the faithful sought to preserve and protect the transparent, crystal vessel that held their faith. The meticulous maintenance of icons and the special tradition used in lighting them (of great interest on the national level) provided a guide by which the faithful might relate to iconic forms. Here was a commitment to symbolic forms that not only unified the faithful through shared experience but also helped Old Believers to find salvation and achieve deification. While these patterns played a part in many popular religious practices, they became elevated to an almost dogmatic status by some Old Believers, as witnessed by the proclamations of their congresses.

Ethnographic data have corroborated the claim that priestless Old Believers viewed the icon somewhat differently from the way their priestly co-religionists did. While the "iconic principle" existed among all Old Believers of this period, attitudes about symbols of the faith did vary from one Old Believer group to another. One contemporary observer, in describing this love for ancient icons, called the Old Believers "zealots for antiquity."[43] Another scholar put it even more strongly, saying that, for the priestless Old Believers, icons took the symbolic place of the Eucharist. This line of reasoning claimed that the presence of the holy person depicted on an icon shadowed the physical manifestation of Christ on earth during the Eucharistic transformation of bread and wine. In addition, this idea connected the reverence paid icons to that given communion vessels, "for [the priestless Old Believers] there is already in the icons—although to a lesser degree than in the Eucharist—the reality of the transfiguration of the flesh by communion."[44] While impressionistic, the analysis touched upon the important task that icons played as physical intercessors between a sinful, natural world and a transfigured state. Through icons, wrote one Old Believer, a soul was enabled "to pass from the dark path and to stand firm in the bosom of the ancient piety."[45] Such a statement more aptly described the priestless Old Believer interaction with icons than it did that of their priestly counterparts, since the latter also had a complete sacramental life to aid their spiritual growth.

Beyond Iconography
Secular Pictures, Old Believers, and Educated Society

Although iconography remained the primary pictorial expression of the Old Belief, it was not the only accepted type of representation. Old Believers had, from the beginning of their struggle, used pictorial representations outside the realm of iconography to bolster arguments against the state and the established church. Woodcuts, illustrations, and text illuminations abounded in Old Believer books, often mixing political statements with religious messages.[46] Clearly, Old Believers did not have any generalized disregard for noniconographic pictures. Yet by the turn of the nineteenth century the predominance of westernized secular art, technological processes of photo and art reproduction, and the rise of portrait photography made many Old Believers uneasy.

Old Believers showed ambivalent attitudes, ranging from outright hostility to complete acceptance, toward both westernized pictorial forms and portrait photography. As in other circumstances, the priestless Old Believers drew a more stringent line against western art forms than did their priestly counterparts. The *Shield of Faith (Shchit very)*, a Pomortsy publication, lamented the necessity of using western-style pictures to illustrate its pages. While regretting that the illustrations did not always conform "to the ideas of the journal and, in the thoughts of the editors, to the ideas of all the old ritual,"[47] *Shchit very* did in fact publish illustrations in a western European style throughout its existence. The editors of the journal hoped that Old Believers, with their post-1905 freedom of religion, would finally produce "clean Christian work[s] of art, with clean Christian ideas, without the tinge of the pernicious influence of human flesh, without the tinge of rationalistic views on the divine traditional prescriptions of the Christian church."[48] This desire, however, rarely bore fruit in the journal's illustrations.

A conference of Chasovenniki, convened in 1912, heard an impassioned speech asking for guidance on many questions, among them "pictorial portraits," "icon painting," and "the painting of nonbelievers."[49] The issues taken up in this conference, including questions of technological change, revealed that the Chasovenniki were often among the most conservative Old Believers. Thanks to modern photographic processes, Russian folk at the turn of the century had the opportunity to commit themselves to posterity in pictorial form. Great consternation was felt by those Old Believers who suspected that the process could confuse secular

Figure 15 An Old Believer illustration of Bishop Paul of Kilomna in traditional icono-graphic style. The bishop wears pre-Nikonian vestments and blesses with the two-fingered sign of the cross. Courtesy of Russkaia Kniga.

portraiture with iconography. Such an attitude, found especially among the faithful in the geographic extremes of Russia, illustrated a peculiar, almost premodern, sensibility about pictorial art. This viewpoint left lit-tle room for distinctions between iconographic forms and secular art, and it invested even secular pictures with an almost iconographic impor-tance. The argument explained that Old Believers must be wary of non-traditional pictorial forms because "the educational meaning of pictures and drawings is very great; many times it affects the mind, will, and heart of a person far more convincingly than the wordy, eloquent argu-ment of a preacher."[50] In other words, secular art could lead to secular ideas. Other Old Believers, however, flatly denied that portraiture was sinful, saying that Christ had his portrait made (albeit without human intervention) and in so doing provided a guide for Christian behavior.[51]

In an attempt to mold photographic portraiture to the "clean works of Christian art" desired by the Pomortsy, some Old Believers used the symbols of iconography to lend an air of sanctity to their own works. In 1909, *Shchit very* (the Pomortsy magazine) published a series of articles called "Material for the History of the Old Rite." One illustration in that series showed Bishop Paul of Kolomna, whom Old Believers asserted had been killed in defense of the old rituals. Paul was never canonized in any liturgical sense but was always considered a martyr by the Old Believers (fig. 15).[52] Note the long face, the shape of the beard, the large eyes, the scroll of holy scripture, and—most important—the prominent blessing made with the two-fingered sign of the cross. In this case the magazine illustrator had decided to use iconographic forms to depict a holy Old Believer. The technique was not new (Old Believers had been painting icons of the archpriest Avvakum for generations), but it did follow the stated desire to illustrate the magazine with pictures not tainted by western styles. Furthermore, in 1913 *Shchit very* also published a pho-

Figure 16 An early twentieth-century photograph of Dionisii Vasil'evich Batov—an Old Believer writer—employs the iconographic techniques shown in Bishop Paul's picture but in a new medium.

Figure 17 A Florentine Madonna, used by liberal Old Believers to show that even the Roman church preferred the two-fingered sign of the cross.

tograph of D. C. Batov, longtime Pomortsy writer and apologist (fig. 16).[53] Compare the photograph to the picture of Paul. Although not dressed in clerical garb, Batov wore a half-cassock popular among the Pomortsy. Like Paul, he held a scroll in his left hand, and his right made the sign of the cross. Since Batov was not a cleric, his hand was not raised in blessing, but there could be no mistaking the similarity between illustration and photograph. Here was proof of an Old Believer style of illustration and of a transferal of iconographic forms to a new technology and medium—the photograph.[54]

Priestly believers generally showed both a more cosmopolitan attitude and a broader interpretation of acceptable pictorial forms, and they made wider use of western artistic styles than did their priestless counterparts. Belokrinitsy magazines often featured illustrations and pictures far removed from traditional iconography, and editors included good examples of western-style pictures based on Christian themes. *Old Ritual Thought (Staroobriadcheskaia mysl')*, for example, published an extraordinary article and a series of reproductions entitled "The History of the Two-Fingered [Sign of the Cross] in Pictures."[55] The journal also printed photo reproductions of paintings and carvings from Paris's Louvre Museum. These included not only ancient Greek icons, in which Christ made the two-fingered sign, but western pictures too. The most surprising illustration may have been the full-page reproduction of a medieval

Florentine Madonna (fig. 17).[56] Only the two-fingered sign in this Madonna could have been acceptable by Old Believer standards: western methods of perspective, dress, composition, and above all the "fleshiness" of the picture starkly contrasted with the religious pictures preferred by Old Believers. Oddly enough, the author paired these western pictorial representations with a classic Old Believer polemical argument against the Russian Orthodox church, claiming that even pictures in the Louvre showed that "the holy apostles did not teach the 'three-fingers,' as the acts of the council of 1666–1667 shamelessly assured. . . ."[57]

Thus, there was no monolithic Old Believer position on the issue of artistic style. On the one hand, the priestly journal printed patently westernized, Renaissance-style sacred images in its text, an action at odds with Old Believer tradition. On the other hand, the editors probably believed that the good end justified the means and hoped to drive home the impropriety of the Russian Orthodox church's attitude on the sign of the cross. In doing so, the priestly Old Believers co-opted western forms for their own use and signaled that western culture was acceptable selectively, so long as it did not confront basic elements of the Old Belief. In some cases, photography firms catered specifically to Old Believer needs, providing photos of old ritualist spiritual leaders (both dead and alive), teachers, children, and brotherhoods, as well as photographic copies of portrayals of events famous in Old Believer history ("Boiarina Morozova," "Argument over the Faith in the Granovityi Palace," and the like).[58]

While disagreeing on the use of new technology and western styles, it was the continued production of old-style icons that began to bring fame to Old Believer communities throughout the empire. Periodicals such as *The Russian Icon (Russkaia ikona)* and committees such as the "Society of Lovers of Spiritual Enlightenment" and the "Committee of Guardians of Folk Iconography" praised Old Believer icons. Educated society's new interest was not connected to the Old Believer community or related to a curiosity about the Old Believer religious experience, although *Russkaia ikona* was probably underwritten at least in part by the Old Believer Riabushinskii family. Authors and scholars viewed the Old Believers as a cultural remnant that preserved the very essence of Russian national identity.[59]

While the public praised Old Believer icons, machine-made icons were increasingly replacing hand-painted ones. Those who appreciated the old styles tended to oppose mass-produced iconography in a struggle against the tradition of painting by hand.[60] The Old Believers were raised up as an example of the survival of Russian national identity in the face of the "exploitation of the spiritual needs of our Russian folk"[61] by foreign firms that flooded the market with inferior quality lithographs or prints. In a market response to machine-made examples, hand-painted icons had become increasingly expensive—far beyond the reach of common believers—and the number of iconographers fell precipitously. N.

P. Kondakov's *The Present State of Russian Folk Icon Painting (Sovremennoe polozhenie russkoi narodnoi ikonopisi)* gained some prominence as an analysis of this decline, especially in the province of Vladimir where fine traditional iconographers had flourished. Kondakov's study noted the Old Believers' retention of ancient styles as one of the few bright spots in an otherwise dire situation for contemporary iconography. Another scholar claimed that the Old Believers' maintenance of tradition showed an "indispensable love for all their Russian kin."[62] Some of the best iconographers using the traditional styles left their villages to be employed by Old Believer communities or wealthy Old Believer industrialists, a phenomenon that both confounded the Russian Orthodox church and secured the Old Believers a reputation as defenders of traditional ways.[63] And, at least one late imperial Old Believer source prohibited buying copper icons from Nikonians.[64]

While they did not explicitly mention it, Old Believers probably accepted only hand-painted icons. Ethnographic texts have not described the presence of machine-printed icons in Old Believer temples. Furthermore, an analysis of present-day Old Believers claims that the photographic reproduction of icons is

> strictly proscribed. Whether the icon is in church or at home, it may under no circumstances be photographed, a prohibition which extends to any other object in the chapel. The only explanation for this provided by my informants emphasized the danger of the photograph's falling into hostile hands and being defaced. Hence there seems to be a postulated transference of identity between a painted original and its mechanical copy.[65]

While this observation does not come from the late imperial period, it does provide some insight into why Old Believers would prohibit reproduction of icons. In the context of Old Believers in the late nineteenth century, however, it would seem more logical to perceive the prohibition against machine-made icons in the context of technological innovation. Since the photographic process was innovative and originated in the West, and since its method provided an unnatural deviation from true painted icons, the process may have been seen literally as an anti-Christian manipulation of the iconic form.[66] Old Believers knew that icons, especially those that preserved the old ritualist style, provided a conduit of grace through which one could become deified. Would not Antichrist strike at that very lifeline and try to deceive the faithful through improper icons? The priestly Old Believers, who generally welcomed technological change, nonetheless led the way in popular education on traditional iconography. Important priestly Old Believer families, such as the Riabushinskii family, continued to hold some of the most important private collections of icons in Russia. Nowhere did even the most liberal priestly magazine condone the use of machine-made icons.

Scholarly publications incorrectly viewed Old Believers as traditionalists, who kept ancient icons out of ignorance, rather than as self-conscious guardians of ancient piety. One scholar said, for example, that "it is better to know about the simple folk, the merchants, holding on to the ancient ways, [and] the old ritualists" than to study the academic aspects of iconography.[67] The Old Believers, however, did not necessarily fall into the realm of "simple folk" in their love for iconography. Instead, they invested energy, time, and wealth into the preservation of artistic forms that bound them to their Orthodox heritage and manifested the presence of God among them.

For whatever reason, though, the educated public at the turn of the century increasingly identified the Old Believers with the best in traditional Russian religious art. In this way, scholars implicitly criticized the Russian Orthodox church for becoming infatuated with western forms, to the point of selling off its ancient icons and replacing them with those in the Italianate style. There was some outcry, at least by Old Believers, over the propriety of a market in ancient icons: "whoever thinks about this question," lamented one author, "who saw these pictures in the bazaars and fairs, then adds sorrow to his aching spirit."[68] Nevertheless, Old Believers—often the wealthy industrialists—bought ancient icons to enrich their places of worship and their personal collections.[69]

The Old Believers of course rejected the idea that iconography was simply a transmittal of the Russian folk aesthetic. For them, an Old Believer icon museum for the study of old Russian art (such as D. K. Trenev proposed) was a profane use of sacred objects.[70] On the other hand, academic interest in Old Believer art—especially among the priestly group expanding its relations with Russian society—dovetailed with the desire to build a self-conscious study of the Old Belief. The priestly cemetery of Rogozhskoe, for example, heralded its Old Believer institute as the first center of higher learning specifically dedicated to the concerns of old ritualism, including iconography.[71] In the end, educated society's revival of interest in ancient iconography only furthered the Old Believers' desire to cement their place as the sole retainers of true Russian Orthodoxy.

Conclusion

Representing the Old Belief was a problematic issue for Old Believers in the late imperial period. On the one hand, their unbending devotion to traditional icon styles offered a link between pre-Nikonian Orthodoxy and the Old Belief that helped legitimize the Old Believers in Russian society. Furthermore, this traditionalism also invited interaction with art historians and enthusiasts interested in iconography as an artifact of Russian culture. On the other hand, the relationship between Old Believer icons and those of the established church remained unclear. Many icons of the ancient piety were kept by the Russian Orthodox church, which, according to the Old Believers, defiled them through its contact. So, while condemning western influences in the iconography of the church, Old Believers at the same time had to acknowledge that the Nikonians maintained some God-given grace through their wonder-working icons. To make matters worse, Old Believers had to contend with the problem of machine-made icons. As conservators of ancient styles, old ritualists had to decide how to combat the dearth of good traditional icons and the flooding of the market by mediocre machine-made examples. The faithful responded by pooling their resources of icons and attracting the best traditional iconographers to the Old Belief. Expanded interest in the care and adoration of icons showed that they remained the primary symbol of the iconic form for Old Believers.

Noniconographic pictorial art also raised problems for Old Believers. Was western-style art acceptable in a pious home? Should Old Believers publish western-style pictures and photographs? Did photographic portraiture act as an unnatural opposite to holy images? These questions revealed a struggle between increasingly secular and modern influences and the traditional Old Believer attitudes toward art. To the extent that Old Believers accepted technical and stylistic innovations, they also accepted modernizing and westernizing society. Urban Old Believers—especially the Belokrinitsy—were most open to outside influences in pictorial art. Others, especially the Pomortsy, hoped to develop a native Old Believer art that could take advantage of new technology while eschewing foreign styles. Many old ritualists, however, simply questioned the sense of receiving any foreign influence at all into their lives.

Ritual Prohibitions

Expanding Boundaries of the Old Belief

About baptism, the Eucharist, confession, marriage,
about prayers with women who recently gave birth,
about the blessing of preceptors, about prayers for
the Sovereign Tsar, about eating with nonbelievers,
about wearing foreign clothes, about tea and
samovars, about drinking wine and sikera (vodka),
about railways, about suicide, about sudden death,
about burials, about domes with eagles and four-
edged crosses that they tread under feet, about tobacco smoking and snuff, about the cutting of hair on
the head and beards, about kerosene lamps, about
potatoes, about the community, about brotherhoods,
about pictorial portraits, about icon painting or the
painting of nonbelievers, about books written by
nonbelievers, about agricultural machines, and many
others.
—*A Chasovennik Old Believer*

Old Believer religious ideology provided a large
number of ritual traditions that defined the relation of a believer to an increasingly secular,
modern Russia. These traditions sometimes
came directly from the writings of the Holy Fathers, sometimes appeared as logical extensions
of holy writings, and sometimes developed in
response to new conditions in Russia. Traditional prohibitions in particular illustrated how Old Believers interacted with their world. Although
scholars have noted "unqualified opposition"[1] by Old Believers to many
activities and substances, documents from the late imperial period show
considerable debate over the nature and role of proscriptive teachings.

Aside from questions on specific prohibitions, an analysis of this debate illuminates three areas of Old Believer life. First, prohibitions were

commitments—interactive symbols—that magnified Old Believer attitudes. Second, differences in opinion regarding prohibitions reflected geographic and philosophical variations among groups of Old Believers. Finally, the debate on prohibitions showed not only how Old Believers combated the influences of modern life but, conversely, how they used modern ideas to reaffirm their own views. At its most extreme, Old Believer ritual bans provided the starting point for an argument in favor of social renewal across all Russia.

In this period, Old Believers themselves held two concurrent yet divergent views on the function of ritual prohibitions. For one group, proscripted behavior provided a method to differentiate the community of believers from the dominant Russian society. This group might be called the traditionalist segment of the Old Belief, since it claimed to conserve ancient rituals. Other Old Believers streamlined prohibitions into more enlightened or rationalized rules. The latter group might be identified as the liberal section of the Old Belief, since it hoped to change the role of ritual prohibitions. The difference in views did not follow clear theological lines, nor was it outwardly acknowledged by the faithful. Nevertheless, the traditional-versus-liberal distinction represented the variation in responses to modernity by Old Believers via their ritual prohibitions. The traditionalists tended to live in the least populated parts of the empire while the liberals were clustered in urban areas.[2]

The outpouring of interest in ritual prohibitions provided the forum for a national debate on the role they played in Old Believer life.[3] Moreover, the newly established rights of the Old Belief both to publish and to assemble opened a floodgate of inquiry by the faithful into their own ritual forms. Previously, only polemicists and missionaries had had the opportunity to consider the issue openly. After the Act of Toleration of 1905, though, old ritualists from all segments of society and from all geographic areas could interact with one another in discussing the ritual forms.

It is not clear to what extent either the traditionalist or liberal views predated 1905. Manuscript evidence from before the Act of Toleration supports the existence of the traditionalist position, but there are few records of any progressive tendencies in the religious writings of Old Believers before 1905. It does seem unlikely, though, that the progressive position would have appeared—fully formed—only after 1905. At any rate, liberals used the freedom to publish as an outlet for their progressive ideas. In addition, the scores of Old Believer conferences held across Russia in the early twentieth century provided the opportunity for both sides to be heard.

The epigraph to this chapter suggests that questions of prohibitions were often tangled. Delegates to a Chasovennik conference did not differentiate between canonical questions (receiving the Eucharist), political questions (praying for the tsar), and ritual prohibitions (eating potatoes, using railroads, taking snuff). Their attitude was typical of Old Believer discourse in the early twentieth century. The Chasovennik speaker illustrated a basic premise prominent in old ritualist thinking—the belief that all modes of human endeavor were to be controlled by ritual prohibitions. Since members of the "apostate" or "heretical" Russian Orthodox faith did not obey the bans, these prohibitions served to set Old Believers apart from the rest of Russian society. By holding some activities to be unacceptable (or even ritually unclean and anti-Christian), Old Believers created a distinction between their community of believers and the rest of the world.

This desire to set apart the remnant of the faithful from the rest of society had deep roots in the Old Belief, due to the group's status as a persecuted faith and to its belief that society was under the power of Antichrist. The priestless Vyg Pustyn', for example, saw itself as both a hermitage and a wilderness, maintaining both meanings of the word *pustyn'*. Confrontation and dissent in that most famous of Old Believer settlements often resulted from differing views on the correct relationship between the monastery and greater Russia. Early adherents of the Old Belief felt sure that the end of the world was at hand and that Antichrist ruled Russian society. As time passed and the apocalypse did not occur, however, Old Believers were pressed to define the correct relationship between themselves and the other Russians. The apocalyptic tradition held fast among Old Believers, though, and manifested itself in the opinion that the outside world had become sullied in its relationship with anti-Christian forces. In time, Russian society's disinterest in ritual proscriptions began to be equated with the apostasy of the three-fingered sign of the cross and the new spelling of Jesus' name.

All of this points to a strongly social understanding of Old Believer prohibitions. The most thorough study according to such an interpretation is the analysis by David Scheffel of Old Believers in Alberta (Canada). His thesis, adapted from that of Mary Douglas, ascribes a dichotomy of purity/impurity to most of the ritual prohibitions he observed among Old Believers in Alberta. The difference between "Christian" and "pagan" practices therefore tended to reinforce distinctions between ritually "clean" Old Believers and the "unclean" world.[4] A good example of this dichotomy (and of variations in opinion) might be seen in one Old Believer's question of whether he could share the *bania* (a north Russian sauna) with the heterodox. The editors of *Shchit very*, a Pomortsy journal, replied that "ancient Christians avoided washing in baths together with heretics" and so probably should he.[5] Some sources absolutely opposed using the bania at all; others prohibited its use on Wednesday and Friday (fast days); while still others associated the bania with prayer, making an explicit connection between bodily cleanliness, health, and religion.[6]

Scheffel has linked ritual prohibitions to the Eastern Orthodox view of purity, especially as it existed in Greek and Russian folk piety. While valid on the local level (among the Alberta Old Believers), Scheffel's thesis on puritanism cannot be universally applied to the Old Belief. First, local communities often constructed their own patterns of bans, leaving no overarching system among all Old Believers. Second, and equally important, many of the clean/unclean differentiations expounded by the Alberta community could have arisen in part from quasi-Christian folk beliefs. For example, the differentiation between types of water described among the Alberta Old Believers (flowing versus stagnant) possibly joined folk ideas of water sprites with Christian traditions of the holy river Jordan and the cleansing of baptismal waters. The syncretism of peasant religion (like some Old Believer prohibitions) proved to be highly variable and did not always lend itself well to wide-ranging analysis.[7]

Some prohibitions, however, did find broad support among many different groups of Old Believers. Among the Pomortsy, for example, the sin of *mirshchenie* (worldliness) forfeited an Old Believer's right to receive the blessing of the censer.[8] Worldliness dramatically illustrated the continuing problem of Old Believers' interaction with society—how much was acceptable? The late imperial period provided the means to argue the question publicly.

As noted earlier, a priestless believer had to make a special prayer of confession to the community after interacting with those who were not a part of Old Believer society. Some Old Believers of this period took an even more stringent line, saying that "it is clear and understood to every God-fearing Christian that . . . having a friendship with nonbelievers" might seem like hospitality but instead actually seduced the faithful into unchristian behavior.[9] One Chasovennik conference concluded that "if one . . . communicates together in eating and drinking with foreigners: the first time [that person is to be] excommunicated from the sobor (of the general prayers) for six days, the second time for one year, and the third time for three years."[10] While these examples seem particularly extreme, many Old Believers regularly abstained from eating and drinking with "foreigners"—those of other faiths.[11] After dining with outsiders, some Old Believers forbade sharing meals or even utensils with family members (semimonastic Old Believers of the upper Kama might not take part in communal prayer for as along as six weeks after breaking bread with outsiders).

By the twentieth century, however, many Old Believers (perhaps the majority) no longer considered it worldly to dine with the heterodox. Fedoseevtsy fathers bemoaned the fact that their flock had begun to sit "at one table" with nonbelievers and so did not say the Lord's Prayer before dining.[12] Some Pomortsy of this period stayed to the middle of the road, saying that "if you eat with a heretic fully to win him over to the church, then you receive no condemnation. . . . Preaching must be accomplished." The converse of the argument, however, was that social dining with non–Old Believers *would* bring down condemnation.[13]

Old Believer dietary rules differed from Old Testament Mosaic law and Jewish kosher regulations. Old Believers kept special plates, glasses, and utensils not to separate various foods but to differentiate between Old Believer and nonbeliever; in many instances, the faithful would not sit at the table with adherents of another faith but would dine elsewhere in the same room. At times, even food touched by non–Old Believers was suspect.[14] In this way, dietary and social prohibitions merged.

Some foods and plants themselves fell under the ritual ban. Although many of these were mentioned in Mosaic laws found in Deuteronomy and Leviticus, other foods—thought to be of foreign origin—were not consumed by the Old Believers.[15] Old ritualists sometimes banned the potato, for example, simply because of its non-Russian source. Otherwise ubiquitous in the Russian peasant diet, the potato was therefore often absent from the Old Believer table. Old Believer magazines generally agreed that the potato could be stricken from any list of prohibitions but realized that many Old Believers still did not accept its use:

> Such an idea was fortified among them because the product arrived to us from the West . . . which the Old Believers do not love up to this very time. The hostile attitude toward this intensified even more since the first [person] who wanted to spread potatoes in Russia was the emperor Peter the Great, who perpetrated so much evil for the old ritualists, imposing the double fine for keeping a beard and wearing old-Russian clothing.[16]

In the middle of the nineteenth century, a certain Chasovennik community, for example, decided to ban the potato. When, however, the local preceptor discovered the "spurious nature" of the manuscript used to promote the ban, he again allowed the potato in the local Old Believer diet.[17] Old Believers went so far as to develop folktales about the origin and development of the potato, placing the tuber at the center of a controversy over the inheritance of a foreign king.[18]

Old Believers once restricted their use of white sugar even more than their eating of the potato, since sugar violated the ancient ban on eating animal blood and because refined sugar had not been known in old Russia.[19] Early bleaching processes, they explained, used blood in sugar whitening. For that reason, many Old Believer manuscripts quoted scripture and the Holy Fathers' writings on animal blood and animal sacrifice under the heading "On sugar." Although many Old Believers began to use sugar once modern refinement procedures had developed, there remained a large manuscript literature that questioned its propriety.[20] One text went so far as to claim that sugar was first imported to Europe from

Siam in the fifteenth century, that the first refinery was built in Venice, and that sugar was now available from plantations in Santo Domingo. Such texts all proved the foreign influence of the substance![21]

Most priestly Old Believers of this period did not accept the bans on worldly interaction or the restrictions on certain foods. Knowing this, Scheffel has interpreted dining segregation as a priestless reaction to "sacramental deprivation," which raised everyday eating to a ritual status previously reserved for the Eucharist itself. Scheffel has noted that in 1910 leaders of the Belokrinitsy lifted all bans on foodstuffs and on eating with nonbelievers.[22] This seems to corroborate the theory that the Belokrinitsy no longer needed the prohibition, since they had ample access to the Eucharist. The theory of sacramental deprivation, however, needs qualification. Another explanation might point to the Belokrinitsa hierarchy's general willingness to integrate themselves into Russian society. That even the Belokrinitsy—most liberal of all old ritualists—waited until 1910 to lift the ban actually illustrates the custom's endurance. Finally, lifting of a ritual ban by the Belokrinitsy assumed that the prohibition had once been in effect, presumably at the time the group still took fugitive priests. Thus, the Belokrinitsy had only briefly been deprived of the Eucharist and so never needed to replace it with food rituals. In fact, the 1910 decision highlighted the changes in attitude prevalent during the period between 1905 and 1917.

Although prohibitions varied among communities, local adherence to ritual bans (based at least formally on Christian themes) created a system of shared values and assumptions that characterized Old Believer communities. While Old Believers might live among other Russians and might even do business with them, peculiar prohibitions helped to differentiate the faithful from all the rest. In short, the process succeeded in creating cohesive, separate units of Old Believers within the dominant Russian society.

Depending on geographic location, Old Believers tended to differ in their views. Old Believers who lived in Siberia or in the forests of north European Russia strongly supported complete ritual separation from the outside world. In the highly autonomous and isolated communities of these regions, the distance between Old Believer and anti-Christian society could, of course, be maintained. Even there, however, the diffusion of agricultural and domestic technology, the advances in communication, and the development of transportation links began to connect Old Believer groups with the rest of Russia. The changes in turn led to a confrontation among various Old Believers—on the definition, importance, and role of ritual prohibitions—that played itself out in the early twentieth century.

In the cities, Old Believers found it more difficult to realize a ritual distinction based on dining prohibitions. There, the faithful had to wrestle more creatively with the question of differentiation between the faithful and the nonbelievers. As a result, many Old Believers came to accept interaction with their neighbors as a way to expand the influence of old ritualist religious ideology into other segments of Russian society. Although the question of differentiation may have predated 1905, manuscript literature does not mention it. Consequently, the period of freedom for Old Believers must have provided the opportunity for the liberal faithful to comment publicly on the question of interaction.

Expanding the Boundaries of Prohibitions

Many Old Believers, seeking to meet modern life on a field defined according to their own religious sensibilities, used prohibitions as a malleable set of rules. These Old Believers hoped to manipulate the rush of innovations in their life—from farm machinery to phonographs—by fitting them into an existing religious structure. Some Old Believers viewed new agricultural and domestic technology with grave doubt. While Russian peasants were generally ambivalent toward mechanization, Old Believers employed religious prohibitions and theologically based arguments to combat perceived threats to their traditional mode of life.

In a largely peasant society, the topic of agricultural machinery provided much fuel for the conflict over technological innovation. One Old Believer conference of this period exemplified the problematic relationship between Old Believers and their machines. Although some delegates wanted to discuss the prohibition of these machines, calling them the "delight of anti-Christians," fellow delegates who already used machinery in their agricultural work successfully tabled the matter.[23] Conferences that took place in European Russia where a preponderance of delegates came from western or central provinces did not mention the question. The issue loomed most large for those Old Believers convening in Siberia, where communities apparently had less familiarity with technology than did their European co-religionists. The question of new farming technology was never really settled because of the decentralized and independent nature of Old Believer communities and the lack of clear scriptural or traditional teaching on the issue. At yet another conference, specifically dedicated to the improvement of Old Believer agriculture, the delegates clearly supported innovations.[24]

While some of the faithful undoubtedly chose to eschew agricultural machines altogether, more often an uneasy truce developed between those who saw the manifest usefulness of machinery and those who felt a vague unease over the potential religious issues involved. Such was the case among a group of Old Believers in Perm, who

> categorically refused to employ a plow for working the earth. It is strange
> that they sow and reap with the help of farm machinery, but yet in tilling

none wants to use the plug [iron plow] and plows instead by sokha [wooden plow], that most primitive method. To [an agronomist's] question they explained that "the [Holy] Writings prohibit deep turning up of soil." The esteemed agronomist reports that he himself repeatedly talked to them about the advantages of the plug, and that his helper talked, and finally he with his helper tried to convince the muzhiks, but the desired results never came: the muzhiks quietly shook their heads and only now and then some 'elder' would utter 'No . . . the Writings prohibit.'[25]

Of course, there were no writings prohibiting particular plowing techniques. Rather, these Old Believers saw the iron plow as a foreign influence and simply used the guise of supposed religious writings to oppose it. The group, however, vacillated in its position—while singling out the iron plow as the implement to be prohibited, these Old Believers accepted other types of agricultural machines. Although the paucity and vagueness of sources leave conclusions unverifiable, the iron plow itself had probably come to symbolize a mechanized order. Other machines appeared in the Old Believer fields, but the plow signified the doubts of the faithful regarding innovative, foreign agricultural machines.

Here indeed was the crux of the problem. On the one hand, Old Believers regularly prohibited goods or actions due to their foreign origin. In the lore of the Old Belief, for instance, Antichrist often appeared as Peter I, and the succeeding westernization of Russia was illustrated by the European style of shaven faces and foreign ("German") clothing and manners.[26] Furthermore, agricultural machines, often designed (though not necessarily built) in western Europe or America, could be included under the prohibition of foreign imports. On the other hand, Old Believers had at the same time developed a well-deserved reputation for good animal husbandry and high agricultural production, not to mention success in industry. Some of the faithful must have embraced more efficient means to achieve higher crop yields than the methods allowed by traditional techniques. Given their predisposition to inject ritual prohibitions into all facets of life, however, it is not surprising that many Old Believers debated the mechanization of agriculture in the context of religious prohibition rather than in economic or social terms.

The prohibition against agricultural technology remained mostly a concern local to Siberian and northern Russian communities. None of the national Old Believer leadership (of any concord) accepted the prohibition, and all Old Believer journals supported the liberal wing of old ritualism, favoring the acceptance of modernization. Some journals, like *Zlatostrui* and *Ural'skii staroobriadets*, actively campaigned against "backwardness" in Old Believer communities. These journals reprinted pieces from more general publications, in which was noted, for example, the difficulty of getting peasants to mow hay with machines. Such articles often did not specifically mention Old Believers but dealt with the problem of technological modernization in broader terms.[27]

Many of the old ritualist faithful also questioned innovations in domestic technology. Debates over the introduction of gramophones in the home often arose in the "Answers from the Editors" sections. Were the machines themselves anti-Christian, and did they lead to improper behavior, or were they actually acceptable in an old ritualist home? Some Old Believers even worried that gramophones might take the place of humans in liturgical singing. Recorded singing would be an unnatural, perverse way to praise God. At the very least, liturgical recordings would leave people mute, and silent prayer was suspect in a culture bound up closely with communal forms of worship.[28] The core of the gramophone problem, therefore, lay both in its innovation (especially its coming from the West) and in its potential to skew the natural, God-given order of things, including the dehumanization of divine services.

Adherents of an expanding canon of prohibitions suspected other innovations as well and produced manuscripts, including "The Golden Chain" ("Zlataia tsep'"), also known as the "Chain of Heaven" ("Tsep' nebesnaia"), to prove that the ancient fathers had warned against using kerosene lamps.[29] "Zlataia tsep'" (which exists only in manuscript form) followed the traditional Russian style of compiling information gleaned from many sources on a variety of religious issues. It mixed together comments on fasting with exhortations on icons, prayer, and heresy. It also apparently made remarks that could be interpreted as recommending the prohibition of kerosene lamps.[30] This prohibition probably developed from previous methods of lighting the home—with tapers and oil lamps—that had provided both light and also a ritual sacrifice to icons. Changing to kerosene in the home could then lead to a variation in ritual lighting, and any change in ritual lamps would surely go against the "natural order" of the old rite. In fact, many Old Believers reportedly did not "make use of kerosene," using instead a torch (luchina) to light their homes. One report claimed that Old Believers even "abhor gunpowder matches, suspecting something antichristianly and unnatural in their quick lighting—and among the old people tinder and flints are used."[31] As could be expected, *Zlatostrui* weighed in heavily for the use of kerosene while also accepting that it could be used improperly:

> God gave man reason, and man invented guns, and with these guns he can protect himself from attack by wild beasts or get food for himself by means of hunting birds and animals. But man can [also] kill his neighbor and even himself with guns. Is it possible that in the latter case we can blame the gun, and not the evil will of a man? Of course, it is the man himself who is culpable of murder or suicide, not the gun. So it is with kerosene. That which was made by God is procured from the earth. The mind of man in-

vented the lamp, which safely burns kerosene, lighting and warming his dwelling. In this where is the sin? See that sin is an action against the commandments of God and against one's neighbor. But in lighting a lamp we do not insult God or people, which makes this action impossible to be called sinful.[32]

The role of modern medicine raised similar doubts about changing the natural order of a divinely organized world. Some Old Believers specifically questioned using the smallpox vaccination to ward off the disease. Was this procedure not a slap in the face of God? Was it not usurping God's power to insure not getting a disease through vaccination?[33] The liberal program replied that

Smallpox was brought to us by the filthy nomadic Tatars, infected from their own cattle. And therefore it is necessary to think of who sins more—the Christian who anticipates a sickness with measures opened to human wisdom by God, or he who through his negligence and ignorance allows the deformity of his children: blindness, crippling, and so on.[34]

This answer turned the age-old suspicion of foreign influence on its head: the *smallpox*, not the vaccination, was to be prohibited since it arrived from the east on the backs of Tatar hordes. The answer, however, did not claim that vaccination did not constitute sin, only that the alternative was more sinful. One magazine received so many letters on this problem that it decided to put a closure to the matter by refusing to continue replying to the question.[35] Other journals showed little enthusiasm for vaccination: one claimed, cryptically, that it was not prohibited just so long as it was "not used against Christianity."[36]

Fear of anticipating the will of God also provided the impetus for prohibitions on innovations such as property insurance. The first Pomortsy conference of 1909 concluded that insuring church buildings—a practice already widespread among Pomortsy Old Believer parishes—was simply "not objectionable." The inclusion of the question on the national agenda, however, showed that the issue was still controversial,[37] as can be seen in a strongly written "Answer from the Editors":

Q: May a Christian insure a home?
A: This question, as it does not concern the salvation of our soul, but touches upon the everyday concerns of the activities of the world, may be permitted [in the question and answer department] dependent on the goals [of those] from which it comes. For example, people may insure their property in order to burn it and then receive a premium. Of course this is a sin. But if a person wishes to protect his property from loss in order to secure his family, etc., then for that [reason] the Lord gave people reason, so that

they may intelligently build their life not only in the relation to the blessing
of eternity, but also to the earthly times.[38]

All these seemingly disparate manifestations of ritual proscriptions
have a common thread in their aversion to "unnatural" innovations of
Christian activities. The idea of an unnatural innovation hearkens back
directly to the iconic form as an influence in Old Believer symbols. If traditional facets of ritual had been accepted as godlike, then any deviation
could be construed as anti-Christian. Even with the exhortations of liberal journals, many Old Believers continued to reject imports from the
West as affronts to religious sensibility. This rejection has already been
discussed in terms of mechanically produced icon prints. It can be seen
as well in the disdain for gramophones that could mechanically repro-
duce human voices, thus leaving mute the living singers of divine songs.
Likewise, kerosene lamps lit by sulfur matches could potentially take the
place of the oil lamps that shone in front of icons. Although no one knew
if kerosene was in itself anti-Christian, the prudent Old Believer held
tight to the old ways to ensure the continuation of the iconic form. In this
context, hating technological innovation could be equated with despising
Antichrist, who was trying to turn traditional Christian symbols into images of evil. While no person might know the final effect of technological
innovation, any Old Believer could realize the possibility of momentous
change spreading like wildfire to all facets of life.

Expanding Boundaries of the Old Belief

While many liberal Old Believers chose to accept the modernization of
society, they continued to retain certain ritual prohibitions associated
with the faith. Some Old Believers in fact sought to build a social program based on pre-existing Old Believer prohibitions. Such a program
diametrically opposed the aims of the more traditional Old Believers discussed above, since any plan for a general social renewal would have to
embrace relations with outside society. Rather than using proscriptions
to differentiate the faithful from their heterodox neighbors, liberal Old
Believers hoped to include all Russia in a prohibition on such things as
tea, tobacco, and alcohol.

The age-old dispute on tea provides a good starting point for an analysis of the new thinking on the prohibition issue. Although its consumption had long been associated with Russian culture, the Old Believers
had often refused tea. Their prohibition of tea derived not only from its
suspect origin (China) and its suspect introduction (during the reign of
Peter I) but also from its status as an intoxicant. The most creative Old
Believers claimed that tea was part of Chinese idolatry and therefore inappropriate for Christian consumption.[39] By the late imperial period,

however, drinking tea had spread among the Old Believers, reflecting a conscious departure from tradition. The Pomortsy conference of 1909, nevertheless, fought against the acceptance of tea by reaffirming the ban, calling tea drinking a "sin of pleasure-loving." Some delegates to the conference actually claimed that tea drinking constituted heresy rather than simply sin.[40]

Other Old Believers, however, seemed to have different ideas on the subject. The Chasovennik journal *Ural'skii staroobriadets*, for example, wrote that no holy books prohibited tea drinking and that tea had been rejected by Old Believers only because of its foreign nature. In an attack on traditionalists, the journal told its readers to follow the teachings of the scriptures and not the "creation of idle minds" that used "dark books" to ban tea drinking.[41] One such dark book claimed that he who drank tea "excommunicates himself from God Himself and thrice opens himself to anathema."[42]

The tea-drinking issue arose frequently in other magazines too. The reaction of *Zlatostrui*, for example, was mixed. On the one hand, it said that no holy scripture ever proscribed tea drinking and agreed with *Ural'skii staroobriadets* in its assessment of spurious holy books—no saints of the church ever wrote a text on tea or potatoes.[43] On the other hand, *Zlatostrui* seemed unwilling to dismiss the ban altogether, since tea drinking did constitute imbibing an intoxicant. Skirting the issue, the editors claimed that any harmful substance should be avoided but that people needed to heed professional doctors who could determine if tea was indeed injurious.[44] The journal finally had to make a general statement referring to previous articles on tea drinking, since it had apparently received as many questions to the editors on this subject as it had on small-pox vaccinations.[45]

The debate on tea drinking revealed the existence of a number of motives typical to discussion of ritual prohibitions. One group of Old Believers retained a traditional posture, saying simply that tea drinking constituted a sin. Another group took a more analytical approach, claiming that tea drinking never *specifically* appeared in scripture. The latter position, however, left the group wondering whether tea drinking should be banned at all. By leaving behind scriptural or quasi-scriptural arguments, these Old Believers turned to scientific data calling tea an intoxicant to reaffirm traditional prohibitions. The process co-opted modern science for the maintenance of tradition and opened the way for liberal Old Believers to take their message of social-renewal-through-abstinence to a larger audience than one willing to accept only traditional religious arguments.

The ambivalent attitude against tea drinking, however, became unequivocal on the prohibition of tobacco. The eradication of this vice, along with that of heavy drinking, turned into a cause célèbre, for Old

Believer ideology had long despised tobacco use as a putrefaction of God's human temple. Snuff was also abhorred, although without the universality accorded the smoking proscription.[46]

In the prohibition of smoking three facets of Old Believer experience interacted. First, the desire to abstain from intoxicants exemplified the "physicalization" of spiritual matters related to the physical forms of worship present among the Old Believers. Consistent with the Old Believer desire to integrate corporeal experience and religious ritual, the prohibition against smoking, like that against tea, also served as a defense against dirtying the body on which the sign of the cross was made, sullying the lips that kissed the cross, and invading the heart of a true believer.[47] "It is necessary," wrote one Old Believer, "to take care of the heart, created by God for the love and all-forgiveness, and not to allow filth going into the mouth to penetrate [the heart] and to pollute it."[48] The author did not differentiate between the physical heart, thought to be affected by smoking, and the metaphysical one, wherein resided love and forgiveness. In his experience as an Old Believer the two intertwined.

Old Believers also equated smoking and tea drinking as sins against temperate behavior. Tobacco acted as a behavior-changing substance, and so its use was classified as an "extraordinary sin."[49] For this reason tobacco was often called a poison, its use suicidal, and its growth or trade prohibited to adherents of the old ritual.[50] As in their position on tea, many Old Believers went so far as to wonder if tobacco smoking constituted heresy rather than simply sin.[51]

Other reasons have been put forth to explain the Old Believers' particular abhorrence to smoking. A rise in the use of tobacco during the westernization of Peter I played an important part in the lore of the subject.[52] An instinctive rejection of western innovations affected Old Believer attitudes toward tobacco, especially during its early dissemination. In itself, however, such an attitude does not adequately explain the vitality and longevity of the tradition, since prohibition of other Petrine innovations did not match the universal scorn given to tobacco use.

Another explanation depended on the perceived polarization between sacred and profane elements of Old Believer life. In this model, each sacred object or action had a profane alternative. Natural versus unnatural, light versus dark, Christian versus pagan, pure versus defiled—all became bound up in the way an Old Believer interacted with the world. Consistent with this theory is the differentiation between incense, a "holy smoke," and tobacco, literally the anti-Christian counterpart. To accept a Christian symbol (often quite literally, as described in the discussion of liturgical ritual in chapter 3), the believer naturally had to abstain from its defiled counterpart.[53]

This argument derived from the well-known belief among Old Believ-

ers that, while incense would bless icons, tobacco smoke would defile
them: after all, tobacco was often attributed to Satan.[54] The exact nature
of the defilement, however, is unclear. Did the Old Believers ban tobacco
smoking in front of icons out of respect for the holy figures portrayed on
them? Or did the physical icon itself become defiled from tobacco
smoke? Perhaps it was impossible to differentiate between these two ex-
planations. Defilement was both physical and spiritual—as interactive
symbols, icons needed to be spiritually and physically clean. Another un-
resolved question related to who actually smoked in front of icons. Since
presumably no Old Believers (even if they did use tobacco) would ever
smoke in a church, chapel, or home, the only possible interaction between tobacco smoke and icons would come from a non–Old Believer.[55]
The very presence of non–Old Believers in front of icons often caused
consternation; a tobacco-smoking nonbeliever would be that much more
unacceptable.

Certainly some Old Believers did fall under the influence of tobacco.
The 1910 report of the Russian Orthodox general procurator claimed, almost gleefully, that "this latest [generation] has begun to become infected with 'heresies' of the spirit and often do not abhor . . . indulging in
'the abominable poison' (tobacco)."[56] Old Believers themselves bemoaned this break from tradition, sometimes blaming it on the bad influences of the cities. "In the remote countryside and villages, where the
folk are whole [and] religious," claimed one observer, "smoking among
these Old Believers is really rare. . . ." When, however, a man left the village to work in industry or in the city, he saw smoking as "civilized."[57]
Unfortunately, statistics regarding Old Believer smoking were never
compiled. As important was the perception that Old Believers did fall
prey to the vice, especially once they left the village for the urban center.

It is notable that Old Believers perceived tobacco to be connected to
interaction with Russian society. One response to that connection was
flight from the offensive influence to a more pure environment. This op-
tion found the most support among Old Believers in Siberia and the far
northern part of European Russia, where separatist traditions remained
very much alive.

For those without the desire to flee into the woods, the influence of
cities had to be confronted. Given the possibility that smoking among
Old Believers was a direct result of their urban life, some old ritualist
leaders attempted to prohibit smoking altogether. The desire to ban
smoking soon expanded beyond the horizons of the old ritual as journal-
ists began to provide innovative arguments against this "filth in the
mouth." Smoking, according to these writers, afflicted every stratum of
society. As one might expect, the journal *Zlatostrui* led the attack on the
widespread smoking that seemed to be present not only among men but
also among women and children. The most unacceptable sight was that

of children smoking openly on the street, for this could only signal debauchery for the coming generations of Russia.[58]

Liberal old ritualists decided that a prohibition against tobacco could best be instituted by eliminating smoking throughout the empire, not just within Old Believer communities. This decision departed from Old Believer tradition by considering the idea that part of the bailiwick of the Old Belief was the spiritual health of the heterodox. Such an idea was just the kind of thing official church leaders had feared would result from the Act of Toleration of 1905—the chance for the Old Belief to compete for a voice of moral authority in Russian society. The fight against tobacco was to be waged among all of Russian society, not simply within the various concords of Old Believers. While not forgetting religious arguments, some Old Believer journals sought to add new weapons to their arsenal. In a step uncharacteristic of the perception of Old Believers as xenophobic and inward looking, a few of these journals promoted foreign examples of tobacco prohibitions. One article, for example, heralded a Russian antismoking league based on similar organizations in European cities.[59] Most news from the international front actually came as examples of antismoking legislation in other lands. European countries, even the United States, led the way in antismoking legislation, according to these articles. Since Michigan, Texas, and Illinois could ban smoking by children, one writer noted, it was hard to understand why Russia could not do the same.[60] It seemed that other nations dealt with such problems more effectively than did the Russians:

> In little Finland a law was passed on the complete prohibition of the manufacture and importation of alcoholic drinks in the land. Thus act true patriots, although most likely there were no fewer members of the Sejm [sic] who drink as there are in our Duma who smoke.[61]

This expansion of interest beyond Russian borders clinched the division between those Old Believers who wanted prohibitions to act as agents of differentiation and those who desired to help integrate Old Believers into wider society. The inclination to change social habits through legislation rather than exhortation or prohibition was new among the Old Believers. Those liberals who extolled this course of action not only accepted the necessity of Old Believer interaction with the state but welcomed the possibility of legislating moral behavior based on an Old Believer model.

Priestless Old Believers—who remained both less centralized and less prolific in publishing—tended to make traditional, religious arguments in defense of prohibitions. The Belokrinitsy, on the other hand, made outward-looking arguments in their campaign against tobacco. *Zlatostrui,* constant in its antismoking theme, provided economic data on the costs of tobacco, statistical evidence on the spread of tobacco use, and discussed the harmful medical effects of nicotine. The journal claimed that "present-day science showed that smoking was no better than heavy drinking."[62]

This mixture of traditional Old Believer proscription and modern scientific thought shows how the Old Believers began to accept the modern world on their own terms. While the layperson might not have defined the prohibition of tobacco as anything more than tradition, Old Believer teachers had begun the process of co-opting the experiences of the scientific world for the sake of a religious heritage. One should not think that these were academic arguments: Old Believer journals prided themselves on being useful, pragmatic publications written for the lay Old Believer. In every sense of the word, these journals were popular magazines. The editors, trying to influence Old Believer behavior, used arguments that their readers were sure to comprehend and with which these readers could identify.

While ritual prohibitions had traditionally provided a way for Old Believers to differentiate themselves from the exterior world, the proscription on tobacco took on a new spin in the post-1905 period. Given that Old Believers themselves increasingly bowed to the vice of smoking, the campaign in the Old Believer press nevertheless broadened into an attack against tobacco use by all Russians. This new point of view was exemplified by *Ural'skii staroobriadets,* which lauded a bishop of the official church for his campaign against smoking by the clergy serving under him.[63] By widening the arguments to include both new methodology and a broader social base, liberal Old Believers yet again signaled their desire to integrate into greater Russian society.

. . .

The prohibition of alcohol was another legislative goal of Old Believers. Liberal Old Believers hoped to follow the standards set by Sweden, Finland (at that time still a Russian grand duchy), and other countries. In time, however, these Old Believers concluded that the problem required more than just legal attention, as they realized that "not only are strong laws needed for this, but also the eradication of the very germ—the attraction to heavy drinking."[64]

Like tea, strong drink had long been associated with Russian culture. Although some Old Believer concords banned the use of spirits, others prohibited only vodka, seen as a post-Petrine introduction to Russia.[65] To the chagrin of all Old Believer leaders, however, the general use of alcohol (as well as tea and tobacco) among Old Believers had increased dramatically by the late imperial period; if tobacco use was rarely seen in Old Believer villages, alcohol was a constant companion to religious holidays (fig. 18). The use of wine had at least a liturgical precedence, but vodka had no scriptural or pre-Nikonian legitimacy. (At least one source claimed that

Figure 18   This late nineteenth- or early twentieth-century verse censures drunkenness. Setting the poem to medieval liturgical chant links social and religious themes and underlines the religious background to ritual prohibitions. Courtesy of Russkaia Kniga.

Christ was the "new wine," making alcoholic wine unnecessary.)[66]

For some Old Believers, the drinking of vodka simply fell under the ritual ban since vodka was allegedly not known during the ancient piety. For others—most notably the Belokrinitsy—the traditional ban on alcohol took on new forms and ultimately expanded into a campaign to stop heavy drinking among all Russians:

> Liquor is the cause of enormous evil to the Russian person. There is no stronger evil than wine. War, plague, and cholera could not affect a person without wine's pernicious strength. Wine does not only kill a person's physical health, but ruinously destroys the strength of the spirit in him, undermining development and economic prosperity as well as agriculture. Crime, poverty, and sickness are all from wine and through wine. The Russian person does not work for that which might increase his prosperity, [nor for that] which would give meaning to living as a person, but [rather] for that which . . . [he] in the end chucks into the hole known as a tavern.[67]

This attack on heavy drinking occurred within the broader context of calls for reform.[68] Tolerance societies had appeared across Russia during the late imperial years. Liberal Old Believers' efforts to join the campaign for abstinence linked them ever closer to groups outside of their religious circle. As the temperance movement gained widespread acceptance in Russian society, the Old Believers intruded into a movement dominated by the Russian Orthodox church and professional physicians. Suddenly, Old Believer ritual prohibitions seemed akin to a mainstream social movement, and the Old Belief appeared as a crusader for Russia's moral and social salvation. Non–Old Believer temperance advocates, however, rarely sought the support of the Old Belief for their cause.[69]

Although not the only publication to decry alcohol use, *Zlatostrui* again led the way in the fight against social ills. The magazine's cause was supported by Old Believer conferences from all those concords that either banned vodka and heavy drinking outright or had at least begun to study ways to eradicate the evil from among Old Believers themselves.[70] One article claimed that

> if the old ritualist pastorate, uniting as one, lifts its voice to the defense of temperance and morality, then it will be possible to say with confidence that the drunken sea has been decreased in its terrible limits and that life in the parish is altered much to the better.[71]

As in other social issues, the Belokrinitsa hierarchy began to compete with the official church for moral authority on these matters. Bishops Innokentii of Nizhni Novgorod and Meletii of Saratov led the Belokrinitsa episcopal fight against alcohol use by comparing Russians to the dead Lazarus, killed by the "demon of drunkenness" yet waiting to be resurrected through the faith. "Religion," explained the bishop, "is the most important factor in the question of counteracting the expansion of heavy drinking. A pious Russian person would most likely yield to the influence of religion [instead of alcohol]."[72] Not content to stop drinking just among Old Believers, the bishops hoped to eradicate it from all Russia. In like manner, *Zlatostrui* published its antidrinking articles not in the

"Old Ritualist Life" section of the journal but rather under the heading "Worldly Life."

Just in case religious arguments did not move drunkards to repentance, some Old Believers turned again to scientific and statistical methods to make their point. As in the fight against tea drinking and (especially) tobacco use, liberal Old Believers saw no contradiction in augmenting religious proscriptions with new and different data. Financial information, demographic data, and authoritative scientific pronouncements on the danger of drinking often appeared side by side with quotations from holy books. *Zlatostrui* dramatically illustrated its claim that "for schooling there is no money, but for vodka it is found" by revealing that the outlay for alcohol in the Moscow province for 1907 was 38,349,715 rubles.[73]

Using scientific and statistical data, Old Believers came to recognize that intemperance was a social problem as well as a religious one. With this recognition (pertaining to tobacco use too), liberal Old Believers, led by the Belokrinitsa concord, distanced themselves from their more traditionalist co-religionists and moved into the mainstream of Russian society. While many traditionalist Old Believers sought to expand the boundaries of ritual prohibitions in order better to circumscribe their social boundaries, the liberal Old Believers hoped to extend the concept of ritual prohibitions until it broke down the walls between Old Believers and other religious or social groups.

Conclusion

On the most local level, the expansion of prohibitions sometimes reinforced solidarity within Old Believer communities (especially those in northern Russia and Siberia), giving them a religious reason to retain traditional modes of agricultural and domestic life. These groups had already developed a ritual distance from the rest of society through a system of apartheid that included food, drink, and social relationships. In this period, however, other Old Believers embraced technological modernization, although even among liberal Old Believers significant differences existed. At one level, members of Old Believer concords agreed that Russia's fast urbanization imperiled traditional values. "In general," wrote one Old Believer, "in the countryside a person becomes closer to God, easier and freer to know the essence of being. In the countryside there are none of those temptations that disastrously influence a person of weakness."[74] Disagreements arose, nevertheless, over the right way to combat those forces that turned Old Believers from the traditional path. Pomortsy leaders, for example, accepted technological change but still thought that Old Believers should maintain a ritual distance from the world.

The Belokrinitsy, on the contrary, welcomed a more active role within the larger Russian society. In doing so, these Old Believers had to construct a social program that would neither compromise their status as Old Believers nor alienate their non–Old Believer neighbors. They did this by including all Russian society as beneficiaries of the ritual prohibitions, arguing that avoidance of tobacco and alcohol (and, to some degree, tea) could help lead Russia into a more enlightened age.

Perhaps the Chasovenniki exemplified the situation of most Old Believers during this period. Many Chasovennik adherents, including the editors of *Ural'skii staroobriadets,* felt drawn toward the liberal opinions epitomized by the Belokrinitsy. Others—especially the multitude of Chasovenniki who lived in isolated parts of Siberia—turned toward the more traditional elements of the Old Belief and tried to use the wilderness as a haven from anti-Christian habits. For them, Old Believer traditions could best be maintained, it seemed, by prohibiting all change.

Yet, the question remains whether disagreement over the form of ritual prohibition tended to divide Old Believers or whether the acceptance of the *idea* of ritual prohibition created unifying common assumptions about the world. Information from the late imperial period would suggest that almost all Old Believers accepted traditional prohibitions such as those against tobacco smoking. This would point to the set of "shared assumptions and points of view" that has been used to define Old Believer communities. Prohibitions did nevertheless divide the priestless from the priestly. Many priestless Old Believers retained the use of prohibitions to define the Old Believer community in opposition to the dominant culture, while their priestly counterparts hoped to expand those same ritual proscriptions to include prohibitions in Russian society as a whole. In the end, although agreement on prohibitions did exist on some level, especially among the local groups and in northern Russia and Siberia, differences in views on ritual issues set the stage for a debate on the nature and existence of the community itself.

The Politics
of Community

> Indeed, on the account of the preservation of the
> community, we are honored to receive eternal bless-
> ings in the kingdom of heaven. Amen.
> —*Al'fa i omega*

Old Believer ideology crystallized in the "community issue" that erupted among the faithful
after passage of the Act on Old Believer and
Sectarian Communities of 17 October 1906,
which defined the rights and responsibilities of
local Old Believer groups. By law, each "community" of Old Believers was, henceforth, to
register its pastors and vital statistics (baptisms,
marriages, and deaths) with the government. In return, each community
would then have the legal right to build temples in whatever manner it
saw fit, to elect its own clerical and lay leaders, and to levy tithes on its
members. In essence, the edict recognized traditional Old Believer organization while integrating it into the government's structure for corporate groups. Response to the act by Old Believers varied widely depending on ideology and geography.

For most Old Believers, legal recognition of their communities was a
cause for celebration. Other Old Believers feared that the state's desire to
define collective Old Believer units would provide a way for the government to control the destiny of the faithful. Indeed, some Old Believers
objected to the word "community" as a legal term proclaimed by the imperial government, and a debate ensued over the existence of the community as an organizational unit. The community question consequently
highlighted many of the issues raised earlier in this work, including the
culture of community and the community as nexus for the dialogue with
modernity.

The Anticommune Argument

Far from presenting an organized front or "party," those Old Believers
who opposed legalization of the community represented scattered rem-
nants of the Old Belief and operated with little formal structure. The an-

ticommune Old Believers were generally marginalized members of the old faith, living in borderlands and professing a particularly conservative ideology. Outside the mainstream and lacking any national organization, these anticommune Old Believers perceived themselves as the remnant of a pure Old Belief rather than as a splinter from it. They included Don Cossacks, peasants from far northern Russia, Siberians, a number of monastics, and some members of particularly strict priestless concords. While separated from one another geographically and theologically (since they came from every concord), anticommunitarians shared a desire to prevent secular elements from influencing religious life. These faithful also shared a sense of being on the periphery of the large Old Believer organizations that had coalesced after 1905. Thus, the anticommunitarians constituted the most extreme segments of the Old Belief both geographically and ideologically.

The anticommunitarians *(protivoobshchiniki)* were moved to action by important concerns. Monastics, for example, questioned the validity of "community" as a legal term because the edict did not recognize the special status of Old Believer monasteries. The word community as defined in the 1906 act connoted a secular as well as a spiritual structure, one made up of both lay believers and clerics. This scheme was essentially different from monastic organization, in which lay believers were not allowed a voice in the governing of affairs.[1] Likewise, some Cossacks also insisted that accepting the community would infringe on their autonomy and liberty. One conference of Old Believer Cossacks stated that

> We, the undersigned Pomortsy of the legal-marriage concord, of the Don Ust-Belokolitvenskii host region and the Ermakovskii stanitsa [village], gathering on the Dubovii khutor [small village], are not united in communities. Having reviewed the holy writings and . . . the ecumenical councils in the Nomocanon [*Kormchaia kniga*] and also having read from the collected acts of the Moscow old rite council of 7417 [1909], leaves 67 and 68 (the speech of the president of that council), we object to receiving the community. [We] wish to administer according to the ancient ways. Making use of the merciful imperial gift in the exercise of divine services, we—[following the] dogmas and rites of the fathers—henceforth shall not mix, shall not pray, not in eating or in drinking, with those united in community; and shall also not marry them, that is, not take of them and not give to them. . . . Moreover, in respect to our population, [if] anyone not united becomes related to communities . . . we dismiss such people from our churches.[2]

By this statement, the Cossacks showed a willingness to address the post-1906 situation on their own terms. Although they accepted the teaching of the 1909 Pomortsy congress, these Cossack groups used the *Kormchaia*—beloved pre-Nikonian compendium of canon law—as a final authority. And while they thanked the emperor, they took the hard line against both Nicholas's edict and that of their own co-religionists who "received the community." Indeed, refusal to pray, to marry, even to eat and drink with procommunitarians provided the harshest excommunication available to these priestless Pomortsy. The Cossacks accepted the gift of freedom of conscience as a political gesture independent of religious ideology, but believed that governmental meddling in their internal organization would destroy the religious identity they had as Old Believers.

The Cossack argument appealed to Old Believers from other fringes of Russia, be they from the northern part of the empire or from Siberia. For centuries, these faithful had fled the centralizing and bureaucratizing force of the state. For them, the community question represented nothing less than the issue of state control over Old Believer life. Whether the community actually existed, however, was beside the point. The real problem was the "pernicious meddling" by the state. In accepting the community, Old Believer spiritual leaders feared they would be bound to the state authorities and thus subject to heretical powers.[3]

Some anticommunitarians felt certain that the law of 17 October would be used to force them into the Russian Orthodox church itself. Others were concerned that registering with the state was the first step toward *edinoverie*. One anticommunitarian revealed the crux of the community issue, asking

> What then is the community? . . . [It is clear] that our Nikonians want to communicate with us and then to build one general church! All true believers do not need to accept the community, otherwise they unite with the antichrist and are tinged with his sign.[4]

Arguing that the state would ultimately lead Old Believers to perdition, anticommunitarians concluded that the community itself (as a unit defined by the government) was by nature sinful, even heretical.[5]

Anticommunitarians advanced two more persuasive points in their argument. First, they claimed that the notion of community had no precedent in the pre-Nikonian Russian church. The new, legal "community" thus constituted an unacceptable religious change.[6] This statement struck a harmonious note among those Old Believers who equated change with heresy.[7] Second, rejection of innovation could be justified legally too. Since the community had not been an issue in pre-Nikonian jurisprudence, it must be de facto a creation of Nikonians. Furthermore, because the "innovative" edict of 17 October had been promulgated by a heretical tsar, anticommunitarians suspected that it was not in accord with the teachings of the church fathers and was, hence, unacceptable.[8] The most extreme anticommunitarians claimed that they needed neither acts promulgated by an anti-Christian emperor nor laws made by a Duma comprised mostly of heretics. Such laws simply confirmed the power of the government over Old Believer religious life.[9]

Anticommunitarians also distrusted the concept of community because of the legal duties that obligated them to the state. Chief among these duties was the registration of all Old Believer parishes (and their pastors) with provincial and imperial authorities. For what reason other than state control, asked the anticommunitarians, would the government want Old Believers to register with it? "State power," claimed one man, "all the more heretical, does not have the right to judge our spiritual leaders as if they committed some criminal offense."[10] If old ritualist communities registered with provincial authorities, as the law stipulated, would they not fall under the control of Nikonian governors? This issue was never resolved: "Thus, in the name 'community,'" one observer commented, the anticommunitarians "perceive not simply church organization of equal legal members of the community, possessing parish property, but as the 'intercourse' with the state church in Russia. . . ."[11] According to the anticommunitarians, this was little different from eighteenth-century poll-tax obligations.

Record books, their suitability and their necessity to Old Believer life, became a major issue in the debate between procommunitarians and anticommunitarians. Always distrustful of ledgers that might be construed as "numbering of the antichrist," anticommunitarians questioned the idea of the registration of vital statistics. Earlier Old Believers had rarely maintained such information and had vigorously opposed inclusion into any imperial census.[12] For some Old Believers, though, the salient issue was really the innovation of the registration after the Nikonian reforms.[13]

While their critique stemmed from a distrust of the state, a number of anticommunitarians simply disagreed with the term "community" itself, claiming the word was vaguely "unsuitable."[14] Others were concerned that, in the 1905 and 1906 laws, the term "old ritualist" had been used to describe Old Believers when the correct name should have simply been "Christian."

> And do you know, brothers, for what and why we are given the community? I shall explain it to you. The community is given to us so that we might . . . voluntarily be called "old ritualists." But this term "old ritualists" means that we are not Christians, that we don't believe in Christ, and believe only in the old rite. . . . If we, brothers, do not call ourselves "old ritualists," but we say "Christians," then we will not allow governmental power to create the community.[15]

Such a statement requires interpretation. The speaker may have been proposing a sly method to circumvent the community act, by defining the faithful as Christians rather than as old ritualists. The speaker also reflected an idea common among Old Believers from remote villages: that they alone were Christians, as opposed to all other Russians. This extremist view maintained a form of apartheid that seemed odd even to most Old Believers, since it drew the line between the faithful and the world not at heresy but at Christianity itself. Finally, the statement hinted that anticommunitarians were unwilling to compete in a religiously pluralistic society: to them, the only acceptable religion was Christianity—that is, old ritualist Orthodoxy.

Although the anticommune argument existed in all groups, the priestless tended to debate the question most vociferously.[16] Members of the Fedoseevtsy, first to decry the act of 1906, denounced the legal acknowledgment of community since it explicitly referred to marriages. How, they asked, could communities register marriages when their interpretation of the Old Belief specifically prohibited matrimony? Instead of seeing the edict as a broadly written act covering exigencies arising among various Old Believers, the Fedoseevtsy regarded it as proof that the imperial government sought to impose secular, anti-Christian influences. The Fedoseevtsy position illustrated once more how fear and distrust of the imperial government remained a potent force among many Old Believers.

The lack of geographic centralization among priestless Old Believers strengthened the anticommune argument in their ranks. Bespopovtsy often lived in the most extreme outposts of the empire and tended to view as suspect the religious ideology of outsiders. Thus, a reporter at one priestless conference noted with surprise that some Siberian Old Believers accepted community registration—since Siberians were usually adamantly opposed to the community idea.[17] The same report claimed, however, that all anticommunitarians came from Siberia, Pskov, far northern Russia, or the area of the Don Cossacks—revealing once again the geographic marginality of anticommune Old Believers.

The Procommune Argument

The anticommunitarians, while vocal in their arguments, constituted a minority of the total Old Believer population. A far larger segment of Old Believers accepted the community as a self-evident unit of organization and therefore applauded the secular government's acknowledgment of it. One Old Believer exclaimed

> Orthodox Christians! You have lived peacefully these years, you have worked honestly for the general Christian good, God granting you peace to live honorably and to govern both the community and the future.
> Where people live peacefully, in accord and love, among them resides God, and where God resides there will be true Christian life.[18]

In response to the anticommunitarian argument, therefore, a large number of authors (like the one quoted above) defended both the term "community" and its legal acceptability. They claimed that the act of October 1906 simply codified and acknowledged the existing structures of Old Believer life and guaranteed legal protection for the faithful.[19] Instead of a method of control, procommunitarians believed that the 1906 act insured them against animosity from local government officials. In fact, according to the procommune argument, registration provided benefits to the Old Believers more significant than any possible infringements on their freedom. The right to open schools, to build temples, and to conduct their own affairs legally outweighed any loss of liberty.[20]

Rather than calling the community an innovation, procommune Old Believers tried to show that it was an ancient and honorable Russian tradition. One author explained that "Old ritualists, for 250 years before the possibility arrived for freedom of religion, were able to organize and create religious communities."[21] These communities, he explained, were both spiritual and juridical constructs, and he said that "community" could be found in Christian writings dating from the Roman period onward, even the in *Kormchaia* itself.[22] According to his argument, the community was nothing more than a "circle of people" who lived, worshipped, and made decisions together.[23] This tradition, according to the procommune argument, existed even among those who foreswore the community.

A major tool in the argument for the community came from the *Alpha and Omega (Al'fa i Omega)*, a pre-Nikonian instructional text popular among Old Believers. The book contained, alphabetically, various important topics for Christian life—confession, penance, love, pride, and hope—as well as a portion devoted specifically to the community. This seven-page section included quotations from both the Gospel and the church fathers regarding the community of believers and the correct attitude of those living within it. Procommunitarians popularized such sayings as the following:

> A brother questions Father Pimen, saying: I want to enter into a common life, and the saint says to him: if you want to enter into common life but not renounce all things and all debate, then it is not possible for you to abide in a common life.[24]

> The Holy Spirit, fulfilling the word of Christ in its appearance, handed down the foundation of the eternal community, as it is said in the book of Acts, 200: the apostolic council.[25]

Armed with quotations from the holy books, procommunitarians sought to disprove, point by point, all the anticommunitarian arguments. The quotations above, for example, proved that the community was a pre-Nikonian phenomenon, both accepted and celebrated by the holy writings. Evidence from irrefutably old ritualist holy books bolstered the communitarian argument.

In general, the procommunitarians' attitude revealed a posture toward the state far different from that of their anticommune counterparts. On the most basic level, procommune Old Believers accepted the state as a legitimate secular power. Even those opposed to the law of 17 October let the secular government, in some fashion, intrude on their lives, by following laws or accepting military protection. Declining to be registered in communities, claimed the procommune Old Believers, did not guarantee freedom from state repression. In fact, submission to the government was a daily fact regardless of religious conviction. Furthermore, the act of 17 October 1906 referred only to secular concerns.[26] Even opponents to the community question had to carry passports, pay taxes, and obey laws made by secular authorities. Registration of communities, therefore, no more constituted submission to the state than did any other activity.[27]

During the period of Tatar domination, the Russian church itself had bowed down before secular authorities, and the procommunitarians claimed that that must have been far more painful than registering with imperial governors. When Orthodox communities interacted closely with Tatar leadership, these communities were simply giving Caesar his due. No one, procommune Old Believers pointed out, considered the church in Tatar times to be heretical. Interaction with non-Orthodox secular authority had ensured survival of the faith.[28] Likewise, registration with the state might cement the rights of Old Believer groups across Russia.

The national Pomortsy congress provided a modicum of centralized direction on the community issue. Its position, as was often the case, lay somewhere between the separatist Fedoseevtsy and the integrative Belokrinitsy. The All-Russian Conference of Pomortsy in 1912 agreed to accept the community as an expression of Old Believer organization but refused to force local Pomortsy groups to follow its lead. The congress stated that "freedom is granted. Communities unwilling [to recognize the law of 17 October 1906] may rule for themselves."[29] Even in granting this latitude, however, the Pomortsy congress referred to "communities" of "anticommunitarians"!

Other concords, such as the highly autonomous Chasovenniki, found their faithful to be split equally and fractiously on the subject.[30] Although the Chasovennik journal *Ural'skii staroobriadets* actively campaigned for the acceptance of the community, the editors acknowledged that large segments of the faithful disagreed with the stance. The split among Chasovenniki illustrated yet again the support of the anticommunitarian movement in the farthest reaches of Russia, since the large majority of Chasovenniki lived either in the Urals or on the Siberian steppe. In the case of the Chasovennik population, the community question received a great deal of attention in print, specifically because the issue was so divisive. *Ural'skii staroobriadets* led the public fight for the community among the Chasovenniki.[31]

The Belokrinitsa hierarchy, which maintained the most regularized and centralized organization of all Old Believer groups, convened in 1912 a council of bishops of the Don diocese about community registration.[32] While the council's decision did not guarantee recognition of the community by all Belokrinitsy, the bishops wielded more authority than did any priestless conference. The fugitive-priestly Old Believers, who by this point had suffered in numbers, seemed generally to accept community legislation. Because they retained a tenuous relationship with the established church, however, the fugitive-priestly continued to fear the intrusion of state authorities more acutely than did their Belokrinitsa counterparts. Given the highly decentralized nature of the group, it seems clear that there must have been at least some anticommunitarians among the fugitive priestly.[33]

Even the most energetic procommunitarian groups found community registration to be problematic. Related to the historic avoidance of census taking, the maintainance of standardized records was both foreign to and suspect among many Old Believers. In response to the problems of registration, a steady stream of magazine articles, editorial comments, and conference proceedings reassured those faithful who were registering that the census information would not be used by agents of Antichrist. Procommune leaders took pains to show community leaders how to keep vital statistics, even providing sample record books as examples. The amount of discussion regarding registration books revealed the novelty of the concept.

Having moved beyond the question of registration, some procommunity Old Believers condemned anticommunitarians as "dark" or "illiterate."[34] Those who forsook legal communities, claimed one author, were often uneducated monks or people who wanted Old Believers to run off and live in the forests.[35] Extreme procommune authors maintained that a lack of education explained the disagreement over terminology, especially regarding the name "old ritualist" instead of "Christian." Although Christians called Jesus "Christ," they asked, did it make him less the son of God to be called "Nazarene" or "Galilean"?[36]

Some procommunitarians claimed that their foes were not true Christians at all but people who used the old ritual as a cover for uncivilized behavior: "Anticommunitarians, disseminating their teachings, sow confusion and cause discord. . . . This is not the activity of God, but of the devil!"[37] The author claimed that an anticommunitarian conference "was not a sobor of believing people, but rather a sobor of dissenters who, up to the promulgation of the law on old rite communities, never had intercourse with the old rite, but rather were always attracted only to false propagandic ideas, enticing others in their delusions."[38]

Anticommunitarians were also condemned as perpetrators of improper acts, such as performing illegal or inappropriate marriages.[39] This vilification labeled anticommunitarians as hooligans and troublemakers. According to extreme procommune writers, refusal to accept the community as a legal entity placed Old Believers beyond the pale of Orthodoxy. "Lord King of Heaven," finished one article, "make wise our brothers the anticommunitarians, and fill their hearts with the love of Christianity!"[40]

Instead of attacking the anticommunitarians, though, some Old Believer polemicists responded to the confusion that existed in Russian Orthodox parish life at the turn of the century. They claimed that Old Believers had a mission to revive community life throughout the empire, not only among old ritualists. The timing of these polemics could not have been better—the established church was in the midst of a long and painful debate on parish reform.[41] One article claimed that old ritualist parishes were "becoming, little by little, famous as community units, unified not only in religious attitudes but, as it is said, having definite outer boundaries that nearly resemble, in the present, ancient Russian Christian parish life."[42] This sort of statement sought to publicize the Old Believer communities as alternatives to the Russian Orthodox parish and to claim the mantle of history for the Old Believers.

Old Believer polemicists entered into a competition with the Russian Orthodox for the moral leadership of a changing Russia. One Old Believer author, for example, reversed the traditional role of Old Believer versus missionary by saying that "the present article is written to the priests of the state church belonging to the so-called progressive pastors, thirsting for the renewal of their church." The Old Believer "missionary" then reviewed the differences between decentralized, democratic Old Believer communities and the centralized, hierarchal system extant in the post-Nikonian Russian church. As one might expect, he claimed that Old Believer communities could heal the "various sicknesses" plaguing the state church—apathy, modernism, secularism, and lack of spiritual bond between priest and parish.[43]

Old Believer writers claimed that social regeneration could be found only in the rebirth of the pre-Nikonian parish, not on flights into modernism, socialism, atheist philosophy, or the unabashed capitalism of the West. Unlike the narrowly defined parish structure of late imperial Russian Orthodoxy, the pre-Nikonian form combined territorial, church, economic, juridical, and administrative functions. Instead of fracturing life into separate and competing spheres, the pre-Nikonian parish fused all facets of social existence into a seamless web. Most importantly, the community acted as both a spiritual unit and a "strong agricultural organization, taking deep part in the life of the folk," helping to provide credit or forms of mutual aid for its members.[44] In this way, Old Believers hoped that the spirit of Christianity might infuse the nonreligious activities of the parish, both adding to the wealth of the community and ministering to the needy. A parish of the old rite model would guide Russians back to "those internal routines that were firmly instituted and invariably observed in the parishes of the ancient holy-paternal church," including democratic management of community affairs, local control of parochial spiritual matters, church-based education (then under attack in the Duma), economic development by the community as a group, and the reversal of the "egoism" that had become an idol of the modern age.[45] Noting the breakdown of Russian society during this revolutionary period, Old Believer writers claimed to have an alternative solution:

> For people who are sincerely devoted to the church, people who ardently love their motherland, the question of the reconstruction of the Russian parish as a judicial unit creates a "conditio sina qua non" for the revival of all Russian life. For the Russian person outside of this there is no and can be no hope for a better future and no return to [a better time]. Outside of religion, outside of the church, there is no salvation for the Russian folk. Presently observing the general disintegration of moral structures—the family, the loss of national feeling, the love for the motherland, etc.—all of this is a direct consequence of the extra-church organization of Russian life.[46]

For this author, the only way to rise above decadence and disintegration was to return to religious forms kept unsullied for centuries by the Old Believers.

The expansive argument on the community question paralleled the liberal Old Believer views on prohibitions. Instead of using the community to insulate Old Believers, the expansion of community organization could in fact help to transform society itself. Not only could Old Believer ritual bans act as agents of social change, but the entire Old Believer community experience could be held up as a means to a better life for Russians everywhere. As well as "going to the people" with their message, these polemicists intrinsically condemned anticommunitarians as Old Believers who themselves had lost the meaning of a communitarian religious life.

Conclusion

The community, its membership, privileges, even its existence, thus provided a source of both pride and tension among Old Believers after the Act on Old Believer and Sectarian Communities of 17 October 1906. Although the existence of Old Believer communities seemed self-evident, the process of legalization and registration scared many of the faithful. To some extent, these faithful were correct: the government did want to control the Old Belief by bringing its membership into the legal structure of the empire. Previously, illegality had provided the kind of freedom to Old Believers that was lost when their communities became legalized. Old ritualists living in remote parts of the empire jealously guarded their independence and were loath to surrender it.

The large majority of Old Believers, however, regarded the law as a legal affirmation of their God-given rights, a legitimization of Old Believer practices of the previous 250 years and a recognition of the peculiar religious characteristics of the Old Belief. In using the community as an organizational model, procommunitarians argued, the law simply codified the reality of Old Believer life. Finally, some claimed that the legal right for Old Believer communities to exist provided the impetus for the regeneration of Russian community life in general. Citing failed reforms of the Russian Orthodox parish system after 1905, Old Believers held out their own organizing principle as the natural choice for all Russians.

Conclusion

 The revolutionary Russia of 1917 was never a "Russia of the Old Believers," although the political issues that brought about revolution necessarily affected the old ritualists, too. All but ignoring the tenets of modern socialist theory, the Old Believers, between 1905 and 1917, developed a social system that linked them to medieval Russian piety. To do this, the faithful manipulated the tools at their disposal—specifically, the symbols and rituals that were second nature to the Old Believers.

The use of symbols and rituals as instruments to change the world came out of the Old Believers' religious experience. Instead of understanding modernity simply through their religious heritage, Old Believers hoped to transform their surroundings to make them fit the experiences and assumptions of the Old Belief. For the Old Believers, the period from 1905 to 1917 constituted a twelve-year oasis in which they were able to strengthen their culture of community by building houses of prayer, adorning them with icons of the ancient piety, and filling them with communal prayer and discussion.

In a time of constant change, however, a complete spectrum of opinion existed on how to link the ancient piety to modern Russia. In the case of the most traditional old ritualists, the symbols of the Old Belief provided a bulwark against westernization—the forces of Antichrist. These believers thought that Russia had strayed so far from the path of orthodoxy that the only hope was to create separate Old Believer communities. For them, symbols and rituals served to solidify Old Believer communities in the face of a heterodox world. Moreover, the most conservative Old Believers sought to manipulate their world according to Old Believer symbols, giving religious answers to such everyday questions as those of kerosene use, photography, or community registration.

Old Believers at this end of the spectrum hoped to develop communities far from the temptations of society. Those old ritualists who lived in Siberia, the Ural Mountains, and in far northern Russia tended to band together against any perceived innovation that threatened their religious communities. Although they may have disagreed on specifics of ideology, even on issues of the priesthood, these geographically remote Old

Believers wanted to stay marginalized; they desired no part of the life of Russian society, and they maintained a distrust of the Russian imperial government.

Old Believers in Siberia and far northern Russia placed high importance on what might be called the monastic aspect of Old Believer life. Through life in the wilderness, these outlying Old Believers replicated a monk's flight from the secular world. In so doing, such Old Believers also developed a faith in local autonomy more pronounced than that of Old Believers living in the center of the empire. The differentiation between procommunitarians and anticommunitarians, between integrators and segregators, between liberals and traditionalists, often correlated more closely with geographic than with theological or ideological characteristics. The Siberian Chasovenniki and Pomortsy, for instance, had more in common with each other than with their co-religionists of the same concord who lived in central Russia.

The more moderate old ritualists sought a halfway point between outright flight from Russian society on the one hand and acceptance of its existence on the other. Changing times had created more opportunities for interaction with nonbelievers through dining, work, and social gathering. For the moderates, rituals and symbols provided a path to strengthen the Old Belief while at the same time giving guidance for interaction with a society undergoing rapid transformation. These Old Believers hoped to use the newly legislated religious freedom to solidify their own communities through building, publishing, and meeting, publicly and frequently. They did not intend to change Russian society, but they did hope to breathe new life into their own communities through the possibilities that emerged after 1905.

The most liberal arm of the Old Belief sought to exploit its freedom to remake Russia in an Old Believer image. To some extent (for example, among the members of the Riabushinskii circle) this was a self-concious decision. Most liberal old ritualists, however, strongly believed that the problems plaguing Russian society could be solved through generous use of the balm of the Old Belief. Russia was rootless, but Old Believers could deliver a link to pre-Petrine piety; Russia had social evils, but old ritualists could show a temperance and antismoking tradition; Russia had lost its identity, but Old Believers could provide a well-defined culture; Russia was chaotic, but Old Believers could offer a community. The community issue itself allowed Old Believers to demonstrate they were the true heirs of Russian spirituality and to legitimize the Old Belief as a regenerative force for Russia. The most liberal procommunitarians hoped that symbols and rituals—liturgy, art, architecture, and prohibitions—could lead Russia both back to its roots and forward to a healthy future.

The desire for the reconstruction of Russian society only existed among those who accepted the role of the secular state. Traditionally, Old Believers had lost little love on the ponderous political system that made the state (instead of the spiritual community) the focus of Russian life. Yet, defenders of the community acknowledged the reality of state power as a legitimate force. To a greater or lesser degree, procommunitarian Old Believers tolerated the secular state as the keeper of peace and order, although they never accepted the state as a defender of Orthodoxy. Those Old Believers who remained wary of the Russian state and of outside society (the Pomortsy, for example) struggled to find the correct balance between integration and isolation. It was the very Old Believers who welcomed Russian society and politics—most notably the Belokrinitsy—who most openly publicized Old Believer ideals of religious and social life.

The greatest proponents of community registration, social integration, and political activity also had the most to gain from such actions. In centrally located parts of the empire integration had already occurred. Some Old Believers held back from total integration while others disavowed all tendencies toward self-segregation. Both groups, however, sought to fortify their communities so that they might survive in a rapidly changing world.

Appendix

Source Note

By the very nature of the sources available, the study of Old Believers in the period after 1905 holds great advantage over the study of other periods in the history of the Old Belief. The Act of Toleration of 1905 opened a floodgate of Old Believer publications, ranging from liturgical texts to popular journals to historical monographs.[1] For the first time, Old Believers had received a legal right to their own voice. Before 1905, Old Believers had had to rely on religious, polemical, and instructional texts that had either been printed abroad and smuggled into Russia, or published underground, or even, in some cases, reproduced by hand-copying.

It is true that Old Believers deserved their reputation as bibliophiles, maintaining as they did a knowledge of the ancient piety revealed in the *starye knigi* (old books). A flowery description of their activity in this regard claimed that the Old Believers had hidden

> in the woods and wilderness . . . a special society of scholarly people, i.e., of the erudite, of well-stocked libraries, of readers, publishers, copyists, and every means for the free communication of thought and word.[2]

This claim, although an exaggeration, did reveal the popular image of the Old Believers' love for books. While liturgical and quasi-liturgical texts comprised only one part of the old ritualist press after 1905, these texts remained the most important books to the Old Believers themselves. Publishers produced liturgical and edifying texts in quarto or folio sizes with high-grade paper, endboards made of wood, and sewn bindings finished with tooled leather covers. These volumes not only replicated the traditional form of liturgical works but also concretely showed that important truths were to be found within such imposing bindings.

Two centers of Old Believer life in Moscow at the turn of the century—the Preobrazhenskoe and Rogozhskoe cemeteries—also housed the two largest liturgical presses. Soon after the Act of Toleration, Old Believers began to publish a range of religious books that had previously been available only through the edinovertsy. Liturgical texts such as the *Divine Liturgy (Sluzhebnik)* and quasi-liturgical works such as *The Book of Truth (Kniga o vere)* and the classic *Son of the church (Syn tserkovnyi)* have great potential for research on the Old Belief in this period, yet have seen little use by contemporary scholars.[3]

Also accessible are the many Old Believer magazines published between 1905 and 1917. In all, various Old Believer groups published more than a dozen different journals during this period. Ranging from the *The Old Ritual Pomorian Magazine (Staroobriadcheskii pomorskii zhurnal)*, two issues only, to the long-running and influential *Tserkov' (Church)*, these journals presented a mix of educational, devotional, and social news. Along with liberal doses of polemic against the Russian Orthodox church, they also contained historical articles on the old ritual. Each journal offered a place for comments, questions, and letters from readers; these communications now constitute one of the few sources of Old Believer popular opinion.[4]

The monthly magazines (except for *Tserkov'*, which appeared weekly) appealed to a broad Old Believer audience and included articles covering a wide range of concerns.[5] *Tserkov'*, for example, had four specific departments to illustrate the magazine's major themes. Its 1909 program listed these as (1) "Present-Day Questions of Church-Society Life," (2) "Theology and Philosophy," (3) "Church-Society (Parish life)," (4) "Chronicle of Church and Governmental News."[6] Additionally, *Tserkov'* hoped to provide bibliographical information (including book reviews), iconography, and illustrations to complement its subject material. The magazine's outreach included articles for children as well as parents.

Each magazine also established its own niche by focusing on a special audience. *Old Believer Thought (Staroobriadcheskaia mysl')*, for example, called itself a "church-social" magazine, but began to include many articles on music, for example, on the ancient chant by signs *(znammenyi raspev)* used among Old Believers. The section on "Church Singing" grew until it became a separate publication, bound with *Staroobriadcheskaia mysl'*, but independently paginated and edited.[7] Likewise, *Shchit very (The Shield of Faith)* targeted a rural audience with articles on popular self-education, as well as news, theology, and polemical stories. The problem of Old Believer education, including staffing schools and training children, was another constant theme throughout different Old Believer publications. Each of these magazines generally reflected the editorial voice of the specific Old Believer organization that published it. While one publication might regularly criticize another, or find fault with its stand on theological and social issues, nevertheless, these Old Believer journals would often advertise in one another's pages, even when the journals represented strongly divergent groups.[8]

Russian Orthodox church publications are a large, if problematic, source for the study of the Old Believers. Although church publications (especially magazines and yearbooks) often carried descriptions of Old Believer communities, the articles were usually tinged by a zeal to convert Old Believers to the Russian Orthodox church. Comments made in church publications (most notably the yearbooks of the general procurator of the Holy Synod) have therefore been regarded in this book as being of secondary importance. While these publications provide reams of material about the Old Believers from the institutional standpoint of the official Russian Orthodox church, they remain of severely limited use as sources on the views of various Old Believer concords.

Archival sources for the study of the Old Belief in the late imperial period also have their limitations. Russian Orthodox church archives—which I have used in this work—provide useful information, but only as seen through the lens of official bodies. Consistory files, for example, often contain information regarding petitions for the building of Old Believer chapels or churches, but only a small percentage of all Old Believer liturgical buildings were built under the aegis of this process, in part because the consistories tended to turn down such requests. In addition, Old Believers themselves were reticent about asking permission from the "schismatic" or "heretical" Russian Orthodox church in matters related to the Old Believers' religious life. While vast amounts of useful information exist for the study of official interaction with the Old Belief, these same myriad files do less to illuminate the Old Believers' own story.

There are some particularly important central repositories of Old Believer materials. At the Russian State Library (formerly the Lenin Library) manuscript division (RGB OR) lie many archival records chronicling the history of the Moscow Old Believer cemeteries. I have used the religious manuscripts from this rich collection, but the significant holdings on economic and social development remain completely unmined. A scholarly investigation of these great centers of the old faith is desperately needed. State Library holdings of the collections of Old Believer bibliophiles and other individuals related to the old ritual similarly lack comprehensive examination.

The Scientific Library of Moscow State University has amassed a major collection of Old Believer writings from the upper Kama river region of central Russia, including some 330 manuscripts and 2000 printed books. The manuscripts and printed works in this library embrace a number of different genres, such as personal diaries, religious texts, and proceedings of Old Believer religious and social conferences. While some of these sources have been preserved in only fragmentary form, all together they furnish an important written record of traditional peasant religious and social life in the twentieth century. Religious texts are particularly abundant and can be used to examine the maintenance (or loss) of religious culture during the period. The Moscow State collection has been made much more accessible by a new book, *Monuments of Old Believer Book Culture of the Upper Kama (Pamiatniki knizhnoi kul'tury staroobriadtsev Verkhokam'ia)*. This guide includes a complete scholarly description and a seven-level index of the collection.

   In St. Petersburg, the Library of the Academy of Sciences (BAN) has much information on the Old Believers. Fortunately, its collection of early manuscripts and old printed books published by the Old Believers has been described in a guide—*Sochineniia pisatelei-staroobriadtsev xvii veka*. Collections in the Novosibirsk and Ekaterinburg university libraries also can provide significant material on the traditional society and culture of the Old Believers. The former collection is now being organized under the leadership of N. N. Pokrovskii. The Ekaterinburg collection, although smaller than its counterparts, has yet to be examined by many western scholars. A guide *(putevoditel')* to its items is listed in the bibliography and gives a useful introduction to the collection there.

Notes

Chapter 1: Studying the Old Believers

1. Michael Scammel, *Solzhenitsyn: A Biography* (New York: W. W. Norton & Company, 1984), 920–23.

2. See V. M. Skvortsov, "Obshchii kharakter staroobriadcheskogo raskola, sushchestvennye priznaki i stepen' vrednosti otdel'nykh ego tolkov," *Missionerskoe obozrenie*, 1896, no. 5–6, bk. 1: 3.

3. Robert Crummey describes the beginning of the polemical debate that engendered the famous Old Believer work *Pomorskie otvety (Pomor'e Responses)* in his work *Old Believers and the World of Antichrist* (Madison: University of Wisconsin Press, 1970), 83 ff. The polemical tradition continued up to the end of the empire, although it waned with the proliferation of published material. See, for an analysis of twentieth-century polemical debates, S. B—v., "Zabytyi zavet," *Zlatostrui*, 1910–1911, no. 9: 22–23.

4. Although the Russian Orthodox perceived these changes simply as variations on a theme, Old Believers claimed that change in form equalled change in meaning. In the prayer "Alleluia, Alleluia, Glory to thee, O God," for example, Nikon added a third "alleluia" to the sentence to make it a threefold glorification of the Holy Trinity. Old Believers, however, claimed that the original meaning of "alleluia" *was* "glory to God," and the addition of one more word would not glorify the Holy Trinity but rather some fourfold godhead.

In the Old Believer sign of the cross, the faithful touched their bodies with the first two fingers of the right hand (signifying the two natures of Christ) while folding over the thumb, ring, and small fingers to commemorate the Holy Trinity. Nikonian innovation moved the thumb to touch the first and second fingers. The Old Believers argued that using three fingers to make the sign of the cross on the body confused the dogmatic statement that both natures of Christ, but *not* the Holy Trinity, hung from the tree. (Others claimed that the three-fingered position too closely resembled the configuration used for pinching snuff!) For the latest semiotic interpretation of the sign of the cross, see Boris A. Uspensky, "The Schism and Cultural Conflict in Seventeenth-Century Russia," in *Seeking God: The Recovery of Religious Identity in Orthodox Russia, Ukraine, and Georgia*, ed. Stephen K. Batalden (DeKalb: Northern Illinois University Press, 1993), 106–43.

5. A good example of the standard church view toward Old Believers is Timofei Tverdynskii [priest], "Kratkie ocherki iz sovremennogo byta pravoslavnykh i raskol'nikov," *Domashnaia beseda*, 1868, no. 30: 746–51; no. 31: 764–67; no. 32: 779–780; no. 33: 782–86; no. 34: 799–805. Michael Cherniavsky is a little harsh in claiming that church historians "published a great deal of source material, and we should not expect anything else," but his basic point is valid—fresh analysis of the Old Belief only began with secular professors' interest in the subject. See Michael Cherniavsky, "The Old Believers and the New Religion," *Slavic Review* 25 (1966): 2.

6. *Vsepoddanneishii otchet ober-prokurora Sviateishego sinoda K. Pobedonostseva po vedomstvu pravoslavnogo ispovedaniia za 1890 i 1891 gody* (St. Petersburg, 1893), 172.

7. Ibid. A few church leaders dissented from this opinion. Bishop Alexander of Vologda maintained that Old Believers were indeed Orthodox, since they "live in peace and accord with the church, baptize their children, were themselves baptized and considered themselves 'Orthodox,'" "Uspekh staroobriadchestva," *Zlatostrui*, 1912–1913, no. 2: 21. An outspoken critic of church policy toward Old Believers was the otherwise conservative Bishop Antonii (Khrapovitskii), who called for legal intermarriage and hoped for a reunion between Old Believers and the Russian Orthodox church. See James W. Cunningham, *A Vanquished Hope: The Movement for Church Renewal in Russia, 1905–1906* (Crestwood, N.Y.: St. Vladimir's Seminary Press, 1981), 300–302.

8. *Vsepoddanneishii otchet za 1890 i 1891*, 175.

9. These populist historians produced the most important contributions: A. Shchapov, *Russkii raskol staroobriadchesvta* (Kazan, 1859), and *Zemstvo i raskol* (St. Petersburg, 1862); V. V. Andreev, *Raskol i ego znachenie v narodnoi russkoi istorii* (St. Petersburg, 1870); I. Iuzov, *Russkie dissidenty: starovery i dukhovnye khristiane* (St. Petersburg, 1881); V. G. Druzhinin, a score of works, especially *Raskol na Donu v kontse XVII veka* (St. Petersburg, 1889); and A. S. Prugavin, noted below. The best overview of Russian historiography on this subject is N. N. Pokrovskii, "Trends in Studying the History of Old Belief by Russian Scholars" (paper presented at Russia's Dissenting Old Believers: An International Conference, Northfield, Minn., Sept. 30–Oct. 2, 1994).

10. A. S. Prugavin, *Raskol i sektantstvo v russkoi narodnoi zhizni: s kriticheskami zamechaniiami dukhovnogo tsenzora* (St. Petersburg, 1905), 9. See also *Raskol-sektantstvo: materialy dlia izucheniia religiozno-bytovnykh dvizhenii russkogo naroda* (Moscow, 1887), *Staroobriadchestvo vo vtoroi polovine xix v.* (Moscow, 1904), and his many articles in *Vestnik Evropy, Russkaia mysl', Istoricheskii vestnik,* and other journals.

11. Prugavin, *Raskol i sektantstvo*, 7.

12. Ibid. The place of Slavophilism in the study of the Old Belief remains obscure. The only explicit treatment of this theme can be found in Ethel Dunn, "A Slavophile Looks at the Raskol and Other Sects," *Slavonic Review* 23 (1964): 167–79. Dunn's study centers on Ivan Aksakov, son of the writer Sergei Aksakov. She claims that Aksakov equated Old Believer economic prosperity with growing westernization. Considering the Old Believers' historically antiwestern bias, this is at best a strange assessment.

13. See Prugavin, *Staroobriadchestvo vo vtoroi polovine xix v.*, and Vl. B., "'Dushila' u russkikh raskol'nikov," *Etnograficheskoe obozrenie*, 1904, no. 2: 160–61.

14. V. G. Senatov, *Filosofiia istorii staroobriadchestva*, 2 vols. (Moscow, 1908). See also M. Davydov, "Kto vinovat," *Shchit very*, 1912, no. 1: 71–77, for an Old Believer view on the historiography of the schism. For a good introduction to the variety of material on the Old Belief, see A. S. Rybakov et al., eds., *Staraia vera: staroobriadcheskaia khrestomatiia* (Moscow: Tipografiia Staroobriadcheskogo Instituta, n.d.), which includes lives of Avvakum and others, histories of the schism, and sections from Mel'nikov-Pecherskii's fictional works on the Old Believers.

15. V. D. Bonch-Bruevich, ed., *Materialy k istorii i izucheniiu russkogo sektanstva i raskola,* 7 vols. (St. Petersburg and Petrograd, 1908–1916). Bonch-Bruevich introduced his project in a pamphlet called *Programma dlia sobraniia svedenii po issledovaniiu i izucheniiu russkogo sektantstva i raskola* (St. Petersburg, 1908).

16. *Bukhtarminskie staroobriadtsy* (Leningrad: Nauka, 1930), and the series *Pamiatniki istorii staroobriadchestva xvii v.,* published throughout the early twentieth century. See also A. Dolotov, *Tserkov' i sektantstvo v Sibiri* (Novosibirsk: Sibkraiizdat, 1930) for a typical early Soviet perspective.

17. V. F. Milovidov, *Staroobriadchestvo v proshlom i nastoiashchem* (Moscow: Izdatelstvo "Mysl'," 1969).

18. The father of this renaissance is N. N. Pokrovskii, whose many works have become standard texts for Old Believer history. Pokrovskii has trained a whole school of young scholars in the study of the Siberian Old Belief. I. A. Pozdeeva has tirelessly led ethnographic and bibliographic work at Moscow State University, whose ethnographic expeditions, now headed by younger scholars, have gathered scores of rare, even unique, volumes by Old Believers. In Ekaterinburg, R. G. Pikhoia has led a team of scholars researching that region's Old Believer history.

19. The latest of these is E. K. Romodanovskaia, ed., *Issledovaniia po istorii literatury i obshchestvennogo soznaniia feodal'noi Rossii* (Novosibirsk: Nauka, Sibirskoe Otdelenie, 1992). This volume includes some scholarship on Old Believer history of the late nineteenth and twentieth centuries. For examples of the work published by the Moscow State group, see I. V. Pozdeeva and E. B. Smilianskaia, eds., *Mir staroobriadchestva: Lichnost', kniga, traditsiia* (Moscow: Izadatel'stvo "Khronograf," 1992, and S. O. Shmidt, ed., *Iz fonda redkikh knig i rukopisei nauchnoi biblioteki Moskovskogo universiteta (Issledovaniia i materiali)* (Moscow: Izdatel'stvo Moskovskogo Universiteta, 1993). A good introduction to the work done in Ekaterinburg is R. G. Pikhoia, ed., *Knigi starogo Urala* (Sverdlovsk: Izdatel'stvo Ural'skogo Universiteta, 1989). Two guides to the material found in Ekaterinburg are the *Putevoditel' po fondam staropechatnykh knig i rukopisei labratorii arkeografiicheskikh issledovanii* (Sverdlovsk: Ural'skii gosudarstvennyi universitet, 1990), and A. T. Shashkov and V. I. Baidin, eds., *Pamiatniki literatury i pis'mennosti krest'ianstva Zaurala* (Sverdlovsk: Izdatel'stvo Ural'skogo Universiteta, 1991).

20. A small but active group of Polish scholars, including E. Iwaniec, I. Grek-Pabis, and others have produced a sizeable amount of ethnographic and linguistic research on Old Believer communities in Poland, some of it describing the twentieth-century Old Believer movement there. An excellent paper on Old Believers in the early twentieth century is I. V. Pozdeeva, "'Serebrianyi vek' russkogo staroobriadchestva, 1905–1917" (paper presented at Russia's Dissenting Old Believers: An International Conference, Northfield, Minn., 1994).

21. A possible exception to this might have been von Haxthausen, who is said to have written an unpublished manuscript on Old Believers and sectarians. See the note in S. Frederick Starr's introduction in August von Haxthausen, *Studies in the Interior of Russia,* ed. S. Frederick Starr, trans. Eleanore L. M. Schmidt (Chicago: University of Chicago Press, 1972), xxvii. (I, too, have been unable to locate the manuscript at the Russian State Library.)

22. See, for example, F. Tetzner, "Die Philipponen in Ostpreussen," *Globus*

76, no. 12 (1899): 181–92, and "Philipponische Legenden," *Globus* 94, no. 8 (1908): 117–19, 241–43; and M. Gerss, "Die Philipponen," *Zeitschrift der Alterumsgesellschaft Insterburg*, 1909, no. 11: 44–84, and "Die Glaubenslehren der Philipponen zur Zeit ihrer Einwanderung in Ostpreussen," *Mitteilungen der Literarischen Gesellschaft Masovia* 15 (1910): 1–27.

23. F. S. Conybeare, *Russian Dissenters* (Cambridge, Mass.: Harvard University Press, 1921).

24. See J. S. Curtiss, *Church and State in Russia: The Last Years of the Empire, 1900–1917* (New York: University of Columbia Press, 1940); and Pierre Pascal, *Avvakum et les débuts du raskol* (Paris: Mouton, 1938).

25. The best overview of western scholarship on the Old Belief is Robert O. Crummey, "Past and Current Interpretations of the Old Belief" (paper presented at Russia's Dissenting Old Believers: An International Conference, Northfield, Minn., 1994).

26. The major exception is Peter Waldron's excellent study on "Religious Reform after 1905: Old Believers and the Orthodox Church," *Oxford Slavonic Papers* 20 (1987): 110–39. In this article Waldron deals primarily with state policy rather than with Old Believer attitudes. Waldron elsewhere places the toleration of the Old Belief into the larger context of imperial policy.

27. Cherniavsky, 3.

28. That many senior historians of Russia attended "Russia's Dissenting Old Believers: An International Conference" (Northfield, Minn., 1994) illustrates the growing interest in Old Believer history among western academics. For useful new interpretations of the Old Believer experience at the turn of the last century, see Ronald Vroon, "The Old Belief and Sectarianism as Cultural Models in the Silver Age" in *Christianity and the Eastern Slavs: Vol. II, Russian Culture in Modern Times*, ed. Robert P. Huges and Irina Paperno (Berkeley: University of California Press, 1994), 172–90; and Barbara Jacobs, *Kleidung als Symbol: das Beispiel der Altgläubigen Südsibiriens im 19. und beginnenden 20. Jahrhundert* (Munich: Lit, 1993). The first attempt at a synthetic history of the Old Belief is Leon Poliakov, *L'epopee des vieux-croyants: une histoire de la Russie authentique* (Paris: Perrin, 1991).

29. See Roy R. Robson, "Recovering Priesthood and the Emigré Experience among Contemporary American *Bespopovtsy* Old Believers," in *Skupiska staroobrzędowców w Europie, Azji i Ameryce, ich miejsce i tradycje we współczesnym świecie*, ed. Iryda Grek-Pabisowa et al.(Warsaw: Polska Akademia Nauk, Institut Slawistiki, 1994), 131–38. Chapter 3 will introduce present-day Western sociological studies of the Old Belief.

30. Joseph R. Gusfield and Jerzy Michalowicz argue persuasively against differentiating between "symbolic" life and "everyday living." See their "Secular Symbolism: Studies of Ritual, Ceremony, and the Symbolic Order in Modern Life," *Annual Review of Sociology* 10 (1984): 418 ff.

31. Maurice Bloch, "Symbols, Song, Dance, and Features of Articulation," *European Journal of Sociology* 15 (1974): 55–81, interprets symbols as the language of domination. His Marxist model, however, cannot explain the Old Believers' devotion to symbols that invited persecution by the Russian state and the Russian Orthodox church. The Marxist approach might be more constructive in identifying the sources of labor control of Old Believer industrialists over their brethren-employees. For a rebuttal to the Marxist model that resonates with

some themes in the present analysis, see Stanley Jeyaraja Tambiah, *Culture, Thought and Social Action: An Anthropological Perspective* (Cambridge, Mass.: Harvard University Press, 1985), 154 ff. The point at which devotion to the old rite became a recognizable movement has yet to be established. It surely happened (at least in some areas) within the first generation of the schism.

32. Emile Durkheim, *Elementary Forms of the Religious Life,* trans. Joseph Ward Swain (New York: Free Press, 1965), 51.

33. See David Z. Scheffel, *In the Shadow of Antichrist: The Old Believers of Alberta* (Lewiston: Broadview Press, 1991), 208–9, for an analysis of Keith Thomas's *Religion and the Decline of Magic,* which makes similar arguments about ritual and belief.

34. Marvin C. Wren, *The Course of Russian History,* 4th ed. (New York: Macmillan Publishing Co., 1979), 149.

35. Timothy Ware, *The Orthodox Church* (New York: Penguin Books, 1976), 236.

36. Peter G. Stromberg, *Symbols of Community: The Cultural System of a Swedish Church* (Tucson, Az: University of Arizona Press, 1986), 13.

37. David Z. Scheffel, *In the Shadow of Antichrist,* 142–43.

38. This is consonant with the view of social theorists who claim that the western European intellect has differentiated between "external reality and internal representations" in a divergent way from that of other cultures. Specifically, scholars argue that classical Greece melded its external and internal interpretations of the world, a practice that carried over into Eastern Orthodoxy. The western church, however, developed a distinction between the "real world" and "symbols." See Paul Rabinow, "Representations are Social Facts: Modernity and Post-Modernity in Anthropology," in *Writing Culture: The Poetics and Politics of Ethnography,* ed. James Gifford and George E. Marcus (Berkeley: University of California Press, 1986), 235.

39. Georg Michels discounts the place of symbol or ritual in the genesis of the Old Believer movement. Michels argues that the schism, during the seventeenth century, should be viewed as a conglomeration of local grievances instead of a well-defined movement. If this is indeed the case, then commitment to old ritualist symbols may have materialized somewhat later as a justification rather than as a reason for the schism. See Georg Michels, "The Solovki Uprising: Religion and Revolt in Northern Russia," *Russian Review* 51 (1992) 1: 1–15.

40. Stromberg, 13.

41. Scheffel, *In the Shadow of Antichrist,* 213–14.

42. Tambiah, 145.

43. Given the evidence and debate engendered by the community issue, we can discount the views of the scholar who said, "the belief that stable and tightly-knit communities existed in the past is [only] an important myth for industrial and highly mobile societies." See Alan Macfarlane, *Reconstructing Historical Communities* (Cambridge, England: Cambridge University Press, 1977), 1. On the other hand, it has been exceedingly difficult for scholars to define the term "community" in any sort of reasonable way. One sociologist analyzed almost one hundred definitions of the term and ended up with a very broad common denominator: "community consists of persons in social interactions within a geographic area and having one or more additional common ties." See G. A. Hillery, Jr.,

"Definitions of Community: Areas of Agreement," *Rural Sociology* 20 (1955): 111–23. Some later social scientists admit that "sociologists have frequently launched into defining community with a will bordering on gay abandon" but with little result. See Colin Bill and Howard Newby, *Community Studies: An Introduction to the Sociology of the Local Community* (New York: Praeger, 1972), 21.

44. This picture of the premodern "community" versus the modern "society" was developed by Ferdinand Tönnies. See his *Community and Society*, trans. and ed. Charles P. Loomis (New York: Harper Torchbooks, 1963), 44 ff.

45. Victor Turner, *The Ritual Process* (Chicago: Aldine Publishing Company, 1969), 126–27.

46. Ibid., 132.

47. The model of communicative action used here derives in part from the work of Jürgen Habermas, *Communication and the Evolution of Society*, trans. Thomas McCarthy (Boston: Beacon Press, 1979). Habermas has become increasingly interested in the development of western civilization in terms of his own views on communicative theory. For example, he proposes an idealized case wherein "participants share a tradition and their orientations are normatively integrated to such an extent that they start from the same definition of the situation and do not disagree about the claims of validity that they reciprocally raise" (Ibid., 208–9). For a historian's response, see, among others, Brian J. Whitton, "Universal Pragmatics and the Formation of Western Civilization: A Critique of Habermas's Theory of Human Moral Evolution," *History and Theory* 31 (1992) 299–313.

48. I have seen ample anecdotal evidence to support Crummey's hypothesis. Old Believers often accept (or reject) each other not on philosophical or ideological grounds but rather on their ability to sing, chant, read, and stand through the lengthy old ritualist divine services.

Chapter 2: Profile of the Old Belief

1. See Michels, "The Solovki Uprising," and his other works, "The First Old Believers in Ukraine: Observations about Their Social Profile and Behavior," *Harvard Ukranian Review* 16 (1992) 3/4: 289–313, and "Some Observations on the Social History of the Old Belief during the Seventeenth Century" (paper presented at Russia's Dissenting Old Believers: An International Conference, Northfield, Minn., 1994). Michels, enthusiastic to use previously unreported archival material and to refute the "myth of the glorious and sacred origins" of the Old Belief ("The First Old Believers," 307), sometimes could analyze the sources produced by the persecuting forces more critically than he does.

2. One attempt at illustrating the various Old Believer concords can be found in the "Tablitsa gl. sekt i soglasii raskola russk. staroobriadstev," *Eniseiskie eparkhial'nye vedomosti*, 1894, no. 6: 103–8. The highly regarded missionary journal *Bratskoe slovo* responded with a critical "Kurëznaia 'tablitsa glavnykh sekt i soglasii' v raskole," *Bratskoe slovo*, 1904, no. 10: 808–15. The importance of this exchange lies in the assistance it offers in following the many names, roots, and permutations of old ritualist concords. By the turn of the nineteenth century, however, only a handful of concords maintained any strong presence nationally.

3. Cherniavsky, 25.

4. Works abound on this subject. One of the more interesting is Modest Musorgsky's opera *Khovanshchina*. The opera ends with pious Old Believers singing praise to the Lord as they burn themselves to death.

5. Cherniavsky, 33–36. The author deals with Petrine legal issues in regard to the Old Believers. A more detailed account can be found in Igor Smolitsch, *Forschungen zur osteuropäischen Geshchichte.* Bd 2 *Geschichte der russischen Kirche,* edited by Gregory L. Freeze (Berlin: Otto Harrassowitz, 1990), 182–88.

6. Cherniavsky, 1.

7. The story of this committee is told in Robert L. Nichols, "The Old Belief Under Surveillance During the Reign of Alexander I" (paper presented at Russia's Dissenting Old Believers: An International Conference, Northfield, Minn., 1994). Unfortunately, there is no similar scholarly analysis of the Secret Committee's actions under Tsar Nicholas.

8. See Anton S. Beliajeff, "The Rise of the Old Orthodox Merchants of Moscow, 1771–1894," (Ph.D. diss., Syracuse University, 1974). Beliajeff analyzes the history of the most famous Muscovite Old Believer merchants and entrepreneurs. See also A. J. Rieber, *Merchants and Entrepreneurs in Imperial Russia* (Chapel Hill: University of North Carolina Press, 1982).

9. The edinoverie, as well as its founder Metropolitan Platon (Levshin), has a substantial historiography. See, for example, V. I. Belikov, *Deiatel'nost' moskovskogo mitropolita Filareta po otnosheniiu k raskolu* (Kazan, 1895); Smolitsch gives a summation and bibliography, 171 ff.

10. *Polnoe sobranie zakonov Rossiskoi imperii,* 3rd series (hereafter *PSZ*), iii, no. 1545, pp. 219–21.

11. Waldron, 114.

12. See, for example, Curtiss, 135–36. For a discussion of the general procurator's views on the Old Belief, see Robert F. Byrnes, *Pobedonostsev: His Life and Thought* (Bloomington: Indiana University Press, 1968), 178–81.

13. *PSZ*, xxv, pt. 1, no. 26126, pp. 258–62.

14. The question of freedom of religion in Russia existed for years before the Act of Toleration of 1905. Most Russian Orthodox leaders (as one might expect) fought against extending freedom of conscience to the Old Believers. See, for example, G. P. Dobrotin, *Zakon i svoboda sovesti v otnoshenii k izucheniiu raskola* (Kiev, 1896[7]), which was critical of "absolute freedom" of religion. A good source for the text of Old Believer laws and regulations after 1905–1906 can be found in *Zakonopolozheniia o staroobriadtsakh i sektantakh* (Khar'kov, 1911).

15. *PSZ*, xxvi, pt. 1, no. 28424, p. 904.

16. Waldron delineates this process thoroughly. See also *Zakonoproekt o staroobriadcheskikh obshchinakh v Gosudarstvennoi dume, Polnyi stenograficheskii otchet o zasedaniiakh 12, 13, 15, 21 maia* (Moscow: 1909). The Old Believer press printed scores of pamphlets on this issue.

17. James L. West, "The Neo–Old Believers of Moscow: Religious Revival and Nationalist Myth in Late Imperial Russia," *Canadian-American Slavic Studies* 26, no. 1–3 (1992): 13. See also his related articles, "The Riabushinskii Circle," in *Between Tsar and People: Educated Society and the Quest for Public Identity in Late Imperial Russia,* ed. Edith W. Clowes et al.(Princeton: Princeton University Press, 1991), 43, and "The Riabushinskij Circle: Russian Industrialists in Search of a Bourgeoisie," *Jahrbucher für Geschichte Osteuropas* 32, H. 3 (1984): 358–77.

18. The earliest published article questioning official census data was *Sbornik pravitel'stvennykh svedenii o raskol'nikakh,* ed. V. I. Kel'siev (London: Trübner & Co., 1860). An early Russian-published analysis of this problem was N. Ivanovskii, "O chislennosti raskol'nikov," *Pravoslavnyi sobesednik,* 1867, no. 2: 257–302. I. V. Pozdeeva, "'Serebrianyi vek'," 1–4, delineates a number of reports on Old Believer population after 1905.

19. P. Mel'nikov, "Schislenie raskol'nikov," *Russkii vestnik,* 1868, no. 2: 403–42.

20. Ibid., 415–16. Later work showed that the lack of change in the number of registered Old Believers could not be explained simply through Old Believer conversions to the Russian Orthodox church. See, for example, E. E. Lebedev, *Edinoverie v protivodeistvii russkomu obriadovomu raskolu* (Novgorod, 1904), which gave explicit data on the number of converts from the Old Belief to edinoverie, starting in 1838.

21. Mel'nikov, 426, 434–35. A more complete history of the statistical expeditions can be found in Ia. Abramov, "Statisticheskie ekspeditsii 50-kh godov (Epizod iz istorii raskola)," *Delo,* 1883, no. 9: 120–45.

22. See A. von Bushen, *Statisticheskie tablitsy Rossiiskoi imperii* (St. Petersburg, 1863), especially 233–43. Kel'siev's famous work, published in London because it was banned in Russia, also provided Mel'nikov considerable material on the Old Believer situation in Russia during the mid-Nikolaevan period.

23. For the poll tax, see *PSZ,* no. 2991, 8 February 1716. Crummey, *Old Believers and Antichrist,* 112, discusses the position of women and the double tax for the Vyg community.

24. Some historians have noted the predominance of women among Old Believers, in terms of raw numbers, spiritual leadership, and growth of the movement. See the short but informative pamphlet by P. S. Smirnov, *Znachenie zhenshchiny v istorii russkogo staroobriadcheskogo raskola* (St. Petersburg, 1902).

25. Von Bushen, 234–35. This number remained conjecture, of course, since it did not take into account apostate Orthodox who were *not* Old Believers. Later Orthodox church documents noted that such practices were indeed common. See, for example, *Vsepoddanneishii otchet za 1888 i 1889,* 79.

26. Such estimates did not sit well with members of the established church. For a rebuttal to estimates by von Bushen, Mel'nikov, and others, see Igumen Pavel, "O chisle raskol'nikov v Rossiiskoi imperii (Pis'mo k redaktsiiu)," *Bratskoe slovo,* 1876, bk. 3: 199–213.

27. Census information from 1897 can be found in the *Pervaia vseobshchaia perepis' naseleniia Rossiiskoi imperii,* 89 vols. (St. Petersburg, 1897–1905), especially table 25 on religion. See also *Pervaia vseobshchaia perepis' naseleniia Rossiiskoi imperii, obshchii svod,* 2 vols. (St. Petersburg, 1905), especially table 12 on religion. An early discussion of the census, Iu. Bunin, "Raspredelenie naseleniia Rossii po veroispovedaniiam," *Russkaia mysl',* 1903, bk. 7: 137–57, also noted discrepancies between the official 1897 reckoning and other sources on the number of Old Believers.

28. Von Bushen, 212. For examples of official estimates, see *Statisticheskie tablitsy Rossiiskoi imperii,* vyp. 2: *Nalichnoe naselenie imperii za 1858 god* (St. Petersburg, 1863), 214–17; *Statisticheskii vremennik Rossiiskoi imperii,* 1866, vol. 1: 34–35; 1871, vol. 2, no. 1: 38–43; 1875, vol. 2, no. 10: 38–43.

29. Missionaries provided a more accurate picture of Old Believer strength than did imperial census takers, but missionaries too had their biases. For Alexandrov's and other related remarks, see "S"ezd edinovertsev v Peterburge," *Zlatostrui*, 1911–1912, no. 7: 74–86. Both the Holy Synod and missionary journals often produced their own estimates of registered Old Believers. See, for example, "Missionerstvo, sekty, i raskol: khronika," *Missionerskoe obozrenie*, 1898, no. 2: 328–34; V. M. Skvortsov, "Obshchii kharakter staroobriadcheskogo raskola," *Missionerskoe obozrenie*, no. 5–6, bk. 1: 4–5; *Obzor deiatel'nosti vedomstva pravoslavnogo ispovedaniia za vremia tsarstvovaniia Imperatora Aleksandra III* (St. Petersburg, 1901), 238–39; *Vsepoddanneishii otchet za 1890 i 1891*, 168; and *Vsepoddanneishii otchet za 1903 i 1904*, 134–36.

30. "Raskol i sekty: chislo raskol'nikov v Rossii," *Strannik*, 1894, bk. 2, no. 5: 182. See also N. N., "Glavneishie tsentry sovremennogo raskola," *Khristianskoe chtenie*, 1890, no. 1–2: 159–73.

31. *Vsepoddanneishii otchet za 1890 i 1891 gody*, 168. See also *Pervaia vseobshchaia perepis' naseleniia*, vol. 31, table 25 (St. Petersburg, 1903) and, for a condensed version of the same information, *Raspredelenie perepisi naseleniia Imperii po glavnym veroispovedaniiam* (St. Petersburg, 1901). One of the few Old Believer comments on the inaccuracy of the 1897 census was "Doklad soveta s"ezdov po povodu predstoiashchei perepisi naseleniia," *Trudy desiatogo Vserossiiskogo s"ezda staroobriadtsev* (Moscow, 1910), 101–4.

32. *Pervaia vseobshchaia perepis' naseleniia*, obshchii svod, table 1.

33. Albert F. Heard, *The Russian Church and Russian Dissent* (New York, 1887. Reprint. New York: AMS Press 1971), 215.

34. N. N. Slybnikov, "Iz dnevnika Vologodskogo eparkhial'nogo missionera za 1903 goda," *Vologodskie eparkhial'nye vedomosti*, 1904, 362.

35. "Pereselenie staroobriadtsev na sever," *Zlatostrui*, 1910–1911, no. 12: 25.

36. See, for example, "Vozvrashchenie v russkoe poddanstvo," *Ural'skii staroobriadets*, 1916, no. 6–7: 33.

37. Information on Old Believer migration in the late imperial period can be found in Kliment Shevtsov, "Staroobriadchestvo v srednem Povolzh'e," *Zlatostrui*, 1911–1912, no. 6: 39–45, as well as in numerous other short articles in the Old Believer press, such as "Khodataistvo amurskikh staroobriadtsev," *Zlatostrui*, 1911–1912, no. 3: 31.

38. *Vsepoddanneishii otchet za 1890 i 1891 gody*, 183 ff.

39. Sibiriak-Altaiskii, "Staroobriadtsy v Sibiri," *Ural'skii staroobriadets*, 1916, no. 1–2: 23–24. For another description of the range of Old Believer groups, see Slybnikov, 530–32.

40. Manuscripts of Old Believer meetings often included signatures of both spiritual fathers and laity. Such manuscripts can be found in RGB OR, *f.* 344, no. 166; information on the election of a spiritual father in 1817 can be found in RGB OR, *f.* 344, no. 210.

41. Richard Stites, *Revolutionary Dreams: Utopian Vision and Experimental Life in the Russian Revolution* (New York: Oxford University Press, 1989), 16.

42. Crummey, *Old Believers and Antichrist*, 108.

43. RGB OR, *f.* 98, no. 685. Although the council made final decisions, a dissenting or additional opinion might also be written down.

44. This claim will be discussed at greater length in chapter 7.

45. *Vsepoddanneishii otchet za 1910 god*, 159.

46. See, for example, *Vsepoddanneishii otchet za 1890 i 1891 gody*, 188 ff., for the reasons given to explain the "steadiness of schism."

47. Crummey, *Old Believers and Antichrist*, 111–13.

48. Smirnov, 14–15. For a review of this work see E. E., [review of] *Znachenie zhenshchiny v istorii russkogo staroobriadcheskogo raskola* by P. S. Smirnov, in *Etnograficheskoe obozrenie*, 1904, no. 1: 153–54.

49. Heard, 213.

50. K. P. Gorbunov, "Sredi raskol'nikov iuzhnogo Urala (iz dnevnika turista)," *Istoricheskii vestnik*, 1888, no. 12: 711. The general well-being of Old Believers prompted Ivan Aksakov to note, a generation earlier, that (as quoted in Dunn, 171)

> the Great Russian raskolnik population [in Starodub] is sharply distinguished, courageous, industrious; they are mature and large, but somewhat rough in appearance. . . . It would be unpleasant to meet them at night, in the forest. But, on the other hand, I have never seen anywhere stouter, more satisfied, fatter women, all white and fleshy, the real type of Russian beauty; and in fact they would be very beautiful if they were not so obese.

51. See "O staroobriadcheskom bogadel'nom dome v Sudislave (1828)," *Russkii arkhiv*, 1884, no. 3: 37–54, for an account of an early almshouse built by the Old Believers. This was a large and prosperous affair, with capital of up to 300,000 rubles, acquired as early as 1812. The project housed up to two hundred people.

52. *Vsepoddanneishii otchet za 1890 i 1891 gody*, 191.

53. *Vsepoddanneishii otchet za 1910 god*, 159–60.

54. See, for examples, "Tserkovno-obshchestvennaia zhizn' v Saratovskom staroobriadcheskom uchilishche," *Shchit very*, 1912, no. 9–10: 850; "Ekaterinburgskie staroobriadcheskie obshchiny i voina," *Ural'skii staroobriadets*, 1915, no. 3: 27; and "Bedstvuiushchie bratiia," *Zlatostrui*, 1910–1911, no. 12: 17.

55. For the bylaws of one such association, see "Ustav staroobriadcheskogo kul'turno-prosvetitel'nogo obshchestva," *Slovo tserkvi*, 1915, no. 17: 405–8.

56. See N. P., "Na miru i smert' krasna," *Ural'skii staroobriadets*, 1915, no. 10: 40–47; and D. M. Sibirskoi, "Pis'mo v redaktsiiu: Koe-chto o kooperatsii," *Ural'skii staroobriadets*, 1916, no. 4–5: 37.

57. R. U., "Nakazannoe nechestie," *Zlatostrui*, 1910, no. 2: 20.

58. "Blagotvoritel'nost'," *Zlatostrui*, 1910–1911, no. 8: 38.

59. The editors of one magazine, for example, promised the traditional "eternal memory" to a certain Ivan Efimovich Selivanov, who was viewed as an outstanding example of Christian charity because he quietly helped the poor at all times. See "Tserkovno-obshchestvennaia zhizn': verkhoturskii zavod, Permskoi gub.," *Shchit very*, 1913, no. 12: 1365. Old Believers did not worry unnecessarily about the depersonalization of charity. Modern scholarship on the issue has shown that corporate management of these Christian duties in the West transformed a personal gift to the "meritorious poor" into an abstraction, wherein an organization cared for the penniless or indigent. See John Bossy,

Christianity in the West: 1400–1700 (New York: Oxford University Press, 1987), 144, for a description of the meritorious poor in early modern times. The poor were later redefined as lawless, not meritorious: "Gradually the attitude evolved that charity was a matter bound by financial stringency, public hygiene, public security, and social stability. This trend was general throughout western Europe, where begging was regulated or prohibited everywhere. . . ." See also R. W. Scribner, *The German Reformation* (Atlantic Highlands, N.J.: Humanities Press International, 1986), 58.

60. See RGB OR, *f.* 344, no. 166, the "Sobornoe uchrezhdenie" of 1809, and RGB OR, *f.* 344, no. 210, for infomation on the councils of 1809 and 1814. K. Popov, *Arkhiv raskol'nicheskogo arkhiereia Amvrosiia* (Stavropol, 1893) provides published reports of mid- and late-nineteenth-century regional councils of priestly Old Believers. Although the most well-publicized conferences were held by the priestly Old Believers, other groups also held conferences throughout much of the imperial period. See also N. N. Pokrovskii, ed., "Rasskaz o Ekaterinburgskom sobore 1884 goda" in Romodanovskaia, 146–59.

61. Significantly, the late imperial period saw Russian Orthodox leaders demanding the restoration of a counciliar tradition in the state-sponsored church. A large number of local conferences took place during Nicholas II's reign, culminating in the general sobor of 1917. At least publicly, the Old Believer and Russian Orthodox conferences were parallel phenomena—it did not behoove the Orthodox to show they were influenced by Old Believers. Instead, Orthodox leaders called for a counciliar revival based on pre-Petrine models without ever mentioning the Old Believers' commitment to the very same principles. It is clear, however, that the counciliar movement that swept across Russia in these years included both Orthodoxy and the Old Belief.

62. The names of specific Old Believer groups will be used so often in this study that they will not be treated as foreign words. The beglopopovtsy often referred to themselves, somewhat awkwardly, as "Old Believers who take priesthood from the official church" (Staroobriadtsy, priemliushchikh sviashchenstvo, perekhodiashchee ot gospodstvuiushchei tserkvi).

63. In this way, the fugitive-priestly Old Believers took on what might be called a more "western" view of ritual and dogmatic distinctions than did their co-religionists, since they accepted the idea that the dogma might be able to be separated from the ritual. Not too much should be made of this "westernization" of Old Believer views, though, since the decision to accept fugitive priests was made under unnaturally difficult circumstances. The beglopopovtsy clearly would have preferred *not* to receive Russian Orthodox clergy, had they believed there was any alternative. Leaders of the Russian Orthodox church complained that the beglopopovtsy simply stole away impoverished priests from the official church, through the promise of higher pay. See *Obzor*, 242–43.

64. See Dmitrii Federov, "Redkostnyi dokument," *Zlatostrui*, 1912–1913, no. 2: 1–5 for a report on the number of beglopopovtsy priests, churches, and believers earlier in the nineteenth century.

65. For a good, concise description of edinoverie, see Smolitsch, 171-82.

66. "Zasedanie soveta Vserossiiskogo staroobriadcheskogo, vo imia sv. Nikoly, Bratstva," *Zlatostrui*, 1911–1912, no. 7: 60–63.

67. Sibiriak-Altaiskii, 24.

68. "Zaselenie chernomorskogo poberezh'ia Kavkaza," *Zlatostrui,* 1911–1912, no. 6: 35–36.

69. *Trudy Vserossiiskogo s"ezda staroobriadtsev, priemliushchikh sviashchenstvo, perekhodiashchee ot gospodstvuiushchei tserkvi, v Nizhnem Novgorode, 15–19 maia, 1908 (7416) goda* (Moscow, 1908), 3. See within the *Trudy,* the "Protokol," 23–83.

70. Ibid., 4, 7–21.

71. Unfortunately, there seem to be no *Trudy* for the 1912 meeting. For reports on the congress, see F. Kruglov, *Poslednie novosti iz zhizni raskolo-staroobriadchestva* (St. Petersburg, 1912), and "Vserossiiskii s"ezd staroobriadtsev v g. Vol'ske," *Zlatostrui,* 1911–1912, no. 11: 40–45. The meeting included 146 representatives from ninety-two parishes and one hundred uncommissioned representatives. For information on the search for a hierarch in this period, see also "K voprosu o priiskanii episkopa," *Zlatostrui,* 1911–1912, no. 4: 49–51, and "S"ezd staroobriadtsev, priemliushchikh sviashchenstvo, perekhodiashchee ot gospodstvuiushchei tserkvi, v donskoi oblasti," *Zlatostrui,* 1910–1911, no. 8: 33–34. A priestless Old Believer report at the 1912 conference expressed dismay at the "impoverished" beglopopovtsy's desire to find a hierarchy. See "S"ezd beglopopovtsev," *Shchit very,* 1912, no. 4: 363.

72. An accessible introduction to the Belaia Krinitsa hierarchy can be found in Smolitsch, 167–71.

73. The Belokrinitsy, with their complete sacramental life and a national organization paralleling that of the state-sponsored church, became the first target of the Russian Orthodox church's ire. Synodal leaders saw in the flowering of the Belokrinitsy the growth of a competitor for the legitimate title of Russian Orthodoxy. In their defense of the established church, these leaders damned the Belokrinitsy as pseudo-Orthodox imposters.

74. A good article on the subject of episcopal versus lay power is "Bor'ba za vlast'," *Zlatostrui,* 1910, no. 2: 52–56.

75. The *Vsepoddanneishii otchet za 1890 i 1891 gody,* 169–71, claimed that most adherents of this concord fell into the *mnimookruzhniki,* who maintained a middle course between the *okruzhniki* and the *protivookruzhniki.* Skvortsov, "Obshchii kharakter," 6–7, noted only the issue of interaction with secular society. I. K. Bykovskii, *Istoriia staroobriadchestva vsekh soglasii* (Moscow, 1906), said that the issue erupted over the use of prosphora in the liturgy to commemorate the tsar. The *protivookruzhniki* refused to make the gesture of accepting imperial authority.

76. "S"ezd staroobriadtsev neokruzhnikov," *Zlatostrui,* 1911–1912, no. 3: 28–30. See also Heard, 230. For descriptions of attempts to reunify the groups, see a series of articles under the heading "Poslednie izvestiia" in *Staroobriadets,* 1906, no. 3: 351–55. The struggle to unify continued, but neither group seemed willing to give ground. In "Arkhipastyrskoe obrashchenie k rasdeliaiushchimsia," *Slovo tserkvy,* 1915, no. 17: 529–31, the *okruzhniki* showed little desire to take steps that would satisfy their *protivookruzhnik* counterparts and instead simply called for reunion between the two. The most famous interchange came from an open letter written by the *okruzhnik* Holy Council. See *Otkrytoe pis'mo Ivanu Ivanovichu Novikovu* (Riazan: Tip. S. N. Khudarovskogo, 1911), and *Otvet na "otkrytoe pis'mo" chlena soveta staroobriadcheskikh vserossiiskikh s"ezdov Fedota Ignat'evicha Maslenikova* (Nizhnii Novgorod: Tip. I. A. Shelemet'eva, 1912).

77. *Cf.* Waldron, 115, who writes that the first all-Russian Belokrinitsa so-bor convened in 1900, while in fact it occurred in 1898.

78. Although viewed as even more marginal than other Old Believer groups in western historiography, the Chasovenniki have received a surprising amount of sociological and anthropological study. This stems from the immigra-tion of three Chasovennik communities to the United States and Canada in the 1960s, where they have subsequently been studied. See, for good examples, Scheffel's work; Richard A. Morris, *Old Russian Ways: A Comparison of Three Rus-sian Groups in Oregon* (New York: AMS Press, 1990); and Michael J. Smithson, "Of Icons and Motorcycles: A Sociological Study of Acculturation Among Russian Old Believers in Central Oregon and Alaska" (Ph.D. diss., University of Oregon, 1976). Each of these works deals with Chasovennik history in some way and of-ten includes valuable oral traditions.

79. *Vsepoddanneishii otchet za 1890 i 1891 gody*, 184–85.

80. *Obzor*, 242.

81. Reports abound of Soviet scientists and military personnel finding hid-den, previously unknown communities of Old Believers in the Siberian forests. If Old Believers could hide themselves away from persecution, why could not a holy hierarch?

82. Sibiriak [Siberian], "Sobor staroobriadtsev 'chasovennykh' v Sibiri," *Zlatostrui*, 1910, no. 4: 33.

83. Ibid.

84. See I., "'Tsarstvo razdelivsheesia na sia'," *Zlatostrui*, 1910, no. 4: 34–35.

85. Bogomolets, "Nevskii zavod: iz zhizni mestnogo staroobriadchestva," *Ural'skii staroobriadets*, 1916, no. 6–7: 36.

86. "S"ezd edinovertsev v Peterburge," *Zlatostrui*, 1911–1912, no. 7: 80. See also Pokrovskii, "Rasskaz," for a description of an 1884 meeting.

87. The journal also published archival documents and related material on the Ural Old Believers. See, for example, "Iz proshlogo staroobriadchestva na Urale," *Ural'skii staroobriadets*, 1915, no. 4–5: 5–22.

88. "K predstoiashchemu Vserossiiskomu s"ezdu staroobriadtsev (Chasovennykh) v g. Ekaterinburge," *Zlatostrui*, 1911–1912, no. 1: 43. The Be-lokrinitsy, as well as the edinovertsy, tried to attract the Chasovenniki to their hi-erarchy. The Pomortsy representative to the all-Russian Chasovennik conference, on the other hand, hoped that the Chasovennik "brothers" would come to under-stand that the only way to the true church of Christ was not through the heretical church but rather through the Pomortsy Old Believers who accepted marriage. See "'Sobor' chasovennykh staroobriadtsev," *Shchit very*, 1913, no. 2–3: 296.

89. "Otvety redaktsii," *Zlatostrui*, 1911–1912, no. 9: 79.

90. See Crummey, *Old Believers and Antichrist*, 122. The ritual itself was not innovative; it used only those parts of the wedding service that did not need priestly activity.

91. See "Sobor staroobriadtsev pomorskogo soglasiia," *Zlatostrui*, 1912–1913, no. 2: 15–21.

92. The 1909 congress referred to decisions made in previous regional con-ferences, especially the 1878 Saratov and 1905 Samara meetings. See, for example, *Deianiia pervogo Vserossiiskogo sobora*, 61.

93. See *Deianiia pervogo Vserossiiskogo sobora*, part one, 69; part five, 3–4. The

creation of a spiritual court was not new. The existence of a "general church court" in another Old Believer concord is noted in RGB OR *f.* 98, no. 685, *l.* 48.

94. "Zapis' zasedanii sobora," 62–63.

95. Local variation occurred among many Old Believer groups. In the upper Kama river region of Perm province, for example, the Pomortsy dealt with the outside world in a particularly novel way: for much of one's life a believer remained "of the world" *(mirskoi)*, which included marriage and interaction with non–Old Believers. Toward the end of one's life, a believer would often become "of the assembly" *(sobornyi)* and accept a life of semimonasticism, contemplation, and flight from worldly interaction (including the use of imperial money and passports). Only these elderly believers held leadership positions in the local Old Believer community. The Archeography Laboratory at Moscow State University has collected a substantial amount of material from the upper Kama region.

96. Issues of ritual distinctions will be explored more fully in chapter 7, while iconographic differentiations will be analyzed in chapter 6. For a list of ritual differences between the Pomortsy and the Fedoseevtsy, see RGB OR, *f.* 344, no. 211, *l.* 96ob–99.

97. Crummey, *Old Believers and Antichrist,* 122.

98. See *Obzor,* 243, for a note on passports or army service among the bespopovtsy; see Slybnikov, 393, for a description of some rural Fedoseevtsy. The most stringent adherents of these practices, however, were the "wanderers" *(stranniki),* who forsook all bonds with society (including money, passports, and official documents) as signs of the Antichrist. Refusing any such contact with the Antichrist, they wandered around Russia, staying at times with fellow-travelers, who hoped to achieve salvation by aiding these most extreme Old Believers and also perhaps to join their midst at a later date. Since stranniki maintained no records at all, little is known about this concord.

99. See Nichols, "Old Belief Under Surveillance," 7–8.

100. "Materialy dlia issledovaniia voprosa o bezsviashchennoslovnom brake," *Shchit very,* 1912, no. 7: 584–91; no. 8: 670–80; no. 9–10: 769–82; no. 12: 1006–12.

101. To make matters worse, the Fedoseevtsy published a short-lived journal named *Staroobriadcheskii pomorskii zhurnal* that had nothing to do with the "*zakonobrachnye*" Pomortsy. The Pomortsy magazine called the Fedoseevtsy the "Staroobriadtsy-Fedoseevtsy staropomorskogo soglasiia." See *Staroobriadcheskii pomorskii zhurnal,* 1909, no. 2: 21. The Belokrinitsa journal *Tserkov'* noted this change in nomenclature as well, *Tserkov',* 1910, no. 51: 1255.

102. Heard, 222.

103. "Obshchee sobranie na Preobrazhenskom kladbishche," *Zlatostrui,* 1911–1912, no. 6: 45. The history of Preobrazhenskoe has had little serious scholarly attention. While some manuscript sources exist (for example, RGB OR, *f.* 344, no. 209. "Akty otnosiashiesia k preobrazhenskomu kladbishchu i moskovskie otecheskie pis'ma"), there has been no attempt to analyze the development of this pivotal community.

104. RGIAgM, *f.* 157 contains financial records for the Preobrazhenskoe almshouse. In the late imperial period, the Fedoseevtsy sought income not only from direct donations but also through the performance of certain liturgical services and from candle sales, much as in any Orthodox parish church. See, for ex-

ample, RGIAgM, *f.* 157, *d.* 11. Prices did not rise with inflation (a memorial service might cost 13 rubles, 50 kopeks) from the late nineteenth into the twentieth centuries. Prices actually dropped, at least in one case, after 1905, RGIAgM, *f.* 157, *o.* 1, *d.* 22.

105. See *Kratkoe izlozhenie trudov obshchego sobraniia khristian drevlepravoslavnogo kafolicheskogo veroispovedaniia i blagochestiia staropomorskogo soglasiia* (Moscow, [1908?]).

106. See "Staroobriadtsy—nepremiemliushchie sviashchenstva," *Zlatostrui,* 1910–1911, no. 9: 31, for a short note on the selection of commissioners.

107. The agenda in these gatherings usually revolved around the possibility of finding marriage without the blessing of a consecrated priest. See, for example, "Tserkovno-obshchestvennaia zhizn': g. Vitebsk," *Shchit very,* 1914, no. 4: 433–34.

108. The name "Spasovtsy" came from the phrase *"Spasova milost',"* meaning that only the "savior has mercy" and not members of the clergy. It is impossible to estimate the number of Spasovtsy after 1905, but Bunin, 140, claims that the group had up to two million adherents in the mid-nineteenth century. Mel'nikov also says that the Spasovtsy were growing by the middle of the century.

109. "Spasova soglasiia staroobriadtsy-bespopovtsy," *Staroobriadcheskii mesiatseslov-kalendar'* (Ural'sk: [Iz] Ural'skoi Staroobriadcheskoi Tipografii, 1910), 79–80.

110. See "Arkhangelskie staroobriadtsy, nepriemliushchie sviashchenstvo," *Zlatostrui,* 1910–1911, no. 7: 40. See also *Krest'ianina Ivana Aleksandrova razgovory o vere s nastavnikom Spasova soglasiia Avvakumom Onisimovym i nastavnikami drugikh soglasii* (Moscow, 1910); and *Rech' skazannaia na sobranii staroobriadtsev Spasova soglasiia malogo nachala, I. Ia. Kuznetsovym* (np., [1916?]). For earlier descriptions of the Spasovtsy, see *Vsepoddanneishii otchet za 1888 i 1889 gody,* 79; and *Beseda staroobriadtsev spasova soglasiia (sleptsa) A.A. Konovalova* (Samara, 1903).

111. See *Letopis' proiskhodiashchikh v raskole sobytii za 1898 god* (Moscow, 1899), 37–46, for a report on the conference.

112. See N. N., "Glavneishie tsentry sovremennogo raskola," for information on Old Believer organization, including the spiritual commission. Numerical breakdown of lay, clergy, and episcopal participation can be found in most reports of Old Believer conferences. See, for example, "Staroobriadcheskii sobor," *Zlatostrui,* 1912–1913, no. 2: 7–12.

113. The best legal history of the Old Belief in the imperial period is still V. I. Iasevich-Borodaevskaia, *Bor'ba za veru* (St. Petersburg, 1912).

114. After 1906, the Belokrinitsy had yearly all-Russian congresses plus regional hierarchal conferences. Fugitive-priestly and priestless groups had fewer national conferences, but made up for that by convening literally scores of regional conferences representing all major concords. Hardly an issue of any Old Believer magazine was published without at least passing notice of yet another conference.

115. "Staroobriadcheskii sobor," *Zlatostrui,* 1911–1912, no. 1: 33.

116. The proceedings of this conference, *Deianiia pervogo Vserossiiskogo sobora khristian-pomortsev, priemliushchikh brak* (Moscow: Moskovskaia Staroobriadcheskaia

Knigopechatnia, 1909) provide a wealth of material on the lifestyle of priestless Old Believers in this period.

117. The Pomortsy and Fedoseevtsy did at times meet to discuss political issues. See for example, *Staroobriadets*, 1906, no. 3: 223; and *Kratkoe izlozhenie*, 3.

Chapter 3: Liturgy and Community

1. Paul Meyendorff, *Russia, Ritual, and Reform: The Liturgical Reforms of Nikon in the 17th Century* (Crestwood: St. Vladimir's Seminary Press, 1991) provides the latest comparison of prominent liturgical texts before and after the schism. The study includes a detailed, side-by-side compilation of the most important changes in the liturgy as found in various *sluzhebniki*. Meyendorff's work, a thorough compilation, makes few attempts to analyze the meaning of textual reforms. The definitive textual comparison may still be Filaret, hieromonk, "Chin liturgii sv. Zlatousta po izlozheniiu staropechatnykh, novoispravlennogo i drevlepis'mennykh sluzhebnikov," *Bratskoe slovo*, 1876, no. 2: 31–80; no. 3: 81–107.

2. Questions about the two-fingered sign of the cross, the number of alleluias, or the spelling of *Isus* or *Iisus* for "Jesus," although significant for the task of following the vagaries of the schism's history, have already received serious attention. For an extensive bibliography of missionary and polemical material regarding Old Believer religious rite, see F. Sakharov, *Literatura istorii i oblicheniia russkogo raskola*, vol. 1 (Tambov, 1887), 160–73; vol. 2 (St. Petersburg, 1892), 191–202; vol. 3 (St. Petersburg, 1900), 274–89.

3. Comparison of Old Believer liturgical texts from before the schism (including a 1630 *sluzhebnik* in the Slavonic Library, University of Helsinki) corroborates the claim that newly printed texts matched their pre-Nikonian counterparts. The Old Believer press became highly active after 1905, publishing liturgical texts, pedagogical and theological works, and more popular books, especially pamphlets. The best-known presses were at the Rogozhskoe and Preobrazhenskoe cemeteries and at the Tipografiia Tovarishchestva na Paiakh Riabushinskikh run by the well-known Old Believer family. Press run information for the last of these publishing houses can be found in RGIAgM, *f.* 1914, especially *o.* 2, *d.* 6, 12, and 17. Some independent groups (brotherhoods and single communities, for example) also published spiritual books and pamphlets. For more information, see Roy R. Robson, "The Old Believer Press" (paper presented at Russia's Dissenting Old Believers: An International Conference, Northfield, Minn., 1994).

4. In text, format, and binding the Book of Hours *(chasovnik)* published at the priestly Rogozhskoe Cemetery in 1912 corresponded perfectly with one printed by the priestless Preobrazhenskoe almshouse in 1908, although the former was intended for a priestly audience and the latter was printed for a priestless group.

5. "O tserkovno-obriadovom vospitanii v shkole," *Slovo tserkvi*, 1916, no. 22: 484. See also "Tserkovnye obriady i staroobriadtsy," *Tserkov'*, 1909, no. 48: 1333–34.

6. "Obriadoverie," *Tserkov'*, 1910, no. 25: 631–32.

7. See, for example, "Bogosluzhenie i intelligentsiia," *Slovo tserkvi*, 1917, no.

1: 9–10. Among the Orthodox (themselves known for their attention to tradition in matters of rite and dogma), Old Believers stood out as particularly zealous adherents to the liturgical cycle. Robert Crummey has shown, for example, that Old Believer spirituality revolved around liturgical devotions rather than individual piety. See his "Spirituality of the Vyg Fathers," in *Church, Nation, and State in Russia and Ukraine*, ed. Geoffrey A. Hosking (New York: St. Martin's Press, 1991): 23–37.

8. I. Kirilov, "Sushchnost' obriada," *Tserkov'*, 1909, no. 51: 1431. "Narushiteliam sviatootecheskikh obychaev i ustavov," *Zlatostrui*, 1912–1913, no. 3: 11 has a similar theme.

9. See "Tserkovnye obriady i staroobriadtsy," *Tserkov'*, 1909, no. 48: 1333–34.

10. Kirilov, 1431.

11. *Trudy o s"ezde staroobriadtsev vsego Severo-zapadnogo, Privislianskogo i Pribaltiiskogo kraev i drugikh gorodov Rossiiskoi imperii, sostoiavshemsiia v gorode Vil'ne 25–27 ianvaria 1906 goda* (Vilnius: Tipografiia Shtaba Vilenskogo Voennogo Okruga, 1906), 199–200, remarks on the importance of thanking the tsar; and "Predsobornoe soveshchanie dukhovnykh ottsov i nachetchikov," *Pervyi Vserossiiskii sobor khristian-pomortsev, priemliushchikh brak* (Moscow: Moskovskaia Staroobriadcheskaia Knigopechatnia, 1909), 30, describes the correct prayer to be said for the tsar.

12. A. I. P., "Protivoobshchinnyi sobor staroobriadtsev, nepriemliushchikh sviashchenstva," *Zlatostrui*, 1910–1911, no. 8: 41.

13. See "Moleben za tsaria i liudi," *Shchit very*, 1914, no. 9: 833–40. Other Old Believers had the same problem. While, for example a *Kanon za tsaria* did appear in a church inventory of 1907, there is no proof of that book ever being used. See RGIAgM, *f.* 2390, *o.* 1, *d.* 7. Prayers for the tsar were rarely included in Old Believer books even after 1905.

14. *Sluzhebnik* (Moscow: Tipografiia Rogozhskogo Kladbishcha, 1912), *l.* 15.

15. Litanies were known among Old Believers only in the priestly communities; those without a hierarchal priesthood did not perform them.

16. *Sluzhebnik* (Moscow, 1912), *l.* 109.

17. *Sluzhebnik* (St. Petersburg, 1913), 99.

18. Like the *litiia* and the litanies, the Great Entry was not celebrated by priestless Old Believers.

19. *Sluzhebnik* (Moscow: 1912), *l.* 133–34.

20. *Sluzhebnik* (St. Petersburg, 1913), 98–99.

21. For the old rite version, see *Liturgii sviatogo Vasiliia Velikogo i prezhdeosviashchennaia* (Moscow: Staroobriadcheskaia Tipografiia Rogozhskogo Kladbishcha, 1912), *l.* 21; and *Sluzhebnik* (St. Petersburg, 1913), 221: "The priest and deacon also do and say [the Great Entry] as in the Liturgy of Chrysostom."

22. Pavlov, "O velikom vykhode za liturgiei," *Tserkov'*, 1910, no. 38: 9. In fact, the late imperial period saw relatively little support for the edinovertsy by church authorities. Although print runs of edinovertsy liturgical books did rise dramatically from 1897 to 1899, many of the books ended up in the hands of Old Believers themselves. Significantly, although *Chasovniki* and *Kanoniki* appeared in runs as large as 3,600, the edinovertsy press published only 720 copies of an old

ritualist catechism. See RGIAgM, *f*. 203, *o*. 399, *d*. 1, *l*. 1 ob. 2, 7, 14; *d*. 19, *l*. 2.

23. Translations from Pimen Simon et al., eds. *Drevnepravoslavnyi molitvennik* / *Old Orthodox Prayer Book* (Erie, PA: Russian Orthodox Church of the Nativity, 1986), 88.

24. "Otvety redaktsii," *Zlatostrui*, 1910–1911, no. 5: 74.

25. See "Besedy o khristianskom bogosluzhenii," *Zlatostrui*, 1910, no. 2: 38, for a good introduction to Old Believer interpretation of liturgical symbolism. The *proshchenie* was also sometimes informally called *proshchat'sia*, or "leave-taking."

26. Ibid.

27. "Otvety redaktsii," *Zlatostrui*, 1910–1911, no. 5: 74.

28. See "Kratkii otchet," *Trudy o s"ezde staroobriadtsev*, 187.

29. These prayers will be discussed at more length below.

30. In the priestly Old Believer tradition, this bowing also took place before each clergy member or parishioner partook of the Eucharist. A few Russian Orthodox church parishes also maintained the tradition.

31. *Chasovnik* (Moscow: Staroobriadcheskaia Tipografiia Rogozhskogo Kladbishcha, 1912), *l*. 110; and *Chasovnik* (Moscow: Khristianskaia Tipografiia pri Preobrazhenskom Bogadelennom Dome, 1908), *l*. 104.

32. *Syn tserkovnyi* (Moscow: Tipografiia Edinovertsev, 1894), *l*. 27–28. For an excellent translation of sections of the *Syn tserkovnyi* see Simon, 372–78. In more serious cases, Old Believer clerics sometimes had to make hundreds of bows to the congregation. See RGB OR, *f*. 98, no. 685, *l*. 48

33. *Chasoslov* (Moscow, 1848), *l*. 50. Emphasis added.

34. *Utrebnyi chasoslov* (St. Petersburg, 1916) 16.

35. For a description of the relation between priest and parish in the state church, and especially of attempts to reform that relationship, see Gregory L. Freeze, *The Parish Clergy in Nineteenth-Century Russia: Crisis, Reform, and Counter-Reform* (Princeton, N.J.: Princeton University Press, 1984), 286 ff. Priestly Old Believers may also have omitted this bow.

36. See ORKiR, NBMGU, no. 809, *l*. 3ob–4 (among other sources) for this practice.

37. *Trudy o s"ezde staroobriadtsev*, 190.

38. This tradition, however, varied from community to community.

39. A concrete, social manifestation of this model could be seen in the scores of Old Believer conferences, wherein clergy and lay believers each comprised about 50 percent of the active participants. These conferences made decisions on organizational, social, and religious issues. Such lay participation was only a dream for liberal Russian Orthodox church leaders.

40. "Otvety redaktsii," *Ural'skii staroobriadets*, 1916, no. 3: 21–22.

41. Arkhimandrit Mikhail, "Nuzhny li obriady," *Tserkov'*, 1911–1912, no. 11: 85.

42. Priestless Old Believers took up this question in the *Trudy o s"ezde staroobriadtsev*, 188. The *Son of the Church*, noted in these deliberations, often mentions the entrance and departure bows. For exact descriptions of entrance bows, see also "Otvety redaktsii," *Zlatostrui*, 1911–12, no. 6: 73–74.

43. *Trudy o s"ezde staroobriadtsev*, 190.

44. The question of Old Believer relations with outside society requires

more extensive research. For a good anthropological view of the problem, see Scheffel, 191–205.

45. See, for example, RGB OR, *f.* 98, no. 1048, *l.* 47, and 1049, *l.* 47 (about 1890 and early twentieth century, respectively). For the Fedoseevtsy, praying with nonbelievers brought on a penalty of three hundred bows to the floor. Those who went to masquerades, theatre, comedies, or simply attended non-Fedoseevtsy icon processions or burials received a less stringent amercement, as reported in RGB OR, *f.* 98, no. 685, *l.* 46ob.

46. *Psaltyr'* (Moscow: v Khristianskoi Tipografii pri Preobrazhenskom Bo-gadelennom Dome, 1909), *l.* 41–42 (translation in Simon, 355). The "Ustav o khristianskom zhitii," RGB OR, *f.* 344, no. 20, *l.* 17ob–24, is another source of bowing protocol.

47. For an Old Believer explanation of bowing protocol, see *Ustav o domash-nei molitve* (Moscow: Khristianskaia Tipografiia pri Preobrazhenskom Bogadelen-nom Dome, 1908), *l.* 22–31; and *Ustav o domashnei molitve* (Moscow: Moskovskaia Staroobriadcheskaia Knigopechatnia, 1909), *l.* 22–31. See also an early *Kanonnik* (Moscow: Tipografiia Edinovertsev, 1822), *l.* 363, published by the edinovertsy. This book would have been identical to later Old Believer imprints, and Old Be-lievers often used edinovertsy publications in lieu of their own.

48. *Syn tserkovnyi*, *l.* 25–27 (translation in Simon, 374). The editors of *Zlatostrui* recommended the *Son of the Church* as a guide for Old Believer spiritual growth in "Otvety redaktsii," *Zlatostrui*, 1910–1911, no. 11: 64.

49. A. Molodov, "Slovo o kreste i o krestnom znamenii," *Shchit very*, 1912, no. 7: 582.

50. *Psaltyr'*, *l.* 51–52 (translation in Simon, 362). The most extensive Old Be-liever use of bows came during the Great Lent, in the service celebrating the Great Canon of Repentance by St. Andrew of Crete; believers typically made about one thousand prostrations. The old-rite service book containing the canon said, "we sing the canticles *(irmosy)* of the great canon in one night. During each song and each verse we make three prostrations, and there are 266 verses. Then we make seven prostrations, then one hundred, then ninety-eight," *Triod' post-naia* (Moscow: Tipografiia pri Preobrazhenskom Bogadelennom Dome, 1910), *l.* 437. See also *Triod' postnaia* (Moscow: Moskovskaia Staroobriadcheskaia Knigopechatnia, 1912), *l.* 437. The Orthodox church eliminated this marathon of bowing but retained the service. *Kanon velikii tvorenie sviatogo Andrea Kritskogo Ierusalimskogo* (St. Petersburg, 1881) did not mention bows to be performed dur-ing the service.

51. Crummey, "Spirituality," 28.

52. *Syn tserkovnyi*, *l.* 24 (translation in Simon, 373–74).

53. "Otvety redaktsii," *Zlatostrui*, 1910–1911, no. 11: 62–63.

54. V. V. Kaurova, "Moia zhizn' v raskole i obrashchenie k pravoslavnoi tserkvi," *Eniseiskie eparkhial'nye vedomosti*, 1904, no. 20: 559. For a discussion of bows—from the state church point of view—with an eye toward the Old Believ-ers, see "Nikol'skogo edinovercheskogo monastyria nastoiatelia, Igumena Pavla, beseda s zashchitnikami avstriiskoi ierarkhii o trekh sveshchakh: ego zhe Pavla beseda s staroobriadtsami o poklonakh," *Bratskoe slovo*, 1876, no. 3: 144–51.

55. See "Skazanie o lestovke ili vervitse po ustavu," *Staroobriadcheskii po-morskii zhurnal*, 1908, no. 1: 3.

56. "Otvety redaktsii," *Zlatostrui,* 1911–1912, no. 11: 85. See also "Ruko-vodstvennye sovety staroobriadcheskim zakonouchiteliam po voprosu o prepodavanii zakona Bozhiia," *Zlatostrui,* 1911–1912, no. 1: 59–61.

Chapter 4: An Architecture of Change

1. Terms such as "church," "chapel," and "prayer house" are not synonymous for Old Believers. In traditional Orthodox nomenclature, chapels and prayer houses did not have a consecrated altar; thus, "chapels" and "prayer houses" are the most precise names to use for priestless liturgical buildings. Churches, also called "temples," had, in the strictest sense, consecrated altars and therefore designated only priestly structures. By the late imperial period, however, Old Believers had begun to call any major liturgical structure a "temple," whether it had a consecrated altar or not. Thus, in the Preobrazhenskoe priestless complex, the Nikol'skaia and Krestovozdvizhenskii buildings were designated as *khram* (temple) and the cemetery building as *chasovnia* (chapel), although none of the structures housed a consecrated altar. In general, the more important and structurally impressive priestless buildings were designated as "temple;" while smaller ones were called "chapels" or "prayer houses." All priestly buildings were called either "church" or, more regularly, "temple."

2. See I. E. Grabar', *Istoriia russkoi arkhitektury,* 4 vols. (Moscow, 1909–1915); and Kathleen Berton, *Moscow: An Architectural History* (London: Macmillan, 1977), 38.

3. Alexander Opolonikov and Yelena Opolonikova, *The Wooden Architecture of Russia: Houses, Fortifications, Churches* (New York: Harry N. Abrams, Inc., 1989), 23.

4. Opolonikov, 24.

5. Crummey, *Old Believers and Antichrist,* 131.

6. Ibid.

7. *PSZ,* 16 August 1864, no. 41199.

8. *PSZ,* 3 May 1883, no. 1545.

9. See the many examples in RGIAgM: *f.* 203, *o.* 544: *d.* 12, 13, 19; *o.* 545, *d.* 21, 23; *o.* 546: *d.* 29; *o.* 548, *d.* 6.2, 12.

10. Curtiss, 141 ff. See also V. I. Iasevich-Borodaevskaia, *Bor'ba za veru* (St. Petersburg: Gosudarstvennaia Tipografiia, 1912), 601–2.

11. Cited in Curtiss, 144.

12. See, for example, N. N., "Glavneishie tsentry sovremennogo raskola," *Khristianskoe chtenie,* 1890, no. 1–2: 163–64. An example of an illegally built Old Believer *pustyn'* can be seen in RGIAgM *f.* 203, *o.* 546, *d.* 29.

13. See, for example, the report on Old Believers in the Suwałki province of Russian Poland claiming Old Believers had erected four ancient Russian-style prayer houses in the area. GARF, *f.* 102, 3 *d-vo* (1885) *d.* 59, *ch.* 54; *l.* 8 ob.

14. See "Po gorodam i vesam: Koz'modem'iansk (Kazan. gub.)," *Staroobriadets,* 1906, no. 4: 209.

15. Ibid. See also, "O staroobriadcheskom kolokol'nom zvone," *Staroobriadets,* 1906, no. 4: 206–8. Later analysis of imperial policy on Old Believer temples can be found in "O staroobriadcheskikh khramakh," *Tserkov',* 1914, no. 2: 44–45.

16. RGIAgM, *f.* 203, *o.* 548, *d.* 17. Traditionally, consistory decisions were

scribbled on the back of the Ministry of Interior *donosheniia* it had received. This bureaucrat, however, underlined his letter's importance by using more formal script on consistory letterhead.

17. See, for example, RGIAgM, *f.* 203, *o.* 548, *d.* 20, 26, 43.

18. William C. Brumfield has noted that Old Believers had "already established the principle of local initiative in construction of churches" before such grassroots support existed on large scale in the dominant church. See "The 'New Style' and the Revival of Orthodox Church Architecture, 1900–1914," in *Christianity and the Arts in Russia,* ed. William C. Brumfield and Milos M. Velimirovic (New York: Cambridge University Press, 1991), 117.

19. "Novyi staroobriadcheskii khram v Moskve," *Zlatostrui,* 1911–1912, no. 5: 53.

20. Brumfield, 112.

21. *Vsepoddanneishii otchet za 1910 god,* 157.

22. See Waldron, "Religious Reform," 128.

23. See V. Kh., "Osviashchenie khrama v s. Zueve," *Shchit very,* 1914, no. 1: 87–103 for a particularly lengthy description of the building of a Pomortsy temple. Also see V. Filippov, "Torzhestvo osviashcheniia khrama," *Shchit very,* 1913, no. 2–3: 254–63.

24. K. Shevtsov, "Vozrazdaiushchaiasia Rossii" in "Sel'skoe khoziaistvo," *Zlatostrui,* 1912–1913, no. 1: 83.

25. See, for example, A. Kuznetsov, "Obshchiny i ikh razvitie," *Ural'skii staroobriadets,* 1915, no. 2: 19.

26. Aleksandr Modolov, "Torzhestvo staroveriia," *Shchit very,* 1912, no. 4: 354–57; no. 5–6: 485–98.

27. The Preobrazhenskoe complex is presently being renovated as the Center for Traditional Russian Culture.

28. Brumfield, 109. RGIAgM, *f.* 1376 (Moskovskoe arkhitekturnoe obshchestvo), *o.* 1, *d.* 25, "Proekt dereviannoi tserkvi dlia pereselenskikh poselkov v Sibiri," dramatically shows how this renaissance in traditional church design spread through the architectural profession.

29. George Heard Hamilton, *The Art and Architecture of Russia* (New York: Penguin Books, 1983), 409.

30. "Pervyi v Moskve khram staroobriadtsev pomortsev brachnogo soglasiia," *Zlatostrui,* 1910, no. 4: 56.

31. Brumfield, 110, also notes that the interior was much less distinctive than the exterior.

32. Ibid.

33. Lev Vladimirovich Dal', "Drevnie dereviannye tserkvi v Rossii," *Zodchii: Architekturnyi i khudozhestvenno-tekhnicheskii zhurnal,* 1875, no. 6: 78.

34. Hubert Faensen, Vladimir Ivanov, and Klaus G. Beyer, *Early Russian Architecture* (London: Paul Elek, 1972), 40.

35. V. P. Ofinskii, *Dereviannoe zodchestvo Karelii* (Leningrad: Izdatel'stvo Literatury po Stroitel'stvu, 1972), 56.

36. Opolonikov, 157.

37. *Bukhtarminskie staroobriadtsy,* 305–11.

38. Scheffel, *In the Shadow of Antichrist,* 164.

39. *Ulozhenie pervogo Vserossiisskogo sobora khristian-pomortsev* (Moscow:

Moskovskaia Staroobriadcheskaia Knigopechatnia, 1909), *l.* 15. In general the Pomortsy did not dictate exterior design. See, for example, "Sooruzhenie ili remont khrama," *Shchit very,* 1916, no. 4: 167. Old Believers in the upper Kama river region agree that their prerevolutionary chapels had neither cupola nor ornament and looked like a large izba.

40. See the maps of the Vyg community in I. Filippov's important *Istoriia vygovskoi staroobriadcheskoi pustyni* (St. Petersburg, 1862).

41. Sviashchenno-inok Serapion, "Khram i molitva," *Tserkov',* 1914, no. 25: 594.

42. The democratic as well as unifying nature of the temple was noted in Modolov, 486.

43. Although at times welcomed to attend services, non–Old Believer visitors could not participate in liturgical celebrations. See "Otvety redaktsii," *Zlatostrui,* 1910–1911, no. 12: 67.

44. Entrance bows, to be made whenever one entered the building, were repeated at the beginning and end of the service and were prescribed for the entrance and departure from one's home.

45. A technologically elaborate message system—with lights to call the pastor back to the narthex—was developed in some places so that the community preceptor would know when to come and lead prayers for the late arrivals.

46. In the upper Kama river region, for example, even today the Old Believers demarcate sacred from secular space when praying in a home. One may move in and out of the eastern corner of the main *izba* room during divine services but never cross that space. Only the celebrant may walk between the *"analoi"* (in this case a rough-hewn table holding service books) and the icons in the corner, and then only from the left. After services, however, the analoi may be moved into another room and the same corner used as an eating area for the faithful.

47. The issue of acceptance or rejection of outside society will receive longer treatment in chapter 6.

48. This arrangement also echoed the benches put around the circumference of the peasant *izba.* Some Old Believers continue to eschew modern furniture for these hard benches, claiming that expensive furniture could "weigh down the soul" until it could not fly to heaven.

49. Crummey, *Old Believers and Antichrist,* 64.

50. Bernard Marchadier, "Les vieux-croyants de Wojonowo," *Cahiers du monde russe et soviétique* 18 (1977), 442.

51. This arrangement served to segregate the eldest, while allowing the youngest parishioners to watch after themselves in the middle of the church. Thus, a young woman and man could stand rather close to each other during the service, making the chapel a social center during long services.

52. The upper Kama river region provided another peculiar variation: there, only the semimonastic faithful (who had withdrawn from the world) celebrated the service, and the rest of the laity did not enter the nave. Since these semimonastics generally numbered only a small portion of the entire community, the rest stood in a gallery *(palata),* a sort of balcony built on the north, south, and west walls of the chapel. Unfortunately, the last of these unique structures was burned down by Soviet authorities during collectivization, because the chapel stood on land owned by a local kulak.

53. A seventeenth-century precedent for this step design can be found in a wooden church of Kopotna, near Moscow. See *Drevnosti: Trudy Komissii po sokhraneniiu drevnikh pamiatnikov Imperatorskogo moskovskogo arkheologicheskogo obshchestva* (Moscow, 1907), XVI. See also David Buxton, *The Wooden Churches of Eastern Europe: An Introductory Survey* (London: Cambridge University Press, 1981), 44.

54. See Dal', 78.

55. Traditional Old Believer liturgical singing, like church design, found new life after 1905. Touring choirs performed to great success, and journals devoted especially to singing began to complement the many other journals in the general Old Believer press. See, for example, *Tserkovnoe penie*, which, as part of the Belokrinitsa journal *Staroobriadcheskaia mysl'*, included articles on the cultural importance of the old-rite singing and its place in Old Believer history, technical articles regarding the method and pedagogy of the old chant, and polemics against "many-voiced" or "italianate" singing.

56. The Nikol'skaia chapel at Preobrazhenskoe cemetery is a pertinent example.

57. There is also a more practical reason for icons being stood on shelves. In poor communities Old Believers would often lend family-owned icons to the temple when it did not own enough itself. This in turn sacramentalized the family icon and reinforced the relationship between home and temple. The Russian Orthodox church banned this custom in the eighteenth century because many icons were judged to be of substandard quality.

58. When segments of bespopovtsy communities decided to receive the full sacramental life (most notably in the diaspora communities of Pennsylvania, Oregon, and Alaska), they maintained their tradition of a front icon wall instead of an icon screen. This persistent tradition—perhaps reinforced by the cost of tearing down a wall to build a screen during the change from priestless to priestly—has given Old Believer churches in these communities a distinct design; since the iconostasis is a wall, there is no air space between it and the ceiling. The altar, instead of being a section screened from the nave, is a completely new room. In design and practice, congregations that accepted priesthood "rebuilt" an altar on the front end of the chapel, converting it to a church. This convention remained faithful to the concept of adding or subtracting *izba* cells as necessary.

59. Scheffel, *In the Shadow of Antichrist*, 134, has noted this phenomenon, even among twentieth-century Old Believers in Alberta, Canada.

60. Examples of these lecterns, also used by Old Believers, can be found in "Drevne-russkaia utvar' i mebel'," *Zodchii* (1879): folio 18, number 6.

61. Eugeniusz Iwaniec, *Z dziejów staroobrzędowców na zemiach polskich xvii-xx w.* (Warsaw: Wydawnictwo Naukowe, 1977), 280. Scheffel, 104–16, describes this in detail.

62. *Cf.* James Billington, *The Icon and the Axe: An Interpretive Study of Russian Culture* (New York: Random House, 1966), 193 ff. An early proponent of this view was Albert F. Heard. Brumfield, 110, makes a similar comment in regard to Old Believer architecture, saying that "the functional, relatively austere design of the interior . . . resembled more closely the simplicity of a Protestant meeting house than the usual Orthodox church."

63. "Minutes of Russian Old Believers' Conference," Erie, Pa., 2 September 1984, 1–2.

64. Marchadier, 442.

Chapter 5: Representing the Old Belief

1. GARF, f. 102, o. 1906, d. 745, l. 74–75.

2. Ibid., l. 31–31ob. Police records do not always differentiate between Old Believer and Orthodox icon processions.

3. GARF, f. 102, II, d. 12, ch. 3, l. 78.

4. "Preobrazhenie Gospodne v ikonografii," Tserkov', 1911, no. 32: 763–67.

5. "Russkiia narodnye reznye ikony," Tserkov', 1910, no. 37: 913–16.

6. Two editions have been published on the Pokrovskii Cathedral's collection: Snimki drevnikh ikon iz staroobriadcheskikh khramov rogozhskogo kladbishcha v Moskve (Moscow, 1913); and Drevnie ikony staroobriadcheskogo kafedral'nogo pokrovskogo sobora pri rogozhskom kladbishche v Moskve (Moscow: Staroobriadcheskaia Arkhiepiskopiia Moskovskaia i vseia Rusi, 1956). For a review of the former, see Russkaia ikona (1914): 33.

7. Although sources remain sketchy on the exact numbers and importance of Old Believer icon collections located outside the major centers, there has been some interest in knowing exactly which icons Old Believers worshipped. See, for example, A. Kuznetsov "Istoricheskie ocherki ural'skogo staroobriadchestva," Ural'skii staroobriadets, 1915, no. 12: 21–30, in which is mentioned a mid-nineteenth-century archival list of Old Believer icons in the Urals. RGIAgM, f. 2390, o. 1, d. 7, l. 3–5ob contains an icon inventory for a Moscow Old Believer congregation in 1907.

8. This Old Testament saying, well known through a favorite Orthodox hymn, was sometimes emblazoned on the walls of a chapel around the icons.

9. The Greek-derived sign, often mistaken for the ancient Russian two-fingered one, was borrowed by Russian iconographers after the schism. In it the pointing finger is straight, next to the bent middle finger, standing for I and C [i.e., the S] in Iisus. Next, the thumb and fourth fingers crossed to make an X, the little finger curving into a C and thus representing Khristi. Sometimes a practiced eye was needed to discern the difference in blessings.

10. Pervyi Vserossiiskii sobor khristian-pomortsev, 16.

11. See for examples of differences between Pomortsy and Fedoseevtsy, RGB OR, f. 98, no. 1200. RGB OR, f. 98, no. 1048, raises the crucifix question a full fourteen times. See, for example, l. 110–110ob. The Fedoseevtsy complained that the Pomortsy inscription of IC KhR was not biblically accurate, even if it was ancient Russian tradition. By the 1890s, however, the Fedoseevtsy did permit the faithful "to bow down and to venerate" Pomortsy-style crucifixes; see, for example, Ibid., l. 45ob–46.

12. "Otvety redaktsii," Zlatostrui, 1911–1912, no. 7: 124.

13. See, for example, "Otvety redaktsii," Zlatostrui, 1910–1911, no. 11: 63; "Otvety na voprosy podpischikov," Shchit very, 1912, no. 12: 1038; and "Khristianskii sobor," Shchit very, 1913, no. 9: 992–94.

14. This is still the case in the upper Kama river region.

15. Vsepoddanneishii otchet za 1888 i 1889 gody, 83.

16. "S"ezd staroobriadtsev Chasovennykh (ne imeiushchikh sviashchen-

stva) v Ekaterinburge," *Zlatostrui,* 1911–1912, no. 6: 5.

17. "Izvestiia i zametki," *Missionerskoe obozrenie,* 1898, no. 2: 360.

18. "Novoe ikonoborchestvo," *Tserkov',* 1910, no. 5: 134.

19. See Nikolay Andreyev, "Nikon and Avvakum on icon-painting," *Revue des études slaves* 38 (1961): 37–44. The Old Believers, unwilling to connect their own struggle with western icons to Nikon, described this as Nikon's "iconoclasm." See "Raskol russkoi tserkvi: ikonoborchestvo patriarkha Nikona," *Slovo tserkvi,* 1916, no. 21: 467–68.

20. D. K. Trenev's *Russkaia ikonopis' i ee zhelaemoe razvitie* (Moscow, 1902) gives not only a concise history of the process of westernization in Russian iconography but also an overview of the state of icon painting at the turn of the nineteenth century.

21. See, for example, "Razlichaiut-li nikonovtsy ikony?" *Shchit very,* 1914, no. 5: 541–43.

22. V. B., "Pered dorogimi, sviatymi portretami," *Tserkov',* 1914, no. 8: 177. Emphasis added.

23. Iwaniec, 28.

24. See "Otvety redaktsii," *Zlatostrui,* 1911–1912, no. 7: 126–27.

25. *Pervyi Vserossiiskii sobor khristian-pomortsev,* 15.

26. Ibid.

27. See RGB OR, *f.* 98, no. 685, *l.* 33ob–34ob.

28. RGB OR, *f.* 98, no. 1948, *l.* 46, 93–93ob.

29. *Staroobriadcheskii vestnik* 1 (1907): 28.

30. "Grabarskaia ikona rozhdestva pres. Bogoroditsy," *Tserkov',* 1914, no. 8: 192–93.

31. *Pervyi Vserossiiskii sobor khristian-pomortsev,* 16.

32. See, for examples of strict interpretation of rules in other circumstances, *Trudy o s"ezde staroobriadtsev,* 200.

33. See, for example, "Sobranie ikon," *Zlatostrui,* 1911, no. 8: 47.

34. "Otvety na voprosy podpischikov," *Shchit very,* 1912, no. 12: 1039.

35. "Letopis' tserkovnoi i obshchestvennoi zhizni v Rossii," *Tserkovnyi vestnik,* 1904, no. 43: 1368.

36. Ibid.

37. Curtiss, 321.

38. Old Believers naturally maintained the tradition and lore of wonder-working icons, even if these icons did belong to Russian Orthodox church. An eighteenth-century manuscript, for example, provided information on various miraculous images: RGB OR, *f.* 344, no. 38.

39. "Sviataia chudotvornaia Kazanskaia ikona Bozhiei Materi, imenuemaia Gubinskoi," *Tserkov',* 1910, no. 47: 1168–70.

40. "O drevlepravoslavnoi sviatyni, nakhodiashcheisia v inovernykh khramakh," *Staroobriadcheskii pastyr',* 1914, no. 5: 406–12.

41. *Pervyi Vserossiiskii sobor khristian-pomortsev,* 15. See also "Otvety redaktsii," *Zlatostrui,* 1911–1912, no. 7: 125–26.

42. Scheffel, *In the Shadow of Antichrist,* 165, notes this use of the word in the Alberta community. In other communities parents might prod their children to venerate an icon by telling them "to kiss God."

43. N. P. Kondakov, *Sovremennoe polozhenie russkoi narodnoi ikonopisi* (n.p., 1901), 1.

44. Marchadier, 442.

45. A. Ozernyi, "Svet znaniia," *Ural'skii staroobriadets*, 1915, no. 3: 22–25.

46. The classic interpretation of such representations is still Cherniavsky.

47. V. Iaskanov, "Opisanie risunkov," *Shchit very*, 1912, no. 3: 267.

48. Ibid.

49. "S"ezd staroobriadtsev chasovennykh (ne imeiushchikh sviashchen-stva) v Ekaterinburge," p. 5, published with *Zlatostrui*, 1911–1912, no. 6.

50. Iaskanov, 467.

51. "Otvety redaktsii," *Zlatostrui*, 1910–1911, no. 12: 67.

52. Illustration of Paul from "Materialy dlia istorii staroobriadchestva," *Shchit very*, 1913, no. 5: 429.

53. "Dionisii Vasil'evich Batov, Pomorskii pisatel' apologet," *Shchit very*, 1913, no. 10: 1034.

54. These pictures illustrate the way that Old Believers manipulated icono-graphic forms for their own use. When the formal lines of canonization were lost to the Old Believers, they turned instead to the icon to beatify their holy ones. By portraying their informal saints in icon form, Old Believers claimed that these teachers exemplified the iconic principle: they had become deified by devoting themselves to the Old Belief. Through this process of beatification, akin to local cults of saints, Old Believers without a hierarchy could approximate canoniza-tion and thus legitimize their own place in Russian Orthodox history.

55. "Istoriia dvuperstiia v kartinakh," *Staroobriadcheskaia mysl'*, 1910, no. 12: 852–55.

56. *Staroobriadcheskaia mysl'*, 1911, no. 8: frontispiece.

57. "Istoriia dvuperstiia v kartinakh," 852.

58. See, for example, *Staroobriadcheskii vestnik* 1 (1907): 30.

59. Trenev, *Russkaia ikonopis' i ee zhelaemoe razvitie*, 25.

60. See *Izvestiia vysochaishe-uchrezhdennogo komiteta popochitel'stva o russkoi ikonopisi*, vol. 1 (St. Petersburg, 1902).

61. D. K. Trenev, *Neskol'ko slov o drevnei i sovremennoi russkoi ikonopisi* (Moscow, 1905), 19.

62. Trenev, *Neskol'ko slov*, 4.

63. Kondakov, 33.

64. RGB OR, *f.* 98, no. 1048, *l.* 46.

65. Scheffel, *In the Shadow of Antichrist*, 149.

66. The part played by "unnatural deviations" will be dealt with at more length in the next chapter.

67. Kondakov, 1.

68. "O prodazhe ikon," *Zlatostrui*, 1912, no. 8: 49.

69. See A. Pankratov, "Pokhishchennaia ikona," *Zlatostrui*, 1911, no. 3: 45; and Trenev, *Neskol'ko slov*, 4–5.

70. Trenev, *Neskol'ko slov*, 5.

71. See "Staroobriadcheskii institut," *Zlatostrui*, 1911–1912, no. 10: 40–43.

Chapter 6: Ritual Prohibitions

1. Scheffel, *In the Shadow of Antichrist*, 200.

2. The two objectives for ritual prohibitions increasingly appeared on the

pages of Old Believer magazines. Although the liberal group of Old Believers had editorial power in these publications, they nevertheless had to answer questions from lay readers, who regarded prohibitions in a more parochial and personal way.

3. Old Believers thus began a critical analysis of their own rituals. The willingness of the Old Believers to question these rituals did not fit into the Russian Orthodox church's portrayal of Old Believers as mindless, ignorant traditionalists.

4. Scheffel, *In the Shadow of Antichrist*, 191–204.

5. "Otvety na voprosy podpischikov," *Shchit very*, 1914, no. 10: 1018–19.

6. See ORKiR, NBMGU, no. 1548, *l.* 1, for the absolute prohibition on *bania* use. RGB OR, *f.* 98, no. 1048 and 1049, *l.* 52, make *bania* use available only on days not requiring a fast. In "Otvety redaktsii," *Zlatostrui*, 1911–1912, no. 7: 118, the relationship of *bania* to prayer is noted.

7. Nineteenth-century Russian ethnographers found the "dual faith" (*dvoeverie*) of Russian Orthodox peasants to be a particularly ripe area for study. Fortunately, western scholars of Russian society have now begun to mine the load of information left by earlier observers. For his analysis of water, cleanliness, and the demons that inhabit unclean water, see Scheffel, *In the Shadow of Antichrist*, 165–68. Eve Levin has called for a reinterpretation of dvoeverie syncretism in her essay, "*Dvoeverie* and Popular Religion," in Batalden, 29–52.

8. "Zapis' zasedanii sobora," in *Pervyi Vserossiiskii sobor khristian-pomortsev*, 64.

9. RGB OR, *f.* 247, no. 430, *l.* 14ob–15. The author also cautioned against foreign (especially French and German) music and dancing, which would "eradicate Christianity."

10. Sibiriak, "Sobor staroobriadtsev 'chasovennykh' v Sibiri," *Zlatostrui*, 1910, no. 4: 32–33.

11. See, for example, RGB OR, *f.* 247, no. 430, *l.* 40b–5ob, which quotes the *Margarit*, a well-known spiritual compendium, regarding the prohibition on eating and drinking with heretics. The quotation was ascribed to St. Ephraim the Syrian. In the same manuscript, see *l.* 6, 6ob for quotations from St. John Zlatoust and St. Joseph of Volokolamsk.

12. RGB OR, *f.* 98, no. 685, *l.* 28 ob.

13. "Otvety na voprosy podpischikov," *Shchit very*, 1912, no. 9–10: 840. The entire article, pp. 834–40, dealt with this subject.

14. In the early years of the schism, Feodosii Vasil'ev—creator of the Fedoseevtsy concord—wanted any food bought from adherents of the official church to be cleansed ritually, because he believed that buying this food constituted interaction with the Antichrist. Although the Pomortsy fathers disagreed—see Crummey, *Old Believers and Antichrist*, 120—the idea never died. "Otvety na voprosy podpischikov," *Shchit very*, 1913, no. 11: 1250 explained that Pomortsy who lived among the heterodox in the western provinces could indeed buy meat touched by Lutherans, Catholics, or Jews without fear of ritual uncleanness.

15. Ethnographic studies have discussed food bans at length. Scheffel, *In the Shadow of Antichrist*, 199–202, provides the best overview of the subject. Some of the prohibited substances, such as tobacco and alcohol, will be discussed below.

16. R. A., "Kartofel'nyi bunt," *Zlatostrui,* 1912–1913, no. 3: 41. This article retold the history of the potato in Russia and described the revolt over its use in terms of the government's imposition of the potato on a reluctant peasantry. For other views, see also "Otvety redaktsii," *Zlatostrui,* 1910–1911, no. 10: 46–47; and K. Shpetsov, "Opyty s kartofelem" in "Sel'skoe khoziaistvo," *Zlatostrui,* 1911–1912, no. 2: 1–6 that went so far as to explain how to increase potato production. *Zlatostrui* kept up its campaign with "Mineral'noe udobrenie pod kartofel'," in "Sel'skoe khoziaistvo," *Zlatostrui,* 1911–1912, no. 10: 1–2.

17. Kaurova, 507.

18. RGB OR, *f.* 247, no. 650.

19. RGB OR, *f.* 247, no. 430, *l.* 15ob claims that sugar was first introduced to Russia through Arkhangelsk.

20. See, for example, RGB OR, *f.* 98, no. 1200, *l.* 379–88ob; ORKiR, NBMGU, no. 1577, *l.* 35ob. Present-day upper Kama Old Believers who live a monastic life still eschew sugar.

21. RGB OR, *f.* 247, no. 649,*l.* 15. See also *l.* 8–9.

22. Scheffel, *In the Shadow of Antichrist,* 204–5.

23. Sibiriak, "Sobor staroobriadtsev," 33.

24. See K. Shvetsov, "Sovet staroobriadcheskikh s"ezdov o sposobakh uluchsheniia sel'skogo khoziaistva," in "Sel'skoe khoziaistvo," *Zlatostrui,* 1911–1912, no. 8: 1–3.

25. "Laia (Gosudareva)," *Ural'skii staroobriadets,* 1915, no. 4–5: 49–50.

26. Old Believer men of this period still generally kept a beard, and women usually wore their hair long. The tradition, however, had become less prevalent among the young. One commentary noted that Old Believers fighting the Germans in World War I refused to cut their beards, while at home the young men wanted to create an urbane look with their shaved faces. See P. D. Lobanov (nastoiatel'), "O bradobritii," *Ural'skii staroobriadets,* 1915, no. 7: 9–12, who wrote, "and we, living with peaceful work, not experiencing the horror occurring before death, should be attending to the fulfillment of those laws of Christianity that our brothers-at-arms so zealously defend."

27. See "Kos'ba travy mashinami," in "Sel'skoe khoziaistvo," *Zlatostrui,* 1911–1912, no. 7: 3–5. See also "Rasprostranenie sel.-khoz. mashin v Rossii," in "Selskoe khoziaistvo," *Zlatostrui,* 1910, no. 4: 18–20, and others in the same journal. One article even showed that, while folk poetry illustrated popular resistance to science and technology, it also reaffirmed, throughout all of Rus', old ritualist religious practices. See "Dukhovnaia poeziia i zhizn'," *Ural'skii staroobriadets,* 1915, no. 12: 10–16.

28. See, for example, the discussion in Slybnikov, 395. Scheffel, *In the Shadow of Antichrist,* 138, says that present-day Alberta Old Believers place similar importance on spoken prayer: "With a few exceptions all prayers . . . are audible. This custom has its genesis in the desire to express as forcefully as possible one's allegiance to God and renunciation of the devil."

29. Any research on *"Zlataia Tsep'"* must begin with the study by M. S. Krutova, *Metodicheskie rekomendatsii po opisaniiu slavianorusskikh rukopisei dlia svodnogo kataloga rukopisei, khraniashchikhsia v SSSR,* vyp. 5, ch. 1 and 2, *"Zlataia Tsep'"* (Novosibirsk, 1990). *Zlatostrui* denounced *"Zlataia Tsep'"* ("Otvety redaktsii," *Zlatostrui,* 1911–1912, no. 7: 118–19.), but a Pomortsy journal took a more

guarded approach, saying simply that it was never published and could only be found in manuscript libraries. See "Otvety na voprosy podpischikov," *Shchit very,* 1916, no. 9: 438–39.

30. RGB OR, *f.* 98, no. 1015, *"Zlataia Tsep'"* had no explicit references to any ritual prohibitions, nor did the extensive index provided by Krutova.

31. Slybnikov, 395. Contemporary upper Kama Old Believers still use flint and steel when preparing food to be eaten at the trapeza, the dinner following divine services. Matches are considered unclean and untraditional.

32. "Otvety redaktsii," *Zlatostrui,* 1911–1912, no. 7: 118–19.

33. Epidemics of smallpox and other diseases were reported among the secluded Old Believers in northern Russia, largely because of their distrust of vaccination and medication. See Slybnikov, 395–96. Scheffel hypothesizes that Old Believers worried that modern medication was ritually impure. Some rural Old Believers continue to question hospitalization as a possible defilement of the body. For passages related to medicine, from the writings of the church Fathers, see RGB OR, *f.* 247, no. 642, *l.* 14ob–15.

34. "Otvety redaktsii," *Zlatostrui,* 1910–1911, no. 5: 77.

35. "Otvety redaktsii," *Zlatostrui,* 1911–1912, no. 7: 115.

36. "Otvety na voprosy podpischikov," *Shchit very,* 1914, no. 8: 826.

37. *Pervyi Vserossiiskii sobor khristian-pomortsev,* 72.

38. "Otvety redaktsii," *Zlatostrui,* 1910–1911, no. 6: 68.

39. RGB OR, *f.* 247, no. 649, *l.* 17ob. There are scores of sources in the manuscript literature on the prohibition of tea for Old Believers. See also Ibid., *l.* 5ob., which claimed that many bishops originally condemned its use; and ORKiR, NBMGU, no. 1577, *l.* 23ob., and *l.* 25.

40. "Zapis' zasedanii sobora," 53–56.

41. "Otvety redaktsii," *Ural'skii staroobriadets,* 1916, no. 1–2: 40–41.

42. See "Otvety na voprosy podpischikov," *Shchit very,* 1914, no. 1: 155. The editors clearly called tea drinking a sin and not a heresy.

43. "Otvety redaktsii," *Zlatostrui,* 1911–1912, no. 9: 78–79.

44. See "Otvety redaktsii," *Zlatostrui,* 1910–1911, no. 8: 68–72. Later on, the same journal included one doctor's prognosis that tea drinking could be as addictive as alcohol. See D., "Pochemu ia brosil pit' chai," *Zlatostrui,* 1910–1911, no. 7: 52–54. The article uses scientific rather than spiritual evidence to bolster the argument of the ill effects of tea drinking.

45. "Otvety redaktsii," *Zlatostrui,* 1911–1912, no. 7: 115.

46. Copies of an early treatise against tobacco use can be found in ORKiR, NBMGU, no. 1415, *l.* 142ob–143ob; no. 1988[1], 70ob; no. 1206, *l.* 52; no. 2152, *l.* 17; no. 1264, *l.* 134ob–35ob; no. 1535, l. 337; and no. 1693, *l.* 39.

47. Often, Old Believer manuscripts tied tea (and coffee) drinking to tobacco use as noxious intoxicants. See ORKiR, NBMGU, no. 810, *l.* 186; no. 1206, *l.* 52; no. 1293, *l.* 173; no. 1409, *l.* 26ob; no. 1577, *l.* 18, 24, 25, 34ob, 35ob.

48. N. St—ko, "Skverna v uste," *Zlatostui,* 1910–1911, no. 5: 50.

49. ORKiR, NBMGU, no. 1413[1], *l.* 50 for "suicidal" use of tobacco, and *Pervyi Vserossiiskii sobor khristian-pomortsev,* 10, for the prohibition on tobacco cultivation or trade.

50. *Pervyi Vserossiiskii sobor khristian-pomortsev,* 10; "Otvety redaktsii," *Zlatostrui,* 1912–1913, no. 5: 51.

51. This attitude was condemned by the Pomortsy at their 1909 conference. See "Predsobornoe soveshchanie dukhovnykh ottsov i nachetchikov," in *Pervyi Vserossiiskii sobor khristian-pomortsev*, 23.

52. "O vrede kureniia," *Zlatostrui*, 1910–1911, no. 11: 44, among other sources, mentions the Petrine "introduction" of tobacco to Russia.

53. David Scheffel develops this theme throughout his *In the Shadow of Antichrist*, especially, pp.199–201.

54. The manuscripts in note 47 all develop the tobacco-Satan connection.

55. This idea was born out in the Erie (Pennsylvania) emigré Old Believer community of this period, where American visitors were specifically prohibited from smoking in front of icons.

56. *Vsepoddanneishii otchet za 1910 god*, 160, parentheses in original.

57. S. B—v., "Vragi chelovechestva," *Zlatostrui*, 1911–1912, no. 2: 33.

58. See, for examples, R. U., "Dlia nekuriashchikh," *Zlatostrui*, 1910, no. 2: 77–78; and V., "O kurenii tabaka," *Zlatostrui*, 1910, no. 4: 73.

59. R. U., "Liga protiv kureniia," *Zlatostrui*, 1910, no. 2: 78.

60. S. B—v., 30–34.

61. R. U., 77–78.

62. "O vrede kureniia," *Zlatostrui*, 1910–1911, no. 11: 45.

63. Oko, "Dukhovenstvo ne dolzhno kurit'," *Ural'skii staroobriadets*, 1916, no. 9–10: 36–37.

64. See "P'ianstvo—zlo," *Ural'skii staroobriadets*, 1916, no. 1–2: 42–49. For an analysis of drinking habits, see Patricia Herlihy, "'Joy of the Rus'': Rites and Rituals of Russian Drinking," *Russian Review* 50 (1991): 131–47. A history of vodka production is found in David Christian, *Living Water: Vodka and Russian Society on the Eve of Emancipation* (New York: Oxford University Press, 1990).

65. A good example from the scores of excoriations on drinking can be found in ORKiR, NBMGU, no. 1525, *l.* 216–21.

66. ORKiR, NBMGU, no. 1395, *l.* 143.

67. "Vino," *Zlatostrui*, 1910, no. 4: 65–66.

68. As proof that the priestless Old Believers too could use nonreligious arguments for their abstinence campaign, see *Staroobriadcheskii mesiatseslov-kalendar'*, 80.

69. Scholarly research on the temperance movement has been increasing in the past few years. See Simon Dixon, "The Church's Social Role in St. Petersburg, 1880–1914," in *Church, Nation, and State in Russia and Ukraine*, ed. G. A. Hosking (New York: St. Martin's, 1991), 167–92. A good introduction to the primary source material on this movement are the *Trudy Komissii po voprosu ob alkogolizme i merakh bor'by s nim, 1900–1909* (St. Petersburg, 1900–1909).

70. See "Saratovskii eparkhial'nyi s"ezd staroobriadtsev," *Zlatostrui*, 1910–1911, no. 12: 25; "Zapis' zasedanii sobora," 53–56; and "S"ezd staroobriadtsev Chasovennykh," 5, for examples. One conference even sent the emperor a letter outlining its "faithful thoughts" regarding the problem. See "Staroobriadcheskii sobor," *Zlatostrui*, 1911–1912, no. 12: 33–38.

71. S. Bystrov, "Vekovoe zlo," *Zlatostrui*, 1910–1911, no. 12: 30.

72. Ibid., 29.

73. See "Vino," 66.

74. Ibid., 68.

Chapter 7: The Politics of Community

1. See "Protiv obshchin . . . ," *Zlatostrui,* 1910–1911, no. 10: 16–27, regarding this argument.

2. A. I. P., "Protivoobshchinnyi sobor staroobriadtsev, nepriemliushchikh sviashchenstva," *Zlatostrui,* 1910–1911, no. 8: 41.

3. One account of this argument can be found in "Sobor staroobriadtsev pomorskogo soglasiia," *Zlatostrui,* 1912–1913, no. 2: 15–21, especially page 19.

4. "Staroobriadcheskie obschiny," *Shchit very,* 1912, no. 7: 594.

5. The words "sinful" and "heretical" were both strong terms to be used by the anticommunitarians and illustrated the importance of this issue to the Old Believer public. For the use of the word "sinful" in this context, see "Tserkovno-obshchestvennaia zhizn': Moskva," *Shchit very,* 1912, no. 2: 189.

6. "Staroobriadcheskie obshchiny," 597.

7. One author, in attacking the anticommunitarians, claimed that the fear of innovation constituted a central concern of the group. See A. T. Kuznetsov, "Staroobriadcheskie obshchiny i protivo-obshchiniki," *Ural'skii staroobriadets,* 1915, no. 6: 27.

8. Ibid., 12.

9. See, for example, "Pervaia v rossii staroobriadcheskaia gazeta," *Staroobriadets,* 1906, no. 4: 215–16.

10. Iv. Kokunin, "Skhizma iz-za obshchin," *Shchit very,* 1913, no. 6–7: 614.

11. "Eparkhial'nyi s"ezd donskoi eparkhii," *Zlatostrui,* 1911–1912, no. 11: 51.

12. Ironically, those who opposed the maintenance of vital statistics unwittingly gave credence to the concept of community that they opposed: registration of marriages, for example, was not necessary in communities that held a corporate memory of such events.

13. "Otvety redaktsii," *Ural'skii staroobriadets,* 1916, no. 6–7: 44–46. The fact that registers of vital statistics did not exist before Nikon arose frequently in the informal question-and-answer section of Old Believer journals.

14. A. Kuznetsov, "Obshchiny i ikh razvitie," *Ural'skii staroobriadets,* 1915, no. 2: 26.

15. "Staroobriadcheskie obshchiny," 597. Note that the speaker never admitted that communities existed independent of governmental action, only that they were created by imperial authorities.

16. See, for example, "Obshchina v staro-pomorskom soglasii," *Tserkov',* 1910, no. 30: 906–8; and "Bespopovtsy-protivoobshchiniki," *Tserkov',* 1910, no. 51: 1255–58, for articles on anticommunitarian tendencies among priestless Old Believers. On the other hand, I. Kokunin, "Staroobriadcheskie obshchiny," *Shchit very,* 1912, no. 7: 592, claimed that the community problem had spread to every corner of the Old Belief.

17. "Sobor staroobriadtsev pomorskogo soglasiia," *Zlatostrui,* 1912–1913, no. 2: 18. Other articles noted that Siberian Chasovenniki and some Siberian Pomortsy also did not accept the community. See Sibiriak-Altaiskii, "Starobriadtsy v Sibiri," *Ural'skii staroobriadets,* 1916, no. 1–2: 23.

18. "Rizhskaia grebenshchikovskaia obshchina staroobriadtsev, nepriempliushchikh sviashchenstva," *Zlatostrui,* 1910–1911, no. 9: 31.

19. Kuznetsov, 19.

20. Ibid., 19–21.

21. A. T. Kuznetsov, "Staroobriadcheskie obshchiny i protivo-obshchiniki," *Ural'skii staroobriadets*, 1915, no. 6: 25.

22. Ibid., 28. See also P. V. Ershov, "Otkrytoe pis'mo somnevaiushchemusia v voprose ob obshchinakh," *Shchit very*, 1912, no. 12: 1031–35.

23. Kuznetsov, "Staroobriadcheskie obshchiny," 26.

24. *Al'fa i omega, l.* 154.

25. Ibid., *l.* 150.

26. "Otvety na voprosy podpischikov," *Shchit very*, 1912, no. 9–10: 832.

27. See Kuznetsov, "Staroobriadcheskie obshchiny," no. 8–9: 13–18, and no. 10: 12–16.

28. Ibid., no. 8–9: 15–18

29. "Sobor staroobriadtsev pomorskogo soglasiia," *Zlatostrui*, 1912–1913 2: 19. See also "Postanovleniia vtorogo Vserossiiskogo khristianskogo sobora," published in *Shchit very*, 1912, no. 11–12.

30. See, for some discussion on the topic, "S"ezd staroobriadtsev chasovennykh (ne imeiushchikh sviashchenstva) v Ekaterinburge," *Zlatostrui*, 1911–1912, no. 6: 5.

31. *Zlatostrui*, on the other hand, viewed itself as a "pan–Old Believer" publication that appealed to the faithful of all concords throughout the empire. This magazine unerringly produced procommunity articles for readers who might have been wavering on the subject.

32. "Eparkhial'nyi s"ezd donskoi eparkhii," *Zlatostrui*, 1911–1912, no. 11: 50–52.

33. Information regarding the fugitive-priestly Old Believers and the community issue is scarce. One conference, however, decided unanimously that opening communities would not constitute heresy. See "S"ezd staroobriadtsev, priemliushchikh sviashchenstvo, perekhodiashchee ot gospodstvuiushchei tserkvi, v donskoi oblasti," *Zlatostrui*, 1910–1911, no. 8: 33–34. For news of another conference that said it would pray for the enlightenment of anticommunitarian Old Believers, see "Vserossiiskii s"ezd staroobriadtsev v g. Vol'ske," *Zlatostrui*, 1911–1912, no. 11: 40–45. An observer of the few beglopopovtsy living in Siberia claimed that they too generally accepted the community, Sibiriak-Altaiskii, 24.

34. See, for example, the proceedings of the "S"ezd staroobriadtsev chasovennykh (ne imeiushchikh sviashchenstva) v Ekaterinburge," included in *Zlatostrui*, 1911–1912, no. 6.

35. See, for example, "Neobshchiniki," *Shchit very*, 1914, no. 10: 1009–10.

36. "Otvety redaktsii," *Zlatostrui*, 1911–1912, no. 6: 76.

37. Kuznetsov, "Staroobriadcheskie obshchiny," 16.

38. Ibid., 12.

39. V. V. Chasovennyi, "Iz zhizni protivoobchinnikov [sic]," *Ural'skii staroobriadets*, 1916, no. 3: 7–8.

40. "Tserkovno-obshchestvennaia zhizn': Rovnoe, Khersonskoi gub.," *Shchit very*, 1913, no. 10: 1124.

41. There is substantial literature on the Russian Orthodox "parish issue." See, for examples, A. G. Boldovskii, *Vozrozhdenie tserkovnogo prikhoda (Obzor*

mnenii pechati) (St. Petersburg, 1903); *Chto sdelano dlia osushchestvleniia mysli ob ustroenii i vozrozhdenii prikhodskoi zhizni* (Orel, 1906); and Ep. Anatolii, *Kanonicheskii prikhod ili prikhod obshchina* (Tomsk, 1916).

42. "Deiatel'nost' pastyria, kak dukhovnika," *Zlatostrui,* 1910–1911, no. 7: 4.

43. "Tserkovnyi prikhod, kak zalog vozrozhdeniia russkoi zhizni," *Tserkov',* 1909, no. 2: 43. For more attacks on modish or lax behavior among priests of the established church, see Staroobriadets, "'Chto ni gorod, to norov; chto ni derevnia, to obychai,'" *Staroobriadets,* 1906, no. 4: 435–40.

44. I. K., "K voprosu o reforme prikhoda," *Ural'skii staroobriadets,* 1916, no. 8: 26.

45. Ibid. See also S. Fomichev, "Idoly nashego vremeni," *Slovo tserkvy,* 1914, no. 1: 3–6; and E. P., "Sel'sko-khoziaistvennye arteli i obshchestva," *Ural'skii staroobriadets,* 1916, no. 3: 25, which linked agricultural commonwealth with the community model.

46. "Tserkovnyi prikhod . . . ," 42.

Appendix: Source Note

1. A complete discussion of post-1905 Old Believer publications can be found in Robson, "Old Believer Press."

2. Dunn, 173, quoting I. Aksakov.

3. The Slavonic Library of Helsinki University holds a particularly rich collection of these books, augmented easily through an interlibrary loan with the library of the Valamo Orthodox monastery in eastern Finland.

4. A preliminary Union list of Old Believer periodicals has been compiled by the Slavic Division of the New York Public Library.

5. *Staroobriadcheskii pastyr'* [1913–1914], however, catered specifically to the concerns of the Old Believer pastorate.

6. *Tserkov',* 1909, no. 2: 80.

7. This journal remains an almost completely unused source for the study of Russian church singing: As well as news of important concerts and conductors, the magazine published pedagogical and theoretical articles. It never failed to jab at the Russian Orthodox church, whose music the Old Believers found operatic, western, and breaking with Russian tradition.

8. *Staroobriadcheskaia mysl',* an organ of the Belokrinitsa hierarchy, often advertised itself in the Pomortsy *Shchit very,* demonstrating that, on some level, all Old Believers saw themselves as co-religionists even though they had major philosophical and ideological differences.

Bibliography

Finding Aids

Ageeva, E. A., I. V. Pozdeeva, E. B. Smilianskaia, et al. *Pamiatniki knizhnoi kul'tury staroobriadtsev Verkhokam'ia: katalog sobranii rukopisei XV–XX vv. biblioteki Moskovskogo universiteta*. Moscow: Izdatel'stvo Moskovskii Universiteta, 1994.

Beliajeff, Anton S. "Articles and Books Relating to the Old Orthodox in Languages other than Russian." *Cahiers du monde russe et soviétique* 21 (1980): 109–21.

Burtsev, A. E. *Slovar' redkikh knig i gravirovannykh portretov*. St. Petersburg, 1905.

Druzhinin, V. G. *Pisaniia russkikh staroobriadtsev*. St. Petersburg, 1912.

Kuz'min, S. A., et al. *Ukazateli soderzhaniia russkikh dorevoliutsionnykh gazet: bibliograficheskii ukazatel'*. Leningrad: Biblioteka Akademii Nauk SSSR, 1986.

Masanov, Iu. I., et al. *Ukazateli soderzhaniia russkikh zhurnalov i prodolzhaiushchikhsia izdanii, 1755–1970 gg.* Moscow: Izdatel'stvo "Kniga", 1975.

Popov, F. *Sistematicheskii ukazatel' statei pomeshchennykh v nizhepoimenovannykh periodicheskikh izdaniiakh s 1830 po 1884 god*. St. Petersburg, 1885.

Popov, K. M. *Novosti bogoslovskoi literatury: sistematicheskii ukazatel' knig i zhurnal'nykh statei*. Sergiev Posad, 1904.

Prugavin, A. S. *Raskol-sektanstvo: materialy dlia izucheniia religiozno-bytovykh dvizhenii russkogo naroda*. Moscow, 1887.

Putevoditel' po fondam staropechatnykh knig i rukopisei laboratorii arkheograficheskikh issledovanii. Sverdlovsk: Ural'skii Gosudarstvennyi Universitet, 1990.

Sakharov, F. *Literatura istorii o oblicheniia russkogo raskola*. 3 vols. Tambov, 1887; St. Petersburg, 1892, 1900.

Shashkov, A. T., and V. I. Baidin, eds. *Pamiatniki literatury i pismennosti krest'ianstva Zaural'ia*. Ekaterinburg: Izdatel'stvo Ural'skogo Universiteta, 1991.

Smolin, I. *Spravochnyi ukazatel' k zhurnalu "Missionerskoe obozrenie" za pervoe piatiletie ego izdaniia, 1896–1900*. St. Petersburg, 1901.

Sochineniia pisatelei-staroobriadtsev XVII veka. Leningrad: Nauka, 1984.

Ukazatel' k "Bratskomu slovu." Moscow, 1896.

"Ukazatel' statei pomeshchennykh v zhurnale '*Shchit very.*'" *Shchit very*, 1913, no. 12: 1379–88.

Manuscript and Archival Sources

Gosudarstvennyi Arkhiv Rossiiskoi Federatsii (GARF), Moscow
    fond 102, Ministry of the Interior, Department of the Police

Otdel' Redkikh Knig i Rukopisei, Nauchnaia Biblioteka Moskovskogo Gosu-
darstvennogo Universiteta (ORKiR, NBMGU), Moscow
Rossiiskaia Gosudarstvennaia Biblioteka, Moscow
    Otdel Rukopisei (RGB OR)
        fond 98, E. E. Egorov Collection
        fond 246, Rogozhskoe Cemetery Collection
        fond 247, Rogozhskoe Cemetery Collection
        fond 344, P. P. Shibanov Collection
Rossiiskii Gosudarstvennyi Istoricheskii Arkhiv goroda Moskvy (RGIAgM),
Moscow
        fond 157, Preobrazhenskoe Almshouse
        fond 203, Moscow Spiritual Consistory
        fond 212, Senior Inspector of Printing Houses and Book Dealers in the
        City of Moscow
        fond 357, Morozov Printing House
        fond 1376, Moscow Architectural Society
        fond 1914, Riabushinskii Printing House
        fond 2390, Bronnitskaia Old Believer Community at the Temple of Holy
        Archangel Michael
"Sobornoe postanovlenie khristian staroobriadtsev spasova soglasiia,"
Manuscript [n.p., n.d.], private collection, Moscow

The Old Believer Press

Shchit very [1912–1916], affiliated with the Pomortsy.
Slovo tserkvi [1914–1917], previously *Tserkov'*; affiliated with the Belokrinitsy.
Staroobriadcheskaia mysl' [1910–1916], affiliated with the Belokrinitsy.
Staroobriadcheskii pastyr' [1913–1914], affiliated with the Belokrinitsy.
Staroobriadcheskii pomorskii zhurnal [1908], affiliated with the Belokrinitsy.
Staroobriadcheskii vestnik [1905–1907], affiliated with the Belokrinitsy.
Staroobriadets [1906–1907], affiliated with the Belokrinitsy.
Staroobriadtsy [1908–1909], affiliated with the Belokrinitsy.
Tserkov' [1908–1914], precedes *Slovo tserkvi,* affiliated with the Belokrinitsy.
Ural'skii staroobriadets [1915–1916], affiliated with the Chasovenniki.
Zlatostrui [1910–1913], probably affiliated with the Belokrinitsy, but with an ecu-
menical Old Believer audience.

Liturgical Sources

Al'fa i omega. Vilna, 1786.
Chasoslov. Moscow: Sinodal'naia Tipografiia, 1848.
Chasoslov utrebnyi. St. Petersburg: Sinodal'naia Tipografiia, 1916.
Chasovnik. Moscow: Khristianskaia Tipografiia pri Preobrazhenskom Bogadelen-
nom Dome, 1908.
Chasovnik. Moscow: Staroobriadcheskaia Tipografiia Rogozhskogo Kladbishcha,
1912.
Kanon velikii: Tvorenie sviatogo Andreia Kritskogo Ierusalimskogo. [St. Petersburg?]:
Sinodal'naia Tipografiia, 1881.

Kanonnik. Moscow: Tipografiia Edinovercheskoi Tserkvi, 1822.

Kniga o vere. Moscow: Khristianskaia Tipografiia pri Preobrazhenskom Bogadelennom Dome, 1910.

Kniga o vere. Moscow: Khristianskaia Tipografiia Pavla Pavlovicha Riabushinskogo, 1914.

Liturgii sviatogo Vasiliia Velikogo i prezhdeosviashchennaia. Moscow: Staroobriadcheskaia Tipografiia Rogozhskogo Kladbishcha, 1912.

Molitvoslov. Moscow: Sinodal'naia Tipografiia, 1912.

Psaltyr'. Moscow: Khristianskaia Tipografiia pri Preobrazhenskom Bogadelennom Dome, 1909.

Simon, Pimen, Theodore Jurewicz [priests], and German Ciuba [hieromonk], eds. *Drevnepravoslavnyi molitvennik/Old Orthodox Prayer Book.* Erie, Pa.: Russian Orthodox Church of the Nativity, 1986.

Sluzhebnik. Moscow: Tipografiia Rogozhskogo Kladbishcha, 1912.

Sluzhebnik. St. Petersburg: Sinodal'naia tipografiia, 1913.

Sluzhebnik. St. Petersburg, 1913.

Syn tserkovnyi. Moscow: Tipografiia Edinovertsev, 1894.

Tipikon and *Ustav.* Moscow, 1885.

Triod' postnaia. Moscow: Tipografiia pri Preobrazhenskom Bogadelennom Dome, 1910.

Triod' postnaia. Moscow: Moskovskaia Staroobriadcheskaia Knigopechatnia, 1912.

Ustav o domashnei molitve. Moscow: Khristianskaia Tipografiia pri Preobrazhenskom Bogadelennom Dome, 1908.

Ustav o domashnei molitve. Moscow: Moskovskaia Staroobriadcheskaia Knigopechatnia, 1909.

Published Source Material

Abramov, Ia. "Statisticheskie ekspeditsii 50-kh godov (Epizod iz istorii raskola)." *Delo,* 1883, no. 9: 120–45.

Akademiia Nauk SSSR. *Pamiatniki istorii staroobriadchestva xvii v.* Leningrad: Nauka, 1927.

Anatolii (ep.). *Kanonicheskii prikhod ili prikhod obshchina.* Tomsk, 1916.

Aristov, N. "Ustroistvo raskol'nichikh obshchin." *Biblioteka dlia chteniia,* 1863, no. 7:1–32.

Arsen'ev, K. *Statisticheskie ocherki Rossii.* St. Petersburg, 1848.

Arsen'ev, K. K. *Svoboda sovesti i veroterpimost'.* St. Petersburg, 1904.

Avvakum [archpriest]. "The Epistles of Avvakum." In *Life and Thought in Old Russia,* edited by Marthe Blinoff. University Park, Pa.: Pennsylvania State University Press, 1961.

Beseda staroobriadtsev spasova soglasiia (sleptsa A.A. Konovalova). Samara, 1903.

Boldovskii, A. G. *Vozrozhdenie tserkovnogo prikhoda (Obzor mnenii pechati).* St. Petersburg, 1903.

Bonch-Bruevich, V. D. *Materialy k istorii i izucheniiu russkogo sektanstva i raskola.* 7 vols. St. Petersburg-Petrograd, 1908–1916.

Bunin, Iu. "Raspredelenie naseleniia Rossii po veroispovedaniiam." *Russkaia mysl',* 1903, bk. 7: 137–57.

Bushen, A. von. *Statisticheskie tablitsy Rossiiskoi Imperii.* 2nd ed. St. Petersburg, 1863.

Bykovskii, I. K. *Istoriia staroobriadchestva vsekh soglasii.* Moscow, 1906.

Chto sdelano dlia osushchestvleniia mysli i vozrozhdenii prikhodskoi zhizni. Orel, 1906.

Deianiia pervogo Vserossiiskogo sobora khristian-pomortsev, priemliushchikh brak. Moscow: Moskovskaia Staroobriadcheskaia Knigopechatnia, 1909.

Dobrotin, G. P. *Zakon i svoboda sovesti v otnoshenii k izucheniiu raskola.* Kiev, 1896[7].

Domostroi. Moscow: "Sovetskaia Rossiia," 1990.

"Drevne-russkaia utvar' i mebel'." *Zodchii: Architekturnyi i khudozhestvenno-tekhnicheskii zhurnal* 8 (1879), l. 18.

Drevnie ikony staroobriadcheskogo kafedral'nogo Pokrovskogo sobora pri Rogozhskom kladbishche v Moskve. Moscow: Staroobriadcheskaia Arkhiepiskopiia Moskovskaia i Vseia Rusi, 1956.

Drevnosti: Trudy Komissii po sokhraneniiu drevnikh pamiatnikov Imperatorskogo moskovskogo arkheologicheskogo obshchestva. Moscow, 1907.

Filaret [hieromonk]. "Chin liturgii sv. Zlatousta po izlozheniiu staropechatnykh, novoispravlennogo i drevlepis'mennykh sluzhebnikov." *Bratskoe slovo,* 1876, no. 2: 31–80; no. 3: 81–107.

Filippov, I. *Istoriia Vygovskoi staroobriadcheskoi pustyni.* St. Petersburg, 1862.

Golubinaia kniga: Russkie narodnye dukhovnye stikhi xi-xix vekov. Moscow: Moskovskii Rabochii, 1991.

Gorbunov, K. P. "Sredi raskol'nikov iuzhnogo Urala (iz dnevnika turista)." *Istoricheskii vestnik,* 1888, no. 12: 709–29.

Gushchin, Il'ia. "Prisoedinenie k pravoslaviiu" *Omskie eparkhial'nye vedomosti,* 1904, no. 15: 38–39.

Iadrintsev, I. M. "Raskol'nich'i obshchiny na granitse Kitaia." *Sibirskii sbornik,* 1886, no. 1: 21–48.

Iasevich-Borodaevskaia, V. I. *Bor'ba za veru.* St. Petersburg: Gosudarstvennaia Tipografiia, 1912.

Instruktsiia pomoshchnikam protivoraskol'nicheskikh missionerov Tobol'skoi eparkhii. Tobolsk, 1897.

Iuzov, I. *Russkie dissidenty: starovery i dukhovnye khristiane.* St. Petersburg, 1881.

Ivanov, Evstafii. "O suval'skikh bezpopovtsakh i moem prisoedinenii k pravoslavnoi tserkvi." *Bratskoe slovo,* 1898, no. 9–10: 567–77.

Ivanovskii, N. "O chislennosti raskol'nikov." *Pravoslavnyi sobesednik,* 1867, no. 2: 257–302.

———. "Staroobriadchestvo i raskol." *Strannik,* 1892, no. 5: 51–81.

"Iz istorii Rogozhskogo i drugikh staroobriadcheskikh kladbishch." *Russkii arkhiv,* 1864, no. 3, 233–62.

"Izvestiia i zametki." *Missionerskoe obozrenie,* 1898, no. 2: 359–61.

Izvestiia Vysochaishe-uchrezhdennogo Komiteta popochitel'stva o russkoi ikonopisi, vol. 1. St. Petersburg: Tipografiia Ministerstva Vnutrennikh Del', 1902.

Kalashnikov, N. "Gania (Ocherk iz byta raskol'nikov)." *Den'* (1891): 1205–13, 1218–20, 1226, 1231, 1259, 1261–68, 1278; (1892): 1296–1315, 1320, 1328, 1338, 1355, 1365, 1371, 1375.

Kaurova, V. V. "Moia zhizn' v raskole i obrashchenie k pravoslavnoi tserkvi." *Eniseiskie eparkhial'nye vedomosti,* 1904, no. 18: 502–8; no. 20: 557–67; no. 21: 573–83; no. 23: 628–32.

Kel'siev, V. I., ed. *Sbornik pravitel'stvennykh svedenii o raskol'nikakh.* London: Trübner & Co., 1860.

Kratkoe izlozhenie trudov obshchego sobraniia khristian drevle-pravoslavnogo kafolicheskogo veroispovedaniia i blagochestiia staropomorskogo soglasiia. Moscow, 1908[?].

Krest'ianina Ivana Aleksandrova razgovory o vere s nastavnikom Spasova soglasiia Avvakumom Onisimovym i nastavnikami drugikh soglasii. Moscow, 1910.

Kruglov, F. *Poslednie novosti iz zhizni raskolo-staroobriadchestva.* St. Petersburg, 1912.

"Kurëznaia 'tablitsa glavnykh sekt i soglasii' v raskole." *Bratskoe slovo,* 1904, no. 10: 808–15.

Lebedev, E. E. *Edinoverie v protivodeistvii russkomu obriadovomu raskolu.* Novgorod, 1904.

Letopis' proiskhodiashchikh v raskole sobytii za 1898 god. Moscow, 1899.

"Letopis' tserkovnoi i obshchestvennoi zhizni v Rossii." *Tserkovnyi vestnik,* 1904, no. 43: 1368.

"Materialy dlia istorii russkogo raskola iz sobraniia A. E. Burtseva." *Khudozhestvenno-bibliograficheskii sbornik,* 1908, no 8: 19–36; no. 12: 1–22; no. 41: 2–45.

Mel'nikov, P. "Schislenie raskol'nikov." *Russkii vestnik,* 1868, no. 2: 403–42.

Ministerstvo vnutrennikh del. Statisticheskii vremennik Rossiiskoi imperii. 1866, vol. 1; 1871, vol. 2; 1875, vol. 2; 1877, vol. 2.

"Minutes of Russian Old Believers' Conference." Typescript. Erie, Pa, 2 September 1984.

"Missionerstvo, sekty, i raskol: khronika." *Missionerskoe obozrenie,* 1898, no. 2: 328–34.

N. N. "Glavneishie tsentry sovremennogo raskola." *Khristianskoe chtenie,* 1890, no. 1–2: 159–73.

"Nikol'skogo edinovercheskogo monastyria nastoiatelia, Igumena Pavla, beseda s zashchitnikami avstriiskoi ierarkhii o trekh sveshchakh: ego zhe Pavla beseda s staroobriadtsami o poklonakh." *Bratskoe slovo,* 1876, bk. 2, no. 3: 144–51.

"O staroobriadcheskom bogadel'nom dome v Sudislave (1828)." *Russkii Arkhiv,* 1884, no. 3: 37–54.

O ukrashenii molitvennykh domov i o sobranii—na molitvu. N.p., 1906.

Obzor deiatel'nosti vedomstva pravoslavnogo ispovedaniia za vremia tsarstvovaniia Imperatora Aleksandra III. St. Petersburg, 1901.

Otkrytoe pis'mo Ivanu Ivanovichu Novikovu. Riazan, 1911.

Otvet na "otkrytoe pis'mo" chlena soveta staroobriadcheskikh vserossiiskikh s"ezdov Fedota Ignat'evicha Maslenikova. Nizhnii Novgorod, 1912.

Pavel [Igumen]. "O chisle raskol'nikov v Rossiiskoi imperii (pism'o v redaktsiiu)." *Bratskoe slovo,* 1876, bk. 3: 199–213.

Pervaia vseobshchaia perepis' naseleniia Rossiiskoi imperii, 1897 g. 89 vols. St. Petersburg, 1897–1905.

Pervaia vseobshchaia perepis' naseleniia Rossiiskoi imperii, obshchii svod. 2 vols. St. Petersburg, 1905.

Pervyi vserossiiskii sobor khristian-pomortsev, priemliushchikh brak. Moscow: Moskovskaia Staroobriadcheskaia Knigopechatnia, 1909.

Polnoe sobranie zakonov Rossiiskoi imperii. 33 vols. St. Petersburg, 1885–1916.

Ponovyi, V. *Tainy raskol'nikov, staroobriadtsev, skoptsov, i drugikh sektantorov.* St. Petersburg, 1871.

"Predsobornoe soveshchanie dukhovnykh ottsov i nachetchikov." In *Pervyi vserossiiskii sobor khristian-pomortsev, priemliushchikh brak.* Moscow: Moskovskaia Staroobriadcheskaia Knigopechatnia, 1909.

Prugavin, A. S. *Raskol i sektantstvo v russkoi narodnoi zhizne: s kriticheskimi zamechaniiami dukhovnogo tsenzora.* St. Petersburg, 1905.

———. *Staroobriadchestvo vo vtoroi polovine xix v.* Moscow, 1904.

Pustozerskaia proza. Moscow: Moskovskii Rabochii, 1989.

"Raskol i sekty: chislo raskol'nikov v Rossii." *Strannik,* 1894, bk. 2, no. 5: 182.

Raspredelenie naseleniia Imperii po glavnym veroispovedaniiam. St. Petersburg, 1901.

"Razsadniki raskola na Urale (otryvki iz arkhivnykh skazanii)." *Russkii arkhiv,* 1915, no. 11–12: 333–76.

Rech' skazanaia na sobranii staroobriadtsev Spasova soglasiia malogo nachala, I. Ia. Kuznetsovym. N.p., 1916[?].

[Review of] *Snimki drevnikh ikon i staroobriadcheskikh khramov Rogozhskogo kladbishcha v Moskve.* In *Russkaia ikona* (1914): 33.

Riabushinskii, V. P. "Staroobriadchestvo i russkoe religioznoe chuvstvo." Typescript, privately printed. Zhuranvil Le Pon, France, 1936.

Russkaia ikona. St. Petersburg, 1914.

Russkii risovannyi lubok kontsa xviii–nachala xx veka. Moscow: Russkaia Kniga, 1992.

Rybakov, A. S., et al., eds. *Staraia vera: Staroobriadcheskaia khrestomatiia.* Moscow: [Tipografiia] Staroobriadcheskogo Instituta, [1914].

Sbornik postanovlenii po chasti raskola (1875–1904). St. Petersburg, 1905.

Selivanova, F. M. *Stikhi dukhovnye.* Moscow: "Sovetskaia Rossiia," 1991.

Senatov, V. G. *Filosofiia istorii staroobriadchestva.* 2 vols. Moscow: I. M. Mashistova, 1908.

Skvortsov, V. M. "Obshchii kharakter staroobriadcheskogo raskola, sushchestvennye priznaki i stepen' vrednosti otdel'nykh ego tolkov." *Missionerskoe obozrenie,* 1896, nos. 5–6, bk. 1: 3–19.

Slybnikov, N. N. "Iz dnevnika Vologodskogo eparkhial'nogo missionera za 1903 goda." *Vologodskie eparkhial'nye vedomosti,* 1904, 36–42, 96–101, 124–26, 155–58, 188–94, 243–47, 317–22, 361–66, 391–98, 413–19, 459–62, 492–97, 529–34, 627–33, 655–60; 1905, 1–5.

Smirnov, P. S. *Znachenie zhenshchiny v istorii russkogo staroobriadcheskogo raskola.* St. Petersburg: Tipografiia A. P. Lopukhina, 1902.

Snimki drevnikh ikon i staroobriadcheskikh khramov Rogozhskogo kladbishcha v Moskve. Moscow: N. N. Kushnerev, 1913.

Staroobriadcheskii mesiatseslov-kalendar'. Ural'sk: [Iz] Ural'skoi Staroobriadcheskoi Tipografii, 1910.

Statisticheskie tablitsy Rossiiskoi imperii. vyp. 2. *Nalichnoe naselenie Imperii za 1858 god.* St. Petersburg, 1863.

Statisticheskii vremennik Rossiiskoi Imperii. St. Petersburg, 1866, 1871, 1875.

"Tablitsa glavnykh sekt i soglasii raskola russkikh staroobriadstev." *Eniseiskie eparkhial'nye vedomosti,* 1894, no. 6: 103–8.

Bibliography 175

Trenev, D. K. *Neskol'ko slov o drevnei i sovremennoi russkoi ikonopisi.* Moscow, 1905.
————.*Russkaia ikonopis' i ee zhelaemoe razvitie.* Moscow, 1902.
Trudy desiatogo Vserossiiskogo s"ezda staroobriadtsev. Moscow, 1910.
Trudy deviatogo Vserossiiskogo s"ezda staroobriadtsev. Moscow, 1909.
Trudy dvenadtsatogo Vserossiiskogo s"ezda staroobriadtsev. Moscow, 1912.
Trudy komissii po voprosu ob alkogolizme i merakh bor'by s nim. St. Petersburg, 1900–1909.
Trudy o s"ezde staroobriadtsev vsego Severo-zapadnogo, Privislianskogo i Pribaltiiskogo kraev i drugikh gorodov Rossisskoi imperii, sostoiavshemsiia v gorode Vil'ne 25–27 ianvaria 1906 goda. Vil'nius: Tipografiia Shtaba Vilenskogo Voennogo Okruga, 1906.
Trudy odinnadtsatogo Vserossiiskogo s"ezda staroobriadtsev. Moscow, 1911.
Trudy sed'mogo Vserossiiskogo s"ezda staroobriadtsev. Nizhnii-Novgorod, 1906.
Trudy shestogo Vserossiiskogo s"ezda staroobriadtsev. Nizhnii-Novgorod, 1905.
Trudy vserossiiskogo s"ezda staroobriadtsev, priemliushchikh sviashchenstvo, perekhodiashchee ot gosudarstvuiushchee tserkvi, v Nizhnem-Novgorode, 15–19 maia 1908 (7416) goda. Moscow, 1908.
Tverdinskii, Timofei [priest]. "Kratkie ocherki iz sovremennogo byta pravoslavnykh i raskol'nikov." *Domashnaia beseda,* 1868, no. 30: 746–51; no. 31: 764–67; no. 32: 779–80; no. 33: 782–86; no. 34: 799–805.
Ulozhenie pervogo Vserossiiskogo sobora khristian-pomortsev. Moscow: Moskovskaia Staroobriadcheskaia Knigopechatnia, 1909.
Viazemskii, P. A. *Polnoe sobranie sochinenii.* 12 vols. St. Petersburg, 1878–1896.
Vsepoddanneishii otchet ober-prokurora Sviateishego sinoda K. Pobedonostseva po vedomstvu pravoslavnogo ispovedaniia za 1888 i 1889 gody. St. Petersburg, 1891.
Vsepoddanneishii otchet ober-prokurora Sviateishego sinoda K. Pobedonostseva po vedomstvu pravoslavnogo ispovedaniia za 1889 i 1890 gody. St. Petersburg, 1891.
Vsepoddanneishii otchet ober-prokurora Sviateishego sinoda K. Pobedonostseva po vedomstvu pravoslavnogo ispovedaniia za 1890 i 1891 gody. St. Petersburg, 1893.
Vsepoddanneishii otchet ober-prokurora Sviateishego sinoda K. Pobedonostseva po vedomstvu pravoslavnogo ispovedaniia za 1896 i 1897 gody. St. Petersburg, 1899.
Vsepoddanneishii otchet ober-prokurora Sviateishego sinoda po vedomstvu pravoslavnogo ispovedaniia za 1903 i 1904 gody. St. Petersburg, 1905.
Vsepoddanneishii otchet ober-prokurora Sviateishego sinoda po vedomstvu pravoslavnogo ispovedaniia za 1903–1904 gody. St. Petersburg, 1909.
Vsepoddanneishii otchet ober-prokurora Sviateishego sinoda po vedomstvu pravoslavnogo ispovedaniia za 1905–1907 gody. St. Petersburg, 1910.
Vsepoddanneishii otchet ober-prokurora Sviateishego sinoda po vedomstvu pravoslavnogo ispovedaniia za 1910 god. St. Petersburg, 1913.
Vsepoddanneishii otchet ober-prokurora Sviateishego sinoda po vedomstvu pravoslavnogo ispovedaniia za 1914 god. St. Petersburg, 1916.
Zakonopolozheniia o staroobriadtsakh i sektantakh. Khar'kov, 1911.
Zakonoproekt o staroobriadcheskikh obshchinakh v gosudarstvennoi dume: polnyi stenograficheskii otchet. Moscow, 1909.
"Zapiska o sovremennom polozhenii raskola v guberniiakh Vitebskoi, Mogilevskoi i Smolenskoi." In *Arkhiv knizhnykh i khudozhestvennykh redkostei, izdavaemyi Aleksandrom Burtsevym,* vol. 3. St. Petersburg, 1905.
"Zapis' zasedanii sobora." In *Pervyi Vserossiiskii sobor khristian-pomortsev,*

priemliushchikh brak. Moscow: Moskovskaia Staroobriadcheskaia Knigopechatnaia, 1909.

Secondary Works

Andreev, V. V. *Raskol i ego znachenie v narodnoi russkoi istorii.* St. Petersburg, 1870.

Andreyev, Nikolay. "Nikon and Avvakum on Icon-Painting." *Revue des études slaves* 38 (1961): 37–44.

Aristov, H. "Ustroistvo raskol'nicheskikh obshchin." *Biblioteka dlia chteniia,* 1863, no. 7: 1–32.

B., Vl. "'Dushila' u russkikh raskol'nikov." *Etnograficheskoe obozrenie,* 1904, no. 2: 160–61.

Balzer, Marjorie Mandelstam, ed. *Russian Traditional Culture: Religion, Gender, and Customary Law.* Armonk, N.Y.: M. E. Sharpe, 1992.

Batalden, Stephen K., ed. *Seeking God: The Recovery of Religious Identity in Orthodox Russia, Ukraine, and Georgia.* DeKalb: Northern Illinois University Press, 1993.

Beliajeff, Anton S., and Richard A. Morris. "Toward a Further Understanding of the Old Believers." *Cahiers du monde russe et soviétique* 28 (1987): 425–28.

———. "The Rise of the Old Orthodox Merchants of Moscow, 1771–1894." Ph.D. diss., Syracuse University, 1974.

Belikov, V. I. *Deiatelnost' moskovskogo mitropolita Filareta po otnosheniiu k raskolu.* Kazan, 1895.

Berton, Kathleen. *Moscow: An Architectural History.* London: Macmillan, 1977.

Bill, Colin, and Howard Newby. *Community Studies: An Introduction to the Sociology of the Local Community.* New York: Praeger, 1972.

Billington James A. *The Icon and the Axe: An Interpretive History of Russian Culture.* New York: Alfred A. Knopf, 1970.

Blackwell, William L. "The Old Believers and the Rise of Private Industrial Enterprise in Early Nineteenth Century Russia." *Slavic Review* 24 (1965): 407–24.

Bloch, Maurice. "Symbols, Song, Dance, and Features of Articulation." *European Journal of Sociology* 15 (1974): 55–81.

Boklevskii, P. *Otzhivaiushchie tipy russkoi narodnosti: krest'iane raskol'niki.* St. Petersburg, 1882.

Bonch-Bruevich, V. D. *Programma dlia sobranii svedenii po issledovaniiu i izucheniiu russkogo sektantstva i raskola.* St. Petersburg, 1908.

Bossy, John. *Christianity in the West: 1400–1700.* New York: Oxford University Press, 1987.

Brumfield, William Craft. "The 'New Style' and the Revival of Orthodox Church Architecture, 1900–1914." In *Christianity and the Arts in Russia,* edited by William C. Brumfield and Milos M. Velimirovic. 105–23. New York: Cambridge University Press, 1991.

Bukhtarminskie staroobriadtsy. Leningrad: Nauka, 1930.

Buslaev, F. *Obshchie poniatiia o russkoi ikonopisi.* Moscow, 1866.

Buxton, David. *The Wooden Churches of Eastern Europe: An Introductory Survey.* London: Cambridge University Press, 1981.

Byrnes, Robert F. *Pobedonostsev: His Life and Thought.* Bloomington: Indiana University Press, 1968.

Cherniavsky, Michael. "The Old Believers and the New Religion." *Slavic Review* 25 (1966): 1–39.

Christian, David. *Living Water: Vodka and Russian Society on the Eve of Emancipation.* New York: Oxford University Press, 1990.

Chrysostomus, P. J. "Die Lage der Altgläubigen in Russland vor dem Ersten Weltkrieg." *Ostkirchliche Studien* 18 (1969): 3–15.

Clem, Ralph S., ed. *Research Guide to the Russian and Soviet Censuses.* Ithaca, N.Y.: Cornell University Press, 1986.

Coneybeare, Frederick C. *Russian Dissenters.* Cambridge, Mass.: Harvard University Press, 1921.

Crummey, Robert O. *Old Believers and the World of Antichrist.* Madison: University of Wisconsin Press, 1970.

Cunningham, James W. *A Vanquished Hope: The Movement for Church Renewal in Russia, 1905–1906.* Crestwood, N.Y.: St. Vladimir's Seminary Press, 1981.

Curtiss, J. S. *Church and State in Russia: The Last Years of the Empire, 1900–1917.* New York: Columbia University Press, 1940.

Demerath, N. J., III, and W. C. Roof. "Religion—Recent Strands in Research." *Annual Review of Sociology* 2 (1976): 19–33.

Dolotov, A. *Tserkov' i sektantstvo v Sibiri.* Novosibirsk: Sibkraiizdat, 1930.

Douglas, Mary. *Purity and Danger: An Analysis of the Concepts of Pollution and Taboo.* London: Routledge & Keegan Paul, 1966.

Druzhinin, V. G. *Raskol na Donu v kontse xvii veka.* St. Petersburg, 1889.

Dunn, Ethel. "A Slavophile Looks at the Raskol and the Sects." *Slavonic and East European Review* 44 (1964): 167–79.

Dunn, Ethel, and Stephen P. Dunn. "Religion as an Instrument of Change: The Problem of Sects in the Soviet Union." *Slavic Review* 23 (1964): 459–578.

Dupront, Alphonse. "Religion and Religious Anthropology." Translated by Martin Thom. In *Constructing the Past: Essays in Historical Methodology,* edited by Jaques Le Goff and Pierre Nora. New York: Cambridge University Press, 1985.

Durkheim, Emile. *The Elementary Forms of the Religious Life.* Translated by Joseph Ward Swain. New York: The Free Press, 1965.

E. E. [Review of] *Znachenie zhenshchiny v istorii russkogo staroobriadcheskogo raskola* by P. S. Smirnov. In *Etnograficheskoe obozrenie,* 1904, no. 1: 153–54.

Faensen, Hubert, Vladimir Ivanov, and Klaus G. Beyer. *Early Russian Architecture.* London: Paul Elek, 1972.

Freeze, Gregory L. *The Parish Clergy in Nineteenth-Century Russia: Crisis, Reform, and Counter-Reform.* Princeton, N.J.: Princeton University Press, 1984.

Geertz, Clifford. *The Interpretation of Cultures.* New York: Basic Books, 1973.

Gerss, M. "Die Glaubenslehren der Philipponen zur Zeit ihrer Einwanderung in Ostpreussen." *Mitteilungen der Literarischen Gesellschaft Masovia* 15 (1910): 1–27.

———. "Die Philipponen." *Zeitschrifte der Altertumsgesellschaft Insterburg,* 1909, no. 11: 44–84.

Goriunov, V. S., and M. P. Tubli. *Arkhitektura epokhi moderna.* St. Petersburg: Stroiizdat, 1992.

Grabar', I. E. *Istoriia russkogo arkhitektura,* 4 vols. Moscow, 1909–1915.

Gromyko, M. M. *Mir russkoi derevni.* Moscow: "Molodaia Gvardiia," 1991.

Gur'ianova, N. S. *Krest'ianskii antimonarkhicheskii protest v staroobriadcheskoi eskhatologicheskoi literature perioda pozdnego feodalizma.* Novosibirsk: Nauka, Sibirskoe Otdelenie, 1988.

Gusfield, Joseph R., and Jerzy Michalowicz. "Secular Symbolism: Studies of Ritual, Ceremony, and the Symbolic Order in Modern Life." *Annual Review of Sociology* 10 (1984): 417–35.

Habermas, Jürgen. *Communication and the Evolution of Society.* Translated by Thomas McCarthy. Boston: Beacon Press, 1979.

Hamilton, George Heard. *The Art and Architecture of Russia.* New York: Penguin Books, 1983.

Haxthausen, August von. *Studies in the Interior of Russia.* Edited by S. Frederick Starr and translated by Eleanore L. M. Schmidt. Chicago: University of Chicago Press, 1972.

Heard, Albert F. *The Russian Church and Russian Dissent.* New York, 1887. Reprint. New York: AMS Press, 1971.

Herlihy, Patricia. "Joy of the Rus': Rites and Rituals of Russian Drinking." *Russian Review* 50 (1991): 131–47.

Hildermeier, Manfred, "Alte Glaube und neue Welt: Zur Sozialgeschichte des Raskol im 18. und 19. Jahrhunderts." *Jahrbücher für Geschichte Osteuropas* 38 (1990): 372–98, 504–25.

Hillery, G. A., Jr. "Definitions of Community: Areas of Agreement." *Rural Sociology* 20 (1955): 111–23.

Hosking, G. A., ed. *Church, Nation and State in Russia and Ukraine.* New York: St. Martin's, 1991.

Iwaniec, Eugeniusz. *Z dziejów staroobrzędowców na ziemiach polskich xviixx w.* Warsaw: Wydawnictwo Naukowe, 1977.

Jacobs, Barbara. *Kleidung als Symbol: das Beispiel der Altgäubigen Südsibiriens im 19. und beginnenden 20. Jahrhundert.* Munich: Lit, 1993.

Kondakov, N. P. *Sovremennoe polozhenie russkoi narodnoi ikonopisi.* [Moscow]: I. N. Skorokhova, 1901.

Krutova, M. S. *Metodicheskie rekomendatsii po opisaniiu slavianorusskikh rukopisei dlia svodnogo kataloga rukopisei, khraniashchikhsia v SSSR.* vyp. 5, ch. 1 and 2. "Zlataia Tsep'." Novosibirsk: n.p., 1990.

Kutuzov, B. *Tserkovnaia reforma xvii veka, ee istinnye prichiny i tseli.* 2 vols. Riga: Izdatel'skii Otdel Drevlepravoslavnoi Pomorskoi Tserkvi Latvii, 1992.

Lenski, G. *The Religious Factor.* Garden City, N.J.: Doubleday, 1961.

Macfarlane, Alan. *Reconstructing Historical Communities.* Cambridge, England: Cambridge University Press, 1977.

Marchadier, Bernard. "Les vieux-croyants de Wojonowo." *Cahiers du monde russe et soviétique* 18 (1977): 435–48.

Meyendorff, Paul. *Russia, Ritual, and Reform: The Liturgical Reforms of Nikon in the 17th Century.* Crestwood, N.Y.: St. Vladimir's Seminary Press, 1991.

Michels, Georg. "The First Old Believers in Ukraine: Observations about Their Social Profile and Behavior." *Harvard Ukranian Review* 16, no. 3/4 (1992): 289–313.

———. "The Solovki Uprising: Religion and Revolt in Northern Russia." *The Russian Review* 51, no. 1 (1992): 1–15.

Milovidov, V. F. *Staroobriadchestvo v proshlom i nastoiashchem.* Moscow: Izdatel'stvo "Mysl'," 1969.

Morosan, Vladimir. "Liturgical Singing or Sacred Music? Understanding the Aesthetic of the New Russian Choral Music." In *The Legacy of St. Vladimir.* Crestwood, N.Y.: St. Vladimir's Seminary Press, 1990.

Morris, Richard A. *Old Russian Ways: A Comparison of Three Russian Groups in Oregon.* New York: AMS Press, 1990.

———. "Three Russian Groups in Oregon: A Comparison of Boundaries in a Pluralistic Environment." Ph.D. diss., University of Oregon, 1981.

Ofinskii, V. P. *Dereviannoe zodchestvo Karelii.* Leningrad: Izdatel'stvo Literatury po Stroitel'stvu, 1972.

Opolonikov, Alexander, and Yelena Opolonikova. *The Wooden Architecture of Russia: Houses, Fortifications, Churches.* New York: Harry N. Abrams, 1989.

Pascal, Pierre. *Avvakum et les débuts du raskol.* Paris: Mouton, 1938.

Pikhoia, R. G., ed. *Knigi starogo Urala.* Sverdlovsk: Izdatel'stvo Ural'skogo Universiteta, 1989.

Pokrovskii, N. N. *Puteshestvie za redkami knigami.* Moscow: "Kniga," 1988.

Pokrovskii, N. N., and R. Morris, eds. *Traditsionnaia dukhovnaia i material'naia kul'tura russkikh staroobriadcheskikh poselenii v stranakh Evropy, Azii i Ameriki.* Novosibirsk: Nauka, Sibirskoe Otdelenie, 1992.

Poliakov, Leon. *L'éopée des vieux-croyants: une histoire de la Russie authentique.* Paris: Perrin, 1991.

Pozdeeva, I. V., and E. B. Smilianskaia. *Mir staroobriadchestva: Lichnost', kniga, traditsiia.* Moscow: Izdatel'stvo "Khronograf," 1992.

Preobrazhenskii, Antonin. *Kul'tovaia muzyka v Rossii.* Leningrad: Academia, 1924.

Prugavin, A. S. *Raskol i sektantstvo v russkoi narodnoi zhizni: s kriticheskami zamechaniiami dukhovnogo tsenzora.* St. Petersburg, 1905.

———. *Staroobriadchestvo vo vtoroi polovine xix v.* Moscow, 1904.

Rabinow, Paul. "Representations are Social Facts: Modernity and Post-Modernity in Anthropology." In *Writing Culture: The Poetics and Politics of Ethnography,* edited by James Gifford and George E. Marcus. Berkeley: University of California Press, 1986.

Rieber, A. J. *Merchants and Entrepreneurs in Imperial Russia.* Chapel Hill: University of North Carolina Press, 1982.

Robson, Roy R. "Recovering Priesthood and the Emigré Experience among Contemporary American Old Believers." In *Skupiska staroobrzędowców w Europie, Azji, i Ameryce: ich miejsce i tradycje we współczesnym świecie,* edited by I. Grek-Pabisowa et al. Warsaw: Polska Akademia Nauk, Institut Slavistiki, 1994.

Romodanovskaia, E. K., ed. *Issledovaniia po istorii literatury in obshchestvennogo soznaniia feodal'noi rossii.* Novosibirsk: Nauka, 1992.

Rovinskii, D. D. *Obozrenie ikonopisaniia.* St. Petersburg, 1903.

Roy, William G. "Class Conflict and Social Change in Historical Perspective." *Annual Review of Sociology* 10 (1984): 483–506.

Scammel, Michael. *Solzhenitsyn: A Biography.* New York: W. W. Norton & Company, 1984.

Scheffel, David Z. *In the Shadow of Antichrist: The Old Believers of Alberta.* Lewiston, N.Y.: Broadview Press, 1991.

———. "There is Always Somewhere to Go. . . .": Russian Old Believers and the State." In *Outwitting the State,* edited by Peter Skalník. New Brunswick, N.J.: Transaction Publishers, 1989.

Scribner, R. W. *The German Reformation*. Atlantic Highlands, N.J.: Humanities Press International, 1986.

Shchapov, A. *Russkii raskol staroobriadchestva*. Kazan, 1859.

———. *Zemstvo i raskol*. St. Petersburg, 1862.

Shmidt, S. O., ed. *Iz fonda redkikh knig i rukopisei nauchnoi biblioteki Moskovskogo universiteta (Issledovaniia i materiali)*. Moscow: Izdatel'stvo Moskovskogo Universiteta, 1993.

Smirnov, S. *Drevne-russkii dukhovnik*. Moscow, 1913.

Smithson, Michael J. "Of Icons and Motorcycles: A Sociological Study of Acculturation Among Russian Old Believers in Central Oregon and Alaska." Ph.D. diss., University of Oregon, 1976.

Smolitsch, Igor. *Forschungen zur osteuropäischen Geshchichte*. Bd 2. *Geschichte der russischen Kirche*, edited by Gregory L. Freeze. Berlin: Otto Harrassowitz, 1990.

Stites, Richard. *Revolutionary Dreams: Utopian Vision and Experimental Life in the Russian Revolution*. New York: Oxford University Press, 1989.

Stromberg, Peter G. *Symbols of Community: The Cultural System of a Swedish Church*. Tucson: University of Arizona Press, 1986.

Tambiah, Stanley Jeyaraja. *Culture, Thought, and Social Action: An Anthropological Perspective*. Cambridge, Mass.: Harvard University Press, 1985.

Tetzner, F. "Die Philipponen in Ostpreussen." *Globus* 76, no. 12 (1899): 181–92

———. "Philipponische Legenden." *Globus* 94, no. 8 (1908): 117–19, 241–43.

Thomas, Keith. *Religion and the Decline of Magic*. New York: Charles Scribner's Sons, 1971.

Tönnies, Ferdinand. *Community and Society*. Translated and edited by Charles P. Loomis. New York: Harper Torchbooks, 1963.

Turner, Victor. *The Ritual Process*. Chicago: Aldine Publishing Company, 1969.

Vroon, Ronald. "The Old Belief and Sectarianism as Cultural Models in the Silver Age." In *Chritianity and the Eastern Slavs: Vol. II, Russian Culture in Modern Times*, edited by Robert P. Huges and Irina Paperno. 172–90. Berkeley: University of California Press, 1994.

Waldron, Peter. "Religious Reform after 1905: Old Believers and the Orthodox Church." *Oxford Slavonic Papers* 20 (1987): 110–39.

———. "Religious Toleration in Late Imperial Russia." In *Civil Rights in Imperial Russia*, edited by Olga Crisp and Linda Edmondson. 103–19. Oxford: Clarendon Press, 1989.

Ware, Timothy. *The Orthodox Church*. New York: Penguin Books, 1976.

West, James L. "The Neo-Old Believers of Moscow: Religious Revival and Nationalist Myth in Late Imperial Russia." *Canadian-American Slavic Studies* 26, no. 1–3 (1992): 5–28.

———. "The Riabushinskii Circle." In *Between Tsar and People: Educated Society and the Quest for Public Identity in Late Imperial Russia*, edited by Edith W. Clowes et al. Princeton: Princeton University Press, 1991.

———. "The Riabushinskij Circle: Russian Industrialists in Search of a Bourgeoisie." *Jahrbücher für Geschichte Osteuropas* 32, H. 3 (1984), 358–77.

Whitton, Brian J. "Universal Pragmatics and the Formation of Western Civilization: A Critique of Habermas's theory of Human Moral Evolution." *History and Theory* 31 (1992): 299–313.

Wren, Melvin C. *The Course of Russian History.* 4th ed. New York: Macmillan Publishing Co., 1979.

Zabylin, M. *Russkii narod: ego obychai, obriady, predaniia, sueveriia, i poeziia.* Moscow, 1880. Reprint. Moscow: "Avtor," 1992.

Zernov, Nicolas. *The Russians and their Church.* London: SPCK, 1954.

Conference Proceedings

Russia's Dissenting Old Believers: An International Conference, Northfield, Minn., Sept. 30–Oct. 2, 1994.

Index